Critical Discourse Analysis

This book provides a comprehensive account of the discipline of Critical Discourse Analysis (CDA) and demonstrates multiple linguistic methods through which it exposes and demystifies ideologies that are present in institutional discourse. The book enables readers to critique the complexities of the relationship between language and power to expose the ideological operation of discourse. Proceeding from a theoretical grounding for CDA in contemporary society, the book comprises analysis of a wide range of discourse examples, including the news media, political speeches, public service leaflets and social media. Readers are guided through a diverse range of models in CDA in order to scrutinise and assess the role of language in society and to consider and challenge the principles of powerful networks, institutions and organisations.

Simon Statham is Lecturer in English Language and Linguistics at Queen's University Belfast, where he teaches and researches in critical linguistics, stylistics and related fields of study.

LEARNING ABOUT LANGUAGE

Series Editors:
Brian Walker, Huddersfield University, UK; **Willem Hollmann**, Lancaster University, UK; and the late **Geoffrey Leech**, Lancaster University, UK

Series Consultant:
Mick Short, Lancaster University, UK

Learning about Language is an exciting and ambitious series of introductions to fundamental topics in language, linguistics and related areas. The books are designed for students of linguistics and those who are studying language as part of a wider course.

Also in this series:

The Earliest English
An Introduction to Old English Language
Chris McCully and Sharon Hilles

Varieties of Modern English
An Introduction
Diane Davies

An Introduction to Psycholinguistics, Second Edition
Danny D. Steinberg and Natalia V. Sciarini

An Introduction to Cognitive Linguistics, Second Edition
Friedrich Ungerer and Hans-Jorg Schmid

Analysing Sentences
An Introduction to English Syntax, Fourth Edition
Noel Burton-Roberts

The History of Early English
An Activity-based Approach
Keith Johnson

An Introduction to Foreign Language Learning and Teaching, Revised Third Edition
Keith Johnson

The History of Late Modern Englishes
An Activity-based Approach
Keith Johnson

Analysing Sentences
An Introduction to English Syntax, Fifth Edition
Noel Burton-Roberts

An Introduction to Sociolinguistics, Sixth Edition
Janet Holmes and Nick Wilson

Critical Discourse Analysis
A Practical Introduction to Power in Language
Simon Statham

For more information about this series please visit:
www.routledge.com/Learning-about-Language/book-series/PEALAL

Critical Discourse Analysis
A Practical Introduction to Power in Language

SIMON STATHAM

Routledge
Taylor & Francis Group
LONDON AND NEW YORK

Cover image: © Getty Images

First published 2022
by Routledge
2 Park Square, Milton Park, Abingdon, Oxon OX14 4RN

and by Routledge
605 Third Avenue, New York, NY 10158

Routledge is an imprint of the Taylor & Francis Group, an informa business

© 2022 Simon Statham

The right of Simon Statham to be identified as author of this work has been asserted in accordance with sections 77 and 78 of the Copyright, Designs and Patents Act 1988.

All rights reserved. No part of this book may be reprinted or reproduced or utilised in any form or by any electronic, mechanical, or other means, now known or hereafter invented, including photocopying and recording, or in any information storage or retrieval system, without permission in writing from the publishers.

Trademark notice: Product or corporate names may be trademarks or registered trademarks, and are used only for identification and explanation without intent to infringe.

British Library Cataloguing-in-Publication Data
A catalogue record for this book is available from the British Library

Library of Congress Cataloging-in-Publication Data
A catalog record has been requested for this book

ISBN: 9780367133696 (hbk)
ISBN: 9780367133702 (pbk)
ISBN: 9780429026133 (ebk)

DOI: 10.4324/9780429026133

Typeset in Sabon
by Newgen Publishing UK

Contents

List of Illustrations ix
List of Examples x

Introduction 1

1 **Power in Language: Principles of Critical Discourse Analysis** 3
   1.1 Introduction 3
   1.2 Key Terms: Power, Discourse and Ideology 4
        1.2.1   Power as Domination and Persuasion 5
        1.2.2   Discourse and Ideology 7
   1.3 Critical Discourse Analysis: In Principle 10
        1.3.1   Manifesto for CDA 15
        1.3.2   Times of Trouble: CDA Today 17
   Summary of Chapter 1 20

2 **Power in Language: Practice of Critical Discourse Analysis** 21
   2.1 Introduction: CDA in Practice 21
   2.2 Key Model: Three-dimensional Model of CDA 22
   2.3 How to Apply the Three-dimensional Model of CDA 24
   Summary of Chapter 2 33

3 **Beginning Analysis: Critical Discourse Analysis and Systemic Functional Linguistics** 34
   3.1 Introduction 34
        3.1.1   CDA and SFL 34
   3.2 The Functions of Language 37
   3.3 The Experiential Function: Transitivity 38
        3.3.1   Material Processes 39
        3.3.2   Mental Processes 43
        3.3.3   Behavioural Processes 44
        3.3.4   Verbal Processes 44
        3.3.5   Relational Processes 46
        3.3.6   Existential Processes 48
   3.4 Transitivity in Action 49
   Summary of Chapter 3 54

CONTENTS

4	Developing Analysis: Evaluation in Text	56
	4.1 Introduction	56
	4.2 Mood	57
	4.3 Modality	61
	4.3.1 Sample Analysis: Modality of Political Speeches	61
	4.4 Evaluation and Appraisal	64
	4.4.1 Affect	66
	4.4.2 Judgement	68
	4.4.3 Appreciation	73
	Summary of Chapter 4	75
5	Strengthening Analysis: Cohesion and Coherence in Text	76
	5.1 Introduction	76
	5.2 Cohesion and Coherence in 'Innovative' Education	77
	5.3 SFL in CDA	84
	5.3.1 Political Leaflets	85
	5.3.2 Public Service Leaflets: Victim Blaming	91
	5.4 Ideological Implications: The Language of Sexual Assault	93
	Summary of Chapter 5	97
6	Voices in Discourse: Media Sources and Institutional Practices	99
	6.1 Introduction	99
	6.2 How to 'Make the News'	100
	6.2.1 Geographical Spectrum of the News	101
	6.2.2 Political Spectrum of the News	102
	6.2.3 Newsworthiness	102
	6.3 Sourcing the News	106
	6.4 Verbs of Saying	109
	6.4.1 Saying It with Style	113
	6.5 Financing the News: Advertisers and Owners	115
	Summary of Chapter 6	117
7	Social Actors: Representing Participants	119
	7.1 Introduction	119
	7.2 Social Actor Analysis	120
	7.2.1 Social Actor Categories	120
	7.2.2 Analysis of Social Actors	126
	7.3 Social Actors in Representations of 'Race'	129
	7.3.1 'Race' in the Media	131
	Summary of Chapter 7	136
8	Politics and Power: Analysing Political Language	138
	8.1 Introduction	138
	8.2 Metaphor	139

	8.3	Strategic Functions of Political Language	142
		8.3.1 Linguistic Features	142
		8.3.2 Coercion	143
		8.3.3 Legitimation	147
		8.3.4 Representation	151
	Summary of Chapter 8		153
9	Political Rhetoric in a Pandemic		154
	9.1	Introduction	154
	9.2	Political Rhetoric	155
		9.2.1 *Ethos*	156
		9.2.2 *Pathos*	157
		9.2.3 *Logos*	157
	9.3	Boris Johnson's Rhetoric	158
	Summary of Chapter 9		166
10	Multimodal Critical Discourse Analysis		167
	10.1 Introduction		167
		10.1.1 Types of Multimodal Discourse	167
		10.1.2 Multimodal Critical Discourse Analysis	168
	10.2 Visual Systemic Functional Linguistics		169
		10.2.1 Visual SFL and Iconography in Media Images	169
	10.3 Salience		173
	10.4 Visual Social Actor Analysis of Immigration		178
		10.4.1 Iconography of Immigration	179
		10.4.2 Salience of Immigration	180
		10.4.3 Visual SFL of Immigration	180
	10.5 Power and Advertising		181
		10.5.1 Advertising Terminology	182
		10.5.2 Analysis of Product Advertising	183
		10.5.3 Analysis of Non-product Advertising	186
	Summary of Chapter 10		189
11	Social Media Language and Power		191
	11.1 Introduction		191
	11.2 Language Online: Brave New World or False Dawn		191
		11.2.1 Online and Offline Links	192
		11.2.2 Computer Mediated Communication and Power	192
		11.2.3 Computer Mediated Communication, Power and Media	193
		11.2.4 Computer Mediated Communication, Power and Social Media	194
	11.3 Evaluation on Twitter: Abortion in Ireland		196
		11.3.1 Together for Yes	198
		11.3.2 Love Both	202

	11.4 Social Media in Context	207
	Summary of Chapter 11	207
12	**Critical Discourse Analysis: Detractors and Defenders**	**209**
	12.1 Introduction: Summarising the Book	209
	12.2 The Development of CDA: Responding to the Critics	210
	12.2.1 Selection and Interpretation of Data	211
	12.2.2 Examples of Real-world Discourse in CDA	212
	12.2.3 Corpus-assisted CDA	212
	12.2.4 Analytical Rigour in CDA	214
	12.3 The Role of the Reader	216
	12.3.1 Ethnomethodology in CDA	216
	12.3.2 Cognition in CDA	216
	12.4 Methodological Diversity of CDA	218
	Summary of Chapter 12	218
	References	220
	Index	228

List of Illustrations

Figures

2.1	Three-dimensional model of CDA	23
3.1	Transitivity processes	49
4.1	Modality	64
4.2	Appraisal	66
5.1	Green Party leaflet	86
5.2	PSNI leaflet	91
7.1	Social actor categories	125
9.1	Boris Johnson letter	159
10.1	Stressed student	170
10.2	*The Guardian* front page	174
10.3	*The Sun* front page	177
10.4	Getty image: France-Britain-Immigration	178
10.5	Rape Crisis Scotland advertisement	188

Tables

4.1	Affect	67
4.2	Judgement	69
4.3	Appreciation	73
6.1	Verbs of saying	110
8.1	Presupposition triggers	143

List of Examples

2.1	'Students at almost every university may have their exams cancelled as lecturers threaten to strike over pensions dispute' – *Daily Mail* 19/02/2018	24
3.1	'Firefight as 90 Brits smash Taliban base' – *The Sun* 11/12/2011	49
4.1	'Just leave Greta Thunberg's Extinction Rebellion groupies glued to the railings to cause a real stink' – *The Sun* 19/10/2019	71
5.1	Zayed University website – www.zu.ac.ae/main/en/explore_zu/index.aspx	77
6.1	'Ian Blackford slapped down by Boris Johnson in fiery PMQs clash over coronavirus sick pay' – *Daily Express* 11/03/2020	112
7.1	'Firefight as 90 Brits smash Taliban base' – *The Sun* 11/12/2011	126
7.2	'Migrants DO take our jobs: Britons losing out to foreign workers, says official study' – *Daily Express* 09/07/2014	132

Introduction

This book provides a comprehensive account of the discipline of Critical Discourse Analysis (CDA) and demonstrates multiple linguistic methods through which it exposes and demystifies ideologies that are present in institutional discourse. The book commences with a theoretical grounding and becomes more analytical and more specialised as it progresses. Chapter 1 presents the principles of CDA and Chapter 2 demonstrates how these principles are pursued in practice through an introductory analysis of the representation of an industrial dispute in the media. The subsequent chapters are a testament to the methodological scope of CDA, with each chapter introducing and applying a new model of analysis. These analyses also illustrate the wide range of discourse arenas which are examined by critical discourse analysts. Chapter 3 examines constructions of war through application of the transitivity framework and Chapter 4 discusses representations of environmental campaigns in the press by presenting and applying the model of Appraisal and introducing grammatical mood and modality. Chapter 5 initially focusses on an example of the discourse which has sought to recast higher education in marketised terms by investigating the cohesion and coherence of a university website. This chapter also analyses two leaflets, one from a recent election and another from governmental and public bodies which exemplifies problematic social constructions of sexual assault, in order to present the simultaneous applications of models for the analysis of the three functions of language in Systemic Functional Linguistics. Chapter 6 analyses the importance of voices in discourse, focussing on the presentation of sources alongside other institutional factors of the media. Chapter 7 considers the role of discourse in the construction of 'race' through a comprehensive account of social actor analysis. Chapters 8 and 9 exemplify the relevance of CDA for the analysis of politics. Chapter 8 deconstructs the strategic functions of a political speech and Chapter 9, in the type of exercise likely to dominate in contemporary critical linguistics, analyses the language of preliminary government responses to the Covid-19 pandemic. CDA is a multimodal discipline, and Chapter 10 illustrates the analysis of visual alongside textual discourses, whilst Chapter 11 discusses language and power online, evaluating the emancipatory potential of the internet and investigating the language used by opposing sides in the Irish abortion referendum on Twitter. In each of these investigations close linguistic analysis is strengthened by a thorough discussion of the socio-political context of the data. Chapter 12 overviews recent developments in CDA which have engaged with corpus, cognitive and ethnomethodological approaches.

As you will read about in more detail in Chapter 1, CDA engages fully with the social and political conditions in which discourse is produced and assesses the potential motivations and institutional factors which underlie this production. CDA is a politically motivated discipline which uses close linguistic analysis to expose the operation of power in societal language. Students and practitioners of CDA are therefore called upon to be both analysts and activists. CDA is a progressive and political discipline which seeks to challenge stratified organisations of society which legitimise capitalism, racism, sexism and classism. By exposing these ideologies we partake in the political process and reject any view of discourse as objective, neutral or disinterested. Chapter 1 will expand upon the role of CDA in contemporary society and will provide you with the theoretical foundation to fully engage with the analytical content of the other chapters in the book. The divisions and conflicts through which much of contemporary society is organised are enshrined in the dialogical relationship between language and power. This book will enable you to critique the complexities of this relationship in order to expose the ideological operation of discourse. The fundamental aim of this book and of the discipline of CDA is that readers will employ linguistic scholarship to scrutinise, challenge and ultimately undermine the principles of powerful networks, institutions and organisations which thrive on these divisions.

1 Power in Language
Principles of Critical Discourse Analysis

KEY TERMS IN CHAPTER 1: power, discourse, ideology

1.1 Introduction

This book is about analysing the various forms of language in society. In particular, it is about investigating power in society and demonstrating how this power is enacted through language. We are interested in powerful institutions in society – think of the government, the media, the legal system or the church as examples of such institutions – and how they can enact influence through language. These institutions draw power through social resources such as wealth and access to knowledge and education, which in turn equip them with status and authority. In this book we will examine the network of power in society and analyse the wide-ranging ways that power is administered through language. The book provides instruction in and endorsement of the scholarly field of Critical Discourse Analysis (CDA). This broad discipline is dedicated to the exposure of the ideological operation of power in the social world. Chapters 1 and 2 will unpack and expand upon the principles and practice of CDA, outlining key terms and practical approaches for students who are committed to discovering, and perhaps challenging, how power and ideology are disseminated through forms of language with which we interact on a daily basis. Language often operates to persuade us of the apparent validity and 'naturalness' of the principles through which powerful groups and institutions wield control in society.

Before embarking upon a more in-depth explanation in this chapter and a practical demonstration of CDA in Chapter 2, it is necessary to offer some explanations of the main theoretical positions which underpin the discipline. CDA is essentially about examining and exposing how power operates through language, but this seemingly simple definition requires a good deal more consideration so that we can fully appreciate what are very significant aspirations.

1.2 Key Terms: Power, Discourse and Ideology

At the very outset of examining the relationship between power and language, it is necessary to first consider what we mean by the concept of **power** itself. Fairclough (2015), a major figure in Critical Discourse Analysis to whose work we will return throughout this book, offers a useful starting point for thinking about power:

> Power is not in itself bad. On the contrary, the power of people to do things is generally a social good. We need to distinguish between the 'power to' do things and 'power over' other people, though we need to see this binary (and others) in a dialectical way: having power over people increases the power to do things; power to do things is conditional (in some cases at least) on having power over people. But 'power over' is not inherently bad either, as long as it is legitimate; we vote in elections for governments or councils which have various forms of legitimate power over the rest of us […] Having and exercising power over other people becomes open to critique when it is not legitimate, or when it has bad effects, for instance when it results in unacceptable and unjustifiable damage to people or to social life.
>
> (Fairclough, 2015:26–27)

Fairclough's explanation essentially makes a distinction between potential and practice: power has the potential to operate in the interests of individuals and society. However, the achievement of this potential depends very much on the practical organisation of power within society itself. As we move through this book, much of what we will uncover will demonstrate that power is very often not enacted in the interests of 'social good'. We will also point out, however, that the very process of uncovering this reality can contribute to a potential for resistance against the 'bad effects' of power.

At the centre of the processes of power is the extent to which power can be considered 'legitimate'. Fairclough's introductory gloss offers the example of democratic elections as a site of legitimate power. However, elections, like all political processes, rather than being thought of as inherently legitimate, should instead be viewed as part of the process of 'legitimisation'. This is because concepts like democracy and practices like elections, whilst generally being viewed as positive, are not inherent or natural. Despite how language might have conditioned us to think that such concepts are natural, rather they are all constructs which contribute, to varying degrees depending on the individual context, to the maintenance of society. It is for this reason, for example, that there are so many different forms of elections and so many varying perspectives on democracy; what unifies these processes is that they all operate to legitimise power. In the United States a president can be elected with fewer votes nationally than those won by an opponent; in the United Kingdom a prime minister usually leads the largest party in the House of Commons, although s/he will only have directly received votes in one of 650 parliamentary constituencies. Both jurisdictions are pointedly different and yet both are often viewed as bastions of democracy, not without irony, as we will discover. As this book proceeds we will begin to appreciate that systems and concepts which appear as legitimate components of the 'natural order of things' are anything but natural.

The perspective which will be taken in this book is that power is directly connected to access to social resources, i.e. the more access to wealth, knowledge and influence possessed by an institution or an individual, the greater the power they will possess. We will primarily be focussed on the power of institutions, and many of the analyses which comprise the subsequent chapters will concentrate on ascendant institutions such as the government or the media and how they maintain, solidify and increase their power. In particular, we will focus on the role of language in these processes, thinking about how institutions use language in various ways to make themselves legitimate in the eyes of society. How power operates in practice can be somewhat more complex than simply the potential for good or bad. Some necessary theory and important terms in the next section will help to explain how power can be viewed as a legitimising process. Once this is established, the principles and practice of Critical Discourse Analysis will make much more sense.

1.2.1 Power as Domination and Persuasion

In order to fully understand the inter-relationship between power and language, it is necessary to first set some theoretical parameters for how power will be understood in this book. We will discuss two very useful types of power in this section, classified by Scott (2001) as 'mainstream' and 'second stream' power. The mainstream view of power correlates with a general, fairly one-dimensional definition of power-as-domination whilst the slightly more complex second stream concentrates on power-as-persuasion.

The mainstream view of power-as-domination represents how many people in non-scholarly contexts might define power and has its origins in traditional perspectives on the power of nation states.

> Actors seek to make others do what they would otherwise not do, and they resist the attempts of others to make them act in ways contrary to their own preferences [...] power relations are seen as asymmetrical, hierarchical relations of super- and sub-ordination in which one agent can gain only at the expense of another. They must be seen in the conflicting interests and goals of the participants and the ability of some to secure the compliance of others.
> (Scott, 2001:6)

This view of power is based on the work of German sociologist Max Weber ([1914] 1978), whose theory of bureaucracy continues to inform social scientific thinking on the power of premodern and modern nation states. Importantly for the understanding of power we are aiming to build here, Weber's focus on the corrective power of the state also recognises the power of institutions such as businesses, the legal system and the church. From a mainstream perspective of power, states and these associated institutions secure the compliance of others through control and dominance. Each of these institutions possesses traditional authority over people and often has the ability to punish non-compliance or resistance.

In order to undertake critical linguistic work, or indeed any critical scholarly work, into the operation of power in society, the second stream view of power-as-persuasion is equally if not more relevant:

> According to this view, power is the collective property of whole systems of cooperating actors, of the fields of social relations within which particular actors are located. At the same time, it stresses not the repressive aspects of power but the 'facilitative' or productive aspects. Of particular importance are the communal mechanisms that result from the cultural, ideological, or discursive formations through which consensus is constituted.
>
> (Scott, 2001:9)

In this definition Scott stresses the importance of power as 'facilitative' and 'communal'. This is a perspective of power relations which transcends the limited notion that power is merely enacted from above by powerful institutions. Instead this view recognises power as persuasive and emanating from consent within society. This is not to say that there is no distinction between influential institutions and those over whom they exert control, rather the second stream view of power stipulates that the processes of this control are much more subtle than a group of powerful organisations bluntly controlling less dominant groups or individuals. This more subtle, persuasive process is represented by the work of Italian communist Antonio Gramsci (1971) and his principle of 'hegemony'. Hegemony refers to the ways in which powerful groups persuade subordinates of the importance and legitimacy of their moral, cultural and economic principles. It is through these principles that powerful groups maintain their position; persuading people that these values are legitimate and natural is much more effective than simply imposing a set of values through control and dominance. In Gramsci's model there is a relationship between powerful and less powerful groups. Powerful groups persuade those with less power of the legitimacy of socio-cultural values which inevitably serve and reinforce their position of control:

> Every State is ethical in as much as one of its most important functions is to raise the great mass of the population to a particular cultural and moral level, a level which corresponds to the needs of the productive forces for development, and hence to the interests of the ruling classes.
>
> (Gramsci, 1971:258)

So, in Gramsci's view the 'interests of the ruling classes' persuade the 'great mass of population' of the legitimacy of principles which essentially maintain a hierarchical status quo. You might consider, for example, how often a significant number of people seriously question the legitimacy of the system of government, regardless of personal political alignments, or genuinely question concepts like 'law and order' or the various prevailing systems of taxation. That is not to say that these forces are malevolent in all contexts, but it is important to acknowledge that neither are they naturally occurring. The second stream view of power recognises that these systems are constructed ideologically through processes which persuade people of their legitimacy and apparent 'naturalness'. Critical discourse analysts therefore refer to the processes of 'legitimisation' and 'naturalisation' in order to note that as power relations are constructed ideologically, they can also be deconstructed to expose and demystify those guiding ideologies. At the centre of Gramsci's theory of hegemony is the fact that these ideologies are routinely ingrained by the institutions of civil society so that they are generally conceived as 'common sense'. The position adopted in this book is that 'common sense' is constructed in a routine fashion to secure the legitimacy and acceptance of ideologies which prop up powerful groups which rely on a hierarchical and largely unfair organisation of the social world. Critical Discourse Analysis is the field of scholarship which recognises that just as language is utilised by powerful groups in securing and maintaining control, so too can linguistic analysis be used to expose this process.

Therefore a critical discourse view of language, which will be explained in more detail shortly, recognises the role which is played by language and other communicative systems in the process of the legitimisation of power. Powerful groups operate consistently to solidify and expand their position. This is achieved through the construction of networks or alliances with other powerful groups, through maintaining institutions which retain a capacity for coercion, such as the police force and the legal system, and through generating consent through language. Consent refers to the fact that subordinate subjects internalise and accept values of powerful groups and hence construct an 'interface at which power is jointly produced' (Statham, 2016:20). Rather than just by dominance and control or through the capacity to restrain and punish, much of the power-building work in this second stream view of power is done through language which is ideologically constructed for the purpose. Critical Discourse Analysis is the tradition of linguistic analysis which seeks to expose how these ideologies have been constructed in language at various levels; viewing language as ideologically loaded and operating persuasively in the interests of powerful groups is to recognise language as 'discourse'.

1.2.2 Discourse and Ideology

So far we have established that power in society operates through a network of domination and consent. As the above outline explains, this is slightly more complex than simply viewing power as something possessed by dominant institutions and exerted over society in general. Instead, society is drawn into the process of power by being persuaded of the common-sense legitimacy of dominant systems and institutions. Discourse plays a key role in this process. As Mayr (2008:8) points out, 'In democratic systems power needs to be legitimate to be accepted by the people. This is generally expressed in symbolic forms by means of language: institutions legitimate themselves with regard to citizens. It is discourse that justifies official action of an institution or the institution itself.'

It should be fairly clear at this early stage, then, that there is an intimate relationship between power and **discourse**, and so it is also necessary to understand discourse as having a somewhat specialised meaning in the context of CDA. In most lay contexts discourse tends to be a synonym of 'language', and the terms are often used interchangeably. However, in critical linguistics, indeed in a range of cognate disciplines such as sociology or politics, discourse is thought of as having a purpose in the social world. Simpson, Mayr and Statham (2018:5) make a clear distinction between 'language' and 'discourse':

> Basically *discourse* is what happens when language 'gets done'. Whereas *language* refers to the more abstract set of patterns and rules which operate simultaneously at different levels in the system (the grammatical, semantic and phonological levels, for example), *discourse* refers to the instantiation of those patterns in real contexts of use. In other words, discourse works above the level of grammar and semantics to capture what happens when these language forms are played out in different social, political and cultural arenas.
>
> (Simpson, Mayr and Statham, 2018:5)

Discourse therefore means somewhat more than how we might use the term 'language'. Whilst the latter is an abstract system which has no meaning *per se* out of context, discourse is interconnected with real contexts of use; it refers to how language is used ideologically in the social organisation of society. Machin and Mayr (2012:20) explain that a 'text's linguistic structure functions, as discourse, to highlight certain ideologies, whilst downplaying or concealing others'. When we view language as discourse we are paying attention to how it operates ideologically and we are questioning the principles which are legitimised through language use. A short, introductory example will make the point clearer.

The headline below is from a British national newspaper in October 2010 and refers to an industrial dispute within the civil service:

Public sector cuts make strikes inevitable, warn unions

Without setting out any specific model of analysis at this stage (although see Chapter 6 for more in-depth examples of this type of analysis), we can say that in this headline the trade unions are represented as attributing clear blame for strike action, and by issuing a warning they have an interest in avoiding the strikes. Before reading on, have a go at the student task.

POWER IN LANGUAGE: PRINCIPLES OF CDA

> **Student Task**
>
> The media, like any institution, has a number of linguistic options available for the representation of an incident. Can you think of any other ways in which the headline could have been represented linguistically? Do you think you could change the ideological position of this headline by changing only one word in the sentence?

The two sentences below are possible responses to the task where only the second verb in the headline has been changed; otherwise the sentence structure and the wording are identical.

Public sector cuts make strikes inevitable, claim unions
Public sector cuts make strikes inevitable, threaten unions

Despite the similarities of the language, the meaning of these sentences has been changed quite a bit. In the first sentence the validity of the unions' position is more uncertain: they are now merely making a claim rather than issuing a warning. The second sentence is a markedly more negative representation of the unions. Rather than an assessment of the situation, they are positioned as the subject of an altogether more aggressive verb phrase by issuing a threat.

You might be able to make an informed guess about which publications would represent trade unions in these ways based on their position on the political spectrum of the media in various jurisdictions (see further Chapter 6). The point is that in all cases the representation of the dispute has come with some form of ideology encoded into the sentence. Regardless of what your own position might be in terms of trade union politics or whether you are more aligned with the principles of the Left or the Right, you cannot claim that any of these sentences is a neutral representation. When you completed the task, you had an ideological agenda in mind, so you have not acted neutrally. The real headline here is from *The Guardian*, a centre-left British publication. So, discourse is about language in context; it is about how we think of language when it comes loaded with ideology. A central aim of CDA is to use linguistic analysis to lay bare the ideological positions which underlie the discourse of powerful institutions such as the media.

It is a central position of this book, and indeed of CDA in general, that language is part of political and socio-cultural contexts. It is influenced by and in turn influences ideology. Therefore a view of language as neutral or merely factual in a political sense is wholly rejected here. The view of **ideology** adopted in this book is that ideology operates in a close inter-relationship with the interests of social groups or institutions. Again, there is a somewhat one-dimensional view of ideology which operates in non-scholarly or non-critical contexts where ideology simply refers to the beliefs of individuals or groups. This view

9

is somewhat inadequate for our purposes because essentially it does not say enough about the role of ideology in light of power relations in society or in terms of the networks of domination and persuasion outlined above.

The view of ideology as operating closely with the interests of powerful groups has its origins in Marxist theory (Marx [1933] 1965), which views ideology as part of the subjugation of the proletariat by the aristocracy or the bourgeoisie. Ideology has come to be viewed slightly more broadly as a belief system possessed by social groups who operate in a range of ways, including linguistically, to maintain and legitimise their power and influence. Often this involves using language to legitimise belief systems so that powerful institutions can continue to flourish. For example, you might consider how your own relationship as students with your higher education institution is consistently cast in a narrative of consumerism, wherein students are encouraged to view themselves as customers who are 'buying' what is increasingly, and euphemistically, billed as the 'student experience'. By reinforcing a belief system in which education is viewed as a commodity instead of a service, universities are in turn strengthening their institutional ability to continue what has in late modernity become a relentless pursuit of profit. Discourse has been at the heart of this strategy. We will return to the marketisation of education in extended examples in Chapters 2 and 5, and consider specifically the linguistic ways in which universities have embraced a dedication to profit over a responsibility to learning. But for now this is a good example of how language operates ideologically to strengthen belief systems which serve the interests of higher education institutions.

1.3 Critical Discourse Analysis: In Principle

The overview above sets out the major theories which underlie the view of language as discourse, in which it operates ideologically in social contexts. Critical Discourse Analysis is a field of study which recognises the interconnectedness of discourse, power and ideology and seeks to expose, and indeed to challenge, the role of powerful networks that maintain and reinforce a hierarchical and stratified organisation of society. Critical discourse analysts investigate the language produced by a wide range of institutions – the media, politics, the legal system, education and advertising, to note just a few – and in a wide spectrum of different textual modes – the visual and the aural alongside the written, and indeed in some cases all three – in order to reveal the ideologies which underpin dominant discourses in the social world. In short, CDA addresses the language which operates to construct the very principles through which we live our lives. This section will set out the origins of CDA and review the main principles which drive its proponents, which Fairclough (2015) has very purposefully called its manifesto. Chapter 2 will demonstrate how close linguistic analysis can achieve these aims.

Using linguistics to examine the ideologies of socio-political texts has its origins in 'critical linguistics', a term coined by Roger Fowler to classify the classic publication *Language and Control* (Fowler et al., 1979). Critical linguistics is generally viewed as the precursor to CDA, as these scholars sought to demonstrate how semantics and grammar in particular operate as ideological tools in social discourse. By focussing on how people and events are classified in texts and by close analysis of foregrounded and backgrounded elements, it is possible to draw quite significant conclusions about the ideologies which are carried by these texts. A classic example of the study of print media, which has come to form the backbone of many studies in CDA, is Tony Trew's chapter in *Language and Control*, 'Theory and Ideology at Work' (Trew, 1979:94–117). In this chapter Trew analyses two divergent media representations of the same event to demonstrate that neither are neutral and that both carry particular ideologies.

We shall not replicate Trew's analysis in full here, but a brief demonstration of his findings makes the point quite clearly. In focussing on two newspaper reports of civil disobedience in pre-independence Rhodesia which appeared on 2nd June 1975, Trew demonstrates that how this event was represented in the discourse of *The Times*, the so-called 'paper of record', which is largely politically conservative in its outlook, was markedly different ideologically from its representation in the left-leaning *The Guardian*. Try the task before reading on.

Student Task

Headline 1: Rioting Blacks Shot Dead by Police as ANC Leaders Meet

Headline 2: Police Shoot 11 Dead in Salisbury Riots

Which headline was produced by *The Times* and which by *The Guardian*? What impressions of the language of each headline contribute to your decision?

You are correct if you attributed Headline 1 to *The Times*. This headline foregrounds the role of 'Blacks', who are placed in the subject-initial position in this passivised sentence. The subject of the verb 'to shoot' is the 'Police', but their role is backgrounded by this syntactic construction. The 'Blacks' are also classified as rioters. Headline 2 is from *The Guardian*. Here the syntax carries a different ideological focus; the active role of the police is given appropriate prominence in the sentence whilst there is no reference whatsoever to rioting. Indeed, in the lead sentence which follows this headline, the phrase 'African demonstrators' is used. *The Times*, as a generally conservative newspaper which is much more ideologically welded to the maintenance of empire and colonialism than the more progressive *The Guardian*, seeks to linguistically reconstruct this event in such a way that culpability lies with the eleven dead demonstrators and not with the police.

This type of analysis, which compares different representations of the same event, is a very useful illustrative tool when explicating the 'critical' principles of CDA and critical linguistics which pre-dates it, and often proves a very popular assignment choice for students. In the years since the publication of *Language and Control*, newspapers and other media outlets remain hugely ideological (see further Chapter 6). With the comments above on how to begin thinking about critical language analysis of newspaper headlines in mind, try the task below. The two headlines were both produced on 22nd February 2018 and relate to industrial action taken by university lecturers whose pensions are under threat by the same market forces which now dominate higher education referred to above. Have a go at the task before reading the analysis below.

Student Task

Headline 1: More than 100,000 university and college students demand £1300 for cancelled classes as the Home Secretary tells striking lecturers to 'get back to work' after pensions walkout

Headline 2: University lecturers begin strike action over pensions. University and College Union sees good turnout on picket lines despite freezing weather

One of these headlines is from *The Guardian* and the other from the right wing *Daily Mail*. Carry out a lexical-semantic analysis of the headlines. What can you say about the ideologies which are present?

In your analysis you might have noted that Headline 1 is very clearly focussed on the financial implications of this industrial action. The headline constructs an opposition between students and lecturers, with the interests of the former being supported by the Home Secretary. You may also have noted here the presence of an ideology which measures education by cost. 'University and college students' are the subject of the verb 'demand', and a link is constructed between these students and the government as the Home Secretary 'tells' lecturers to 'get back to work'. Students and government are linked by similar verbal acts; they both require some sort of restitution. Students and government seem to be on the same side. The phrase 'pensions walkout', linked later in the article to the phrase 'mass walkout', suggests that the lecturers' actions are somewhat less considered and more abrupt than the long period of ballots, campaigns and negotiations which precede strike action would suggest. Our analysis can conclude, then, that this publication constructs a view of an industrial dispute which is selfish on the part of lecturers and ultimately detrimental to students, whose first priority is to recoup lost fees rather than 'cancelled classes'.

Headline 2 is focussed exclusively on lecturers and the initial success of the action. 'Strike action' and 'picket lines' cast the incident in much more official terms than 'walkout'. This action was preceded by the usual process of balloting members of the University and College Union, and giving this official title also serves to legitimise the strike. Lecturers are presented as measured and essentially dedicated to their position in this headline. It is always necessary when carrying out discourse analysis, even a brief and introductory one such as this, to consider what is omitted as well as what is present in a text. Whilst Headline 1 is focussed on the cost to students, there is no reference to either of these elements in the second headline, which is more ideologically approving of the action undertaken by lecturers. The divergent ideologies in these headlines are reinforced throughout the subsequent articles. Taking account of these features of language in the student task should have made it relatively easy for you to decide which of these headlines is from the *Daily Mail* (Headline 1) and which is from *The Guardian* (Headline 2).

A key principle which was developed in critical linguistics and remains at the core of CDA is the theory of language as a social practice. Hodge and Kress (1988, 1993) consistently argue that language is at the centre of how societies are regulated and maintained, and part of the way institutions naturalise and legitimise their principles and values. They point out that the 'rules and norms which govern linguistic behaviour have a social function, origin and meaning' (Hodge and Kress, 1993:204). This position mirrors closely the conclusions reached by Trew in his seminal analysis outlined here:

> A complete understanding of the ideological nature in the coverage of the media must in the end be based not only on an understanding of what the sources in the news are, and their relation to the state and other powers, but also on an understanding of the engagement of the newspapers and other media with social relations and processes.
>
> (Trew, 1979:116)

Trew explains that an important part of discourse, such as that produced in the media, is its 'engagement' with the wider social world. Critical Discourse Analysis has developed this notion of engagement somewhat further so that language is now understood as part of the social process itself. Rather than merely a relationship of engagement, we think of powerful institutions as having an internal and dialectical relationship with social realities. They engage with the social world through language, and this shapes, maintains and reinforces both society and in turn this language itself. As Fairclough (2001) puts it:

> What exactly does this [language as a form of social practice] imply? Firstly, that language is part of society and not somehow external to it. Secondly that language is a social process. And thirdly, that language is a socially conditioned process, conditioned that is by (non-linguistic) parts of society.
>
> (Fairclough, 2001:19)

Fairclough insists at several points throughout his work on CDA that a fundamental tenet of the discipline is that linguistic phenomena are social and social phenomena are linguistic; language does not exist externally to the social world which it constructs and maintains but rather it must be thought of as an integral part of that world. So when critical discourse analysts and proponents of CDA refer to the 'dialectical relationship' between language and society, they mean that society is affected by the language which describes it and that the form of this language is in turn affected by this function.

Think about this relationship when considering the negative position of the *Daily Mail* towards the higher education pension strike in the task and discussion above. The discourse is constructed in such a way that readers of the *Mail* will adopt an unsympathetic view of lecturers. In turn, the unsympathetic and ideologically driven view of the *Mail*, and of its owners and advertisers (see further Chapter 6), accounts for the negative discourse. The ideology drives the linguistic representation at the same time as the linguistic representation reinforces the ideology. CDA is therefore particularly focussed on how and why linguistic features are produced in institutional discourse.

So CDA builds significantly upon the foundations laid by critical linguistics in viewing language itself as a form of social practice and is motivated to set discourse in context. This motivation points to another of the fundamental principles of CDA, that it is openly committed to political intervention and social change. As you may have been able to extrapolate already from some of the short examples and tasks in this chapter and will appreciate quite clearly by the end of this book, CDA does not cling to the concept of objective or neutral analysis but rather it is committed to using linguistic analysis in a way that contributes to the potential redressing of the imbalances which pervade society. Bloor and Bloor (2007:4) state that the 'critical discourse analyst does not attempt the type of objectivity that is sometimes claimed by scientists or linguists, but recognises that such objectivity is likely to be impossible because of the nature of their experience'. In investigating the ideological role of language and in proffering linguistic analysis as a way to increase awareness of and present potential change to prejudice and the misuse of power, it would be somewhat naïve to claim that an analyst is a disinterested or objective participant who is engaged in a solely scholarly process. Fairclough (2010:10) is adamant that, despite the practice of CDA being somewhat broad in its application, this motivation to political intervention is one of three general characteristics which unites work in the field. He suggests that 'research and analysis counts as CDA in so far as it has all of the following characteristics':

1. It is not just analysis of discourse (or more concretely texts), it is part of some form of transdisciplinary analysis of relations between discourse and other elements of the social process.
2. It is not just general commentary on discourse, it includes some form of systematic analysis of text.

3. It is not just descriptive, it is also normative. It addresses social wrongs in their discursive aspects and possible ways of righting or mitigating them.

(Fairclough, 2010:10)

These characteristics of CDA confirm much of what this introductory chapter has set out so far; essentially that CDA proceeds through close textual analysis which recognises the position of language in the social world and that this analysis should not merely focus on the description of prevailing 'social wrongs' but should also look to contribute to correcting them.

1.3.1 Manifesto for CDA

In a seminal paper which demonstrates that CDA is both 'engaged and committed' to pursuing change in a social world hierarchically organised by the powerful, for the powerful, as it were, as well as being 'careful, rigorous and systematic' in the scholarship and analysis it undertakes, Fairclough and Wodak (1997:271–280) set out the central methodological and theoretical principles of CDA:

1. *CDA Addresses Social Problems*: Rather than be an analysis of the use of language alone, CDA focusses on the 'partially linguistic character of social and cultural processes and structures'. Using the neo-capitalist discourse of Thatcherism as an example, Fairclough and Wodak demonstrate that a CDA approach to this discourse develops a critical awareness of its principles – unashamedly approving of free market capitalism and committed to the weakening of institutions of social democracy, particularly trade unions – which in turn provides the analyst with a potential resource to challenge these principles.
2. *Power Relations Are Discursive*: In acknowledging the linguistic nature of power relations, CDA also notes that 'power relations are exercised and negotiated in discourse [...] Discursive aspects of power relations are not fixed and monolithic.' Fairclough and Wodak point to the example of a media interview with a politician; whilst the power in such an interaction rests with the interviewer, who asks questions and should control the topic, politicians also possess what Bourdieu (1997) calls 'cultural capital' of their own. They possess social assets such as education, intellect and influence. Encounters such as a political interview are therefore about 'power in discourse' as well as the more general 'power over discourse'. Resisting and challenging institutional norms in an interview might contribute to an increase in a politician's general grasp on power and influence.
3. *Discourse Constitutes Society and Culture*: This position refers to the dialectical relationship between discourse and society explained above; discourse both constitutes society and culture and is constituted by them. Fairclough and Wodak state that any part of a text simultaneously constitutes representations, relations and identities. This aspect of CDA will be expanded in Chapters 3, 4 and 5 in particular, which set out the relationship between CDA and Systemic Functional Linguistics (SFL).

4. *Discourse Does Ideological Work*: Again, this feature of CDA has been well established already in this chapter, and in Chapter 2 we will see the ideological operation of discourse in action. Fairclough and Wodak state that ideologies are 'particular ways of representing and constructing society which produce unequal relations of power, relations of domination and exploitation'. A key element of CDA, which should be part of the conclusion of any CDA analysis you undertake, is to consider social effects of the ideological work which is done by discourse. Much work in CDA has adopted this approach to expose how discourse constructs dominant ideologies such as racism, classism and sexism in society.
5. *Discourse Is Historical*: This principle essentially reminds the analyst that discourse comes accompanied by context and therefore that context must be taken into consideration when examining the ideological implications of a text. As well as with accompanying socio-cultural knowledge, discourse should also be considered intertextually; that is, with appropriate recognition that discourse is connected to other discourse which has been produced earlier. You might consider aspects of a text like a direct quotation in a media article or reference to the words of an elite or celebrated figure in a political speech. Political discourse will be addressed specifically in Chapters 8 and 9, but generally this type of intertextuality serves to add legitimacy to a speech and to a speaker.
6. *The Link between Text and Society Is Mediated*: CDA is focussed on the connections between text and society, which we have already seen in operation in this chapter. Fairclough and Wodak say that text is characterised by a range of institutional practices. For example, in a hospital the discourse of medical records and patients' notes, and increasingly of administrative documents and managerialist discourse marked by registers of accountancy instead of health and science, characterise the general discourse of the institution. So we can say that the language produced by institutions is mediated by various institutional practices.
7. *Discourse Analysis Is Interpretive and Explanatory*: Fairclough and Wodak acknowledge that the audience of a discourse and the amount of accompanying contextual information can affect the interpretation of that discourse. Aspects like class, gender and age demonstrate that 'understanding takes place against the background of emotions, attitudes and knowledge'. The fact that CDA proceeds by a 'systematic methodology and a thorough investigation of context' means that interpretations take into account the social conditions of the text and its ideological role in organising power relations. CDA is explanatory as well as interpretive because this process inevitably involves self-reflection from the analyst, who is a critical reader rather than a disinterested audience. The example of CDA in Chapter 2 demonstrates that description, interpretation and explanation are all necessary parts of a thorough analysis of discourse.
8. *Discourse Is a Form of Social Action*: CDA is a 'socially committed scientific paradigm' and many proponents and scholars undertake CDA with the intention of changing discourse and patterns of power in certain institutions. Van Dijk (1993) for example exposes potentially racist

language in schoolbooks in the Netherlands, which led directly to the production of new educational materials. Critical discourse analysts have also been actively involved in the analysis of power relations in doctor–patient communication (West, 1990), in exposing and combating sexist language (Cameron, 2001), in examining wrongful convictions in the legal system (Coulthard, 1992; Eades, 1997) and more recently in examining the language of social media (Seargeant and Tagg, 2014) and post-truth politics (Simpson, Mayr and Statham, 2018). And these are only a few of very many examples. CDA has a clear concern about the exercise of power in society.

These principles make it clear that CDA pursues a critical focus on discourse with a politically motivated agenda to expose and challenge the actions of powerful groups. Language is used to disseminate and legitimise, reinforce and naturalise the ideologies of these groups, and critically focussed linguistic analysis can be used in turn to reveal both the processes and motivations of ideological discourse.

As a scholar based in the UK, Fairclough has engaged extensively with the British political environment. The first edition of his influential CDA book *Language and Power* (1989) was written at a time when the malign principles of the Thatcher administration held sway in British politics and had found an ideological bedfellow in the presidency of Ronald Reagan in the United States. When the second edition emerged (Fairclough, 2001) a regime change in Britain had seen the election of a Labour administration, which came to power under the leadership of Tony Blair in 1997. CDA was then focussed on the neo-liberalism and new capitalism of the Blair years, when many of the inequalities which had been concretised under successive Tory regimes were essentially maintained. Fairclough (2000) examines how language was used to construct the perception of change in this period. By the time Fairclough wrote the third edition of *Language and Power* (2015), the financial crash and subsequent global recession had thrust society into a further crisis. The individualist Thatcherite mantra 'There is no such thing as society' was gone and replaced with 'We are all in this together', the disingenuous justification of the Conservative–Liberal Democrat coalition government for austerity aimed at paying off the huge debts of bankers and various forms of venture capitalists. The same mantra has been used by the British government to characterise the response to the coronavirus pandemic in 2020 and 2021 despite the consistent failures of the government to manage the crisis (see further Chapter 9).

1.3.2 Times of Trouble: CDA Today

At the beginning of the global recession in the autumn of 2008, Fairclough (2010) considered the role of CDA in a 'time of crisis'. He suggests that CDA should be focussed not just on the negative critique of systems such as neo-liberalism but also on a positive critique which 'seeks possibilities for transformations which can overcome or mitigate limits on human well-being' (Fairclough, 2010:14). Fairclough rightly viewed the financial crash as not a crisis *in* neo-liberal capitalism but *of* neo-liberal capitalism, and speculated as to the future of the great gulfs in power and influence that had opened up in the years of its prominence. As it turns out, the result of the financial crisis led not to any bridging of these gulfs but rather to their solidification. George Osborne, British Chancellor of the Exchequer in 2010, said that it is 'those who had least to do with the cause of the economic misfortunes who are the hardest hit'. Osborne presumably intended his audience to interpret this statement as a pledge that this time it would be different rather than see it as description of what would happen again under the government of which he was a part. The coalition government poured billions of pounds into the financial institutions which caused the crash whilst poorer sections of society were hit with unemployment and a sustained attack on the welfare system. Welfare claimants and immigrants were vilified across public discourse and massive tuition fees limited access to higher education in a move to re-gentrify the university sector so that critical thinking would be limited. Whilst austerity was aimed squarely at less powerful groups in society, those who caused the financial crisis 'have been allowed to get away with murder' (Fairclough, 2015:4).

In a prophetic speculation as to the long-term effects of this recession, Fairclough (2010:17) considers the possibility of a 'resurgent extreme right' as a consequence of the 'absence of a coherent progressive alternative' in post-recession politics. Reactionary right wing governments have been propelled into power across much of the developed world in the last decade. Even in the worst throes of austerity across Europe and the United States in this period, the most critical and contextually aware amongst us probably could not have predicted the decision of the British electorate in June 2016 to leave the European Union or the election of property developer and reality television personality Donald Trump as forty-fifth President of the United States in November of the same year. In the years since then, right wing populism has grown to a worrying degree in Austria, the Netherlands, France and Italy. The Trump administration in the US, ejected from office in the general election of November 2020, pursued policies from the questionable to the openly racist, and the ruling Conservative Party in Britain has moved so far to the Right that a withdrawal agreement with the European Union proved almost impossible to negotiate. If 2010 was a 'time of crisis' in Fairclough's terms, over a decade later we remain in times of trouble. It is also likely that the effects of the Covid-19 pandemic will make things even worse.

The pandemic has thrown into sharp focus the economic priorities of the Right, where the decisions of politicians to place economic concerns ahead of public health in some jurisdictions have caused hundreds of thousands of deaths. The pandemic has exposed the dangers of underfunding of public health services and the insecure foundations of economic principles which champion the disproportionate distribution of wealth. There is a clear correlation between the level of devastation caused by Covid-19 and the longstanding priorities of elite groups across the world. Much of the more optimistic discourse in this time of emergency has focussed on the need for deep societal change. CDA endorses this need strongly; indeed the message for change is one upon which the discipline was founded. However, this book will also explore the enormous power of institutions and organisations that will continue to stand against the type of change really needed in society and demonstrate that much of the success of such institutions in this period has been achieved through persuasive discourse.

As students beginning to explore the principles and motivations of CDA, you may be forgiven for wondering, given the uncomfortable realities described here, if CDA has perhaps outlived its usefulness. After all, critical discourse analysts have been rallying for decades against injustices in society which seem only to have grown stronger. I would suggest however that a political emergency driven by powerful reactionary forces or a global pandemic which will have long-reaching implications is the worst time for progressive voices to choose to fall silent. Perhaps more so than at any time since its emergence as a scholarly discipline, CDA has a responsibility to continue to expose and challenge the ideologies which underpin the discourse of powerful groups.

This call to continued action also places a burden of responsibility onto the shoulders of new students of linguistics, such as the readers of this book. It has been suggested here that part of the strategy of reactionary regimes to effectively privatise higher education through tuition fees, and indeed to fatten university management systems with people who have been unwaveringly prepared to transform learning into earning, has been to reduce the capacity for and indeed the desire to embrace critical thinking. The fewer people who can access progressive schools of thought like CDA, the better the interests of ascendant groups are served. The interests of these groups are served even more strongly if university students are once again disproportionately representative of socio-economically privileged groups in society. Therefore it is an aim of this book to remind students and new readers of CDA of the importance of the discipline as a progressive alternative to the more divisive forces presently in power across the most powerful countries in the world. This book will enable you to look beyond the surface of the discourse you will encounter, in the media, from the government and political parties, from advertisers, from capitalist university vice chancellors, from instruments of church and state, so that you can access the ideologies which permeate them. In this scenario it is hoped that as critical readers and scholars you will perhaps act not necessarily in line with principles which strengthen division, sexism, racism or classism but instead will look to challenge and undermine them.

Summary of Chapter 1

This chapter has introduced some key terms in CDA. We have discussed the concepts of power and ideology and addressed how discourse plays an important part in their operation in society. CDA is a scholarly approach to the analysis of discourse which pays particular attention to this social role. The manifesto for CDA overviewed in this chapter makes it clear that as critical discourse analysts we also play a part in the political process. It is an inherently political act to analyse discourse with the intention of exposing the ideologies which it constructs and reinforces in society, and Chapter 2 will present Fairclough's three-dimensional model as an important approach to this type of analysis. In the final part of this introductory chapter we make a *cri de coeur* to readers of this book to keep the principles of CDA central to your studies. Chapter 2 and the analyses which follow throughout the remainder of the book will demonstrate how to do this in practice.

Further Reading

Fairclough, N. (2015) *Language and Power*, 3rd edition. London and New York: Routledge.
Fairclough, N. and Wodak, R. (1997) 'Critical Discourse Analysis', in van Dijk, T. (ed.) *Discourse as Social Interaction*. London: Sage, pp.258–285.

2 Power in Language
Practice of Critical Discourse Analysis

KEY TERMS IN CHAPTER 2: text, discursive practice, social practice, intertextuality, interdiscursivity, lexical cohesion, overlexicalisation

MODELS OF ANALYSIS IN CHAPTER 2: three-tiered model of Critical Discourse Analysis

2.1 Introduction: CDA in Practice

In this chapter we will demonstrate how to analyse language as ideologically loaded discourse so that a close description of a text can be developed to also consider interpretation and explanation. By the end of the chapter you will be set firmly on the practical path to Critical Discourse Analysis. There is no one, singular model which is exclusive to CDA. Kress (1990:85) states that the discipline has a 'critical focus, broad scope and overtly political agenda'. Analysts do not claim to be neutral overseers but are motivated by the examination of the ideological operation of institutional discourse. CDA is an inevitably interested and political process, and many critical discourse analysts are actively involved in progressive political movements. Whilst the discipline is generally unified on its overarching principles, there are a number of approaches which are used to pursue the aims of CDA. Fairclough, Wodak and van Dijk are perhaps the most prominent critical discourse analysts, and their influence in the establishment of the discipline has been significant. However, a multitude of approaches to CDA has emerged in the last three decades especially, and the discipline continues to be modified for the analysis of many types of institutional discourse across several modes, such as the analysis of images (see Chapter 10) and the examination of social media (see Chapter 11).

Throughout this book each chapter will introduce a new model of analysis through which the manifesto for CDA overviewed in Chapter 1 can be serviced. These models will demonstrate the analytical diversity of CDA whilst also reinforcing the discipline's core focus on the ideological operation of institutional discourse. As the book proceeds you will engage with a wide range of different types

DOI: 10.4324/9780429026133-3

of discourse; examples will be drawn from diverse areas like the media, political speeches, websites, social media and different types of advertising. Chapters 3, 4 and 5 will provide an in-depth account of the three functions of language in Systemic Functional Linguistics (SFL) (Halliday, 1994). Chapter 6 analyses the use of sources in text and offers a case study of the media to demonstrate the importance of contextual and institutional factors when analysing institutional discourse, which will be discussed throughout the book. Chapter 7 addresses 'race', and Chapters 8 and 9 examine political language, the latter beginning CDA's inevitable engagement with the language of Covid-19. Chapters 10 and 11 will analyse semiotic arenas which transcend text, examining how meaning is communicated in images and online. You will be instructed in several models of analysis in every chapter so that even when the thematic focus of chapters is more specific, they will remain model-led. The main models of analysis and some key terms to which you should pay particular attention are highlighted at the start of each chapter. The analyses are intended to expose the ideological agenda of powerful groups in society and to demonstrate how they are achieved through the use of language. Students will be able to replicate the exercises carried out throughout the book to examine the discourse you encounter in your own lives. Therefore there is no single, homogenous version of CDA, but a number of approaches unified by general, guiding principles. To start us off, a fundamental model offered by Fairclough (1989, 1992, 1995) will be demonstrated.

2.2 Key Model: Three-dimensional Model of CDA

A seminal model for CDA developed by Fairclough (1989, 1992, 1995) operates by a three-stage procedure which accounts for language as **text, discursive practice** and **social practice**. Each of these interrelated levels of analysis corresponds with **description, interpretation** and **explanation**, which are necessary elements in an analysis which recognises the social role of language. We can describe each element and its role in Fairclough's model as follows:

> **Description** is the stage which is concerned with formal properties of the text. Description corresponds to the **text** dimension of the model. This essentially refers to identifying the formal features of a text, such as lexical choices, pronouns and metaphor, for example, and grammatical features, like the favouring of one aspect of a verb over another.
>
> **Interpretation** specifies the **discursive practice** section of the three-tiered model. Interpretation is about viewing text as a product of the processes of production and consumption. Particular attention should be paid here to the different ways in which interaction is achieved in text, specifically through **intertextuality** and **interdiscursivity**. Intertextuality means the presence, either implicitly or explicitly, of other texts. Interdiscursivity refers to strategies for using both formal and informal language in a text. If you

consider these features in terms of the model's requirement to pay appropriate attention to elements of production and consumption, the focus on intertextuality and interdiscursivity should make perfect sense. In a newspaper article, for example, intertextuality comes in the form of sources who are quoted or referred to in the text. This is a quintessential feature of the production of news which must rely on sources to construct the impression of credibility. Of course, the privilege of certain sources over others is itself an ideological choice. Interdiscursivity is important in the consumption of a text by readers. Formal language constructs newsworthy events with an appropriate level of gravitas, whilst more informal language is used to build an alliance with readers.

Explanation refers to the **social practice** dimension of the model. It is concerned with the relationship between interaction and social context. This stage of the analysis considers how the text interacts with ideologies and power relations in wider society. It considers the social context of the discourse and asks about the wider societal effects of its linguistic structures.

Figure 2.1 summarises the basic features of this model. This is a very useful starting point for CDA for a number of reasons. Firstly, the model is very versatile. It is self-contained in that, whilst it requires knowledge of the levels of language (being able to identify verbs and nouns, for example) and assumes some knowledge of grammar, it does not necessarily require knowledge of additional models of analysis, such as transitivity, which will be introduced in Chapter 3, or the Appraisal system, which will be accounted for in Chapter 4. That being said, models of analysis such as transitivity or Appraisal can be integrated into this three-dimensional model of CDA. This book will introduce new models of

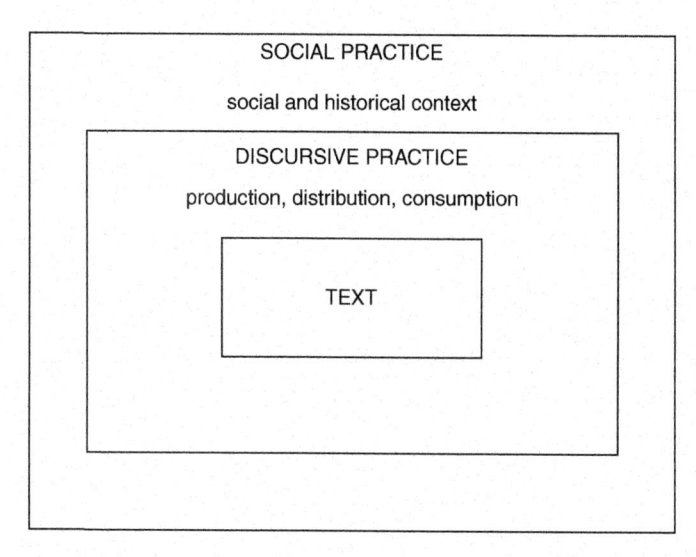

Figure 2.1 Three-dimensional model of CDA

analysis in each chapter. As well as being applied independently, these models can also be integrated into Fairclough's three-dimensional model.

The versatility of this model extends also to the data which is being analysed. Whilst initially focussed on written and spoken textual analysis, contemporary CDA now accounts for the transmission of ideologies through a range of discourse modes, such as the visual and the aural. Institutional discourse, be it in the context of advertising, politics or news, for example, is therefore considered to be 'multimodal', and much of CDA is necessarily multimodal as a result. Kress and van Leeuwen (1996) have a developed a grammar of visual discourse which has been used extensively by critical discourse analysts in carrying out CDA, and Machin and Mayr (2012) provide a comprehensive overview of the importance of visual as well as verbal semiotic choices in contemporary discourse. Chapter 10 of this book will examine Multimodal CDA specifically, and visual meaning is also considered in Chapter 5. Fairclough's three-dimensional model can be applied to visual, spoken and time-based texts as well as to written language.

The most important feature of this model is that its structure is all-encompassing; it transcends the descriptive and pays particular attention to the social role of language. A discursive event is analysed not just as a text but, in line with the principles in the manifesto for CDA, the production of a text and its interpretation within a larger social context are also addressed.

2.3 How to Apply the Three-dimensional Model of CDA

The article below was published in the *Daily Mail* on 19th February 2018 and relates to the industrial action undertaken by university lecturers in February and March 2018 over cuts to a higher education pension scheme. Read carefully the application of the three-dimensional model which follows the article. Alongside the analysis of the article's text, pay particular attention to how the commentary addresses elements of production and expands the discussion to consider how discourse plays a tangible role in society at large.

> **Example 2.1 Students at almost every university may have their exams cancelled as lecturers threaten to strike over pensions dispute**
>
> Union leaders say they will call 'unprecedented' industrial action this summer
>   It's being done deliberately to coincide with exam season as they issue demands

Up to 45,000 academics could walk out at 64 universities, causing cancellations

Students at almost every mainstream university could have their final year exams cancelled or disrupted this year because of striking academics.

Union leaders say they will call 'unprecedented' industrial action in the summer to coincide with exam season if university bosses do not meet their demands in a dispute over pensions.

Up to 45,000 academics could walk out at 64 universities, causing countless exams to be called off.

Students who are unable to take exams may find that their final degree grade is based instead on coursework or exam performance from previous years.

Alternatively, universities may be able to draft in agency staff to replace some of the strikers, or else reschedule exams for later in the summer.

More than 200,000 students in their final years could be affected.

Yesterday some students said it was unfair of academics to bring them into the dispute. Geography student Nick Sundin said: 'I thought it was pensions this was about? Seems selfish to prioritise those over an entire generation of students.'

Chris Price added: 'As always, it's the students who bear the consequences of this selfish action. I have sympathy with their pension situation but striking is not the answer.'

Students across many campuses are demanding compensation of tuition fees and say the lost 14 days will equate to £1,295 worth of lost teaching per person.

Proposed changes to the sector pension scheme mean academics are set to lose up to half their retirement income, according to analysis by experts.

The University and College Union (UCU), which represents academics and campus staff, is already holding four weeks of strikes beginning this Thursday which they say will affect one million students in the institutions covered by the action.

Lecturers will refuse to teach on 14 strike days spread across this period, with classes cancelled and marking left undone. The strikes will take place in mostly older, research-intensive universities, including 22 out of 24 in the elite Russell Group.

Academics will walk out from institutions including Cambridge, Oxford, UCL, Bristol, Cardiff, Durham, Exeter, Glasgow, Imperial College, Leeds, Manchester, Newcastle, Queen's Belfast, Sheffield, Southampton, Warwick and York.

If the union does not have a concession from the universities by March 2 it will consider 'further action' in the summer, since the strike mandate lasts six months.

> Students are already threatening to sue universities for the potential damage the strike will cause to their education.
>
> UCU general secretary Sally Hunt urged new Education Secretary Damian Hinds to intervene to end the strikes by telling vice-chancellors to give her members a fair deal.
>
> She said: 'I'm devastated students will be affected by this. They're in the middle because we haven't had a negotiation. What we've had is an imposition.'
>
> Universities UK, which represents vice-chancellors, said in November it would stop offering staff traditional 'defined benefit' pensions, which offer a certainty of income in retirement. Instead, it wants to shift staff into a riskier, less generous 'defined contribution' plan, to help deal with rising costs as many private sector companies have done.
>
> A Universities UK spokesman said: 'We hope employees recognise changes are necessary to put the scheme on a secure footing, and the proposed strike action will only serve to unfairly disrupt students' education.'
>
> (*Daily Mail*, 19th February 2018)

Text

Analysis of text logically commences with a focus on the headline of an article. Headlines are defined by Bell (1991:189) as 'part of news rhetoric whose function is to attract the reader', and Iarovici and Amel (1989:443) state that headlines have a dual function, 'a semantic function regarding the referential text and a pragmatic function regarding the reader (the receiver) to whom the text is addressed'. So, headlines operate semantically to indicate the content of an article; they give the essence of what it is about. Connected to this, they perform a pragmatic function which attracts the reader. Interestingly, headlines are not usually written by the journalist who writes the accompanying copy, but normally they are written by sub-editors who abstract the story to a short summarising sentence or group of sentences with both the semantic and pragmatic function of the headline in mind. Thus, the production of headlines is a significantly ideological process. In this article the headline is thematically focussed on the effect of the impending industrial action on students. The verb 'threaten' is attributed to lecturers, who are therefore cast as aggressive actors from the beginning of the article. Lecturers also 'walk out' and 'issue demands' in the sub-headlines. Linguistic strategies which are prevalent throughout this article commence in the headline and sub-headlines. The ideological position of the publication on the issue of industrial action is established clearly and augmented throughout the article. The industrial action being proposed is 'unprecedented' and 'being done deliberately to coincide with exam season'; the strike is constructed as an action taken by lecturers to the specific detriment of students. The word 'pensions' is only mentioned once amidst the disproportionate focus on examinations.

An important function of vocabulary in an article is that it constructs **lexical cohesion**. Lexical cohesion refers to the repetition and reiteration of words which are linked in meaning and which serve therefore to consistently define certain features of an incident or event (see further Chapter 5 for an extensive account of cohesion). 'Unprecedented' and 'demands' are repeated in the second paragraph, whilst the cohesive focus of effect on examinations is also consistent throughout the article, with 'cancelled', 'cancellations', 'called off' and 'disrupted' all appearing in the first three paragraphs of the piece. Cohesion is also achieved by the use and repetition of selective statistics in this article; '45,000 academics' and '64 universities' appear in the sub-headlines and are repeated immediately at the top of the main text. There are also references to '200,000 students', 'lost 14 days', '£1,295 worth of lost teaching', 'one million students', '14 strike days' and '22 out of 24 in the elite Russell Group'. Again, note the lexical focus on the effect of the action on students and, very tellingly, student fees. In an article ostensibly about lecturers' pensions, one might expect some financial explanation of that issue or that a monetary value might be attributed to the lost pension income at the core of this dispute, but instead there are no statistics offered on these points whatsoever. It is acknowledged in the tenth paragraph that 'academics are set to lose up to half their retirement income', but the changes to the pension scheme are qualified as being 'proposed', and the effect on academics is 'according to analysis by experts' who the *Mail* specifically chooses not to imbue with the status of even a name.

This vague and unattributed assessment of the higher education pension dispute is textually important for a number of reasons. In terms of the structure of the article, this information is only offered after a clear narrative of 'selfish' and aggressive academics has been constructed. The singular focus on the effect of the strike on student examinations is also an example of **overlexicalisation**, a pragmatic strategy which encodes ideologies in news discourse by a lexical focus on an aspect of a particular event which is disproportionate to reality. The reason that this focus is disproportionate is not because student examinations are not important but rather it is because this outcome is wholly hypothetical. Potential industrial action in the summer term of the 2017/18 academic year was one of several tactics of the University and College Union (UCU) if an agreement could not be reached between the parties after or during the strike action. This context is not provided until the eleventh paragraph, after a cohesive and overlexicalised, statistics-heavy narrative of 'unprecedented' action by 'demanding' and 'selfish' lecturers at 'elite' institutions has been constructed. As it happens, a tentative agreement was reached following the fourteen days of strike action, and summer examinations in 2017/18 were in no way affected by the strike. The beginning of the article does come with the appropriate modality, with modal verbs such as 'may' and 'could' (see further Chapter 4); however, the ideological position of the publication is clear.

Our analysis of the text of this article reveals that a structural opposition between students and lecturers is constructed. The publication attempts to establish that the former will be adversely affected by the actions of the latter. Structural oppositions refer to the construction of distinctions between classes or concepts. Halliday (1978, 1985) reminds us that, as well as words possessing their own meaning in context, the lexicon of a text also forms a network of meaning; words can bring with them 'related clusters of concepts' (Machin and Mayr, 2012:39). The overlexicalisation of this article constructs an opposition between lecturers and students, between the apparent self-interest of academics and the financial value of examinations and degrees. Consider for example the first paragraph of the main body of the article:

> Students at almost every mainstream university could have their final year exams cancelled or disrupted this year because of striking academics.

The syntax or sentence structure here is somewhat non-standard. The sentence is an example of what Chapter 3 will define as a Relational process, in which one entity in a sentence – 'Students at almost every mainstream university' in this case – is 'related' in some way to another entity by equivalence, possession or circumstance – 'their final year exams cancelled or disrupted' in this sentence. Throughout the article students' education is related consistently to exams, which will be noted in the social practice commentary below. The threat to these exams is attributed directly to 'striking academics' through the causal phrase 'because of'.

Student Task

Thinking again about the sentence 'Students at almost every mainstream university could have their final year exams cancelled or disrupted this year because of striking academics', can you rewrite this sentence in a way that represents a different ideology?

You might consider changing the focus from examinations to education or attributing the blame for the industrial dispute elsewhere.

Often a useful exercise in CDA, especially given the motivation for the analysis to expose ideology in a text, is to consider other ways in which sentences might be rendered. Try the student task before reading the commentary on sentences i, ii and iii, which are suggested solutions.

Here are some examples of how you might have addressed the task:

i. Student examinations could be affected this summer because of the decision of Universities UK to devalue academic pensions.
ii. The education of university students is affected as academics are forced to strike over devaluation of pension scheme.

iii. Students at almost every mainstream university could have their final year examinations cancelled or disrupted because of the refusal of wealthy vice chancellors to compromise over academic pensions.

The first sentence offers a somewhat more innocuous verb in 'affected' than 'cancelled' or 'disrupted'; it retains the causal phrase and maintains the structural opposition but this time attributes culpability to Universities UK (UUK). The second sentence focusses on the 'education' of students rather than assessing the value of university merely in terms of fees and examinations, and mitigates academics as being 'forced' to strike. Through 'devaluation' it also offers some context to the dispute, which does not come until the tenth paragraph in the article. The third sentence replicates the original but attributes responsibility to the ideologically driven actions of university managers rather than to aggressive academics. Each of these sentences refers to the same event but each carries a very different ideological position. An exercise like this reminds the analyst to acknowledge that no sentence in discourse is neutral, including ones with which you might feel allegiance. The sentences above might perhaps appear in a more left-leaning publication, but they are ideological nonetheless, constructed with a particular motivation in mind. Examining how a publication has *not* constructed an event can be very useful in exposing for the analyst the ideological position which is being taken.

The clear agency attributed to lecturers in this article is also constructed grammatically. Lecturers are the subject of active verbs throughout the piece, 'Lecturers will refuse...' and 'Academics will walk out...', for example. Students are also given agency in some ideologically important sentences in the article, 'demanding compensation of tuition fees' and 'threatening to sue universities'. Clauses like these appear to attribute some blame to institutions for the strike, but even here a certain ideological position is reinforced. Universities are cast as businesses and education as a commodity. The construction of 'learning-to-earn' which has dominated higher education in late modernity and has been aggressively pursued by successive governments in Britain and beyond in recent decades is clear in this article.

The analysis of the first dimension of Fairclough's three-dimensional model should be focussed on identifying important features of the text, such as the nouns and verbs used, as in the discussion above. Obviously not every article will include every feature which may be textually significant. The article here proceeds largely by a strategy of overlexicalisation at the level of text, for example, but there are a number of other features which may be important in the analysis of other discourse examples. These will all be addressed in relevant parts of the book, but you should also consider whether or not metaphors are used (see further Chapter 8), and consider the evaluative meanings of certain words. This is addressed somewhat in the account above but will be elaborated on in Chapter 4. In terms of grammar, whilst the majority of sentences in this article are active, that is, they follow a standard subject-verb-object (SVO) structure with the agent of the verb clearly identifiable, it is also important to note patterns of passive sentences in discourse. The process of passivisation, in which the object of a verb is moved to the sentence-initial position and the subject to the usual object position after the verb, is often very ideological. This process will be discussed in greater detail in Chapter 3. Patterns of pronouns are also important in many pieces of discourse; how 'we' and 'you' are used to construct alliances and oppositions within a text and between a writer and a reader – the 'text encoder' and the 'text decoder' respectively – can suggest a lot about the ideological position of the text.

Discursive Practice

We have been able to offer a detailed description of the *Daily Mail* article at the first stage of the CDA model and to make some well-informed contentions about the dominant ideological position of the newspaper on this industrial action, industrial action in general and, particularly, about education as a marketised commodity. The second stage of the model, discursive practice, considers the processes involved in the production, distribution and consumption of, in this case, news discourse. These considerations can be slightly more complex than you might assume and will be examined at length in Chapter 6. Obviously, there is a straightforward enough trajectory which can be drawn from a journalist who compiles a story to a reader who consumes it; however, these actors in the process are only part of a network of production and consumption. Bell (1991) reminds us that multiple parties contribute to the production of the product which appears in print as a newspaper or online article. The ideological finished product, as it were, emerges with other concerns, such as the likely position of advertisers or a newspaper's corporate owners, in mind (see further Chapter 6).

One important process of production in the media is the gathering of information from a range of sources. A reporter may interview or attend the news conferences of a multitude of sources, for example. Usually not all of these, and certainly not in their full unedited form, will appear in an article, but rather sources can be chosen to reinforce the ideological position of the piece. Quotations from sources is the main way in which intertextuality is realised in the media. In keeping with the casting of this strike as less about the devaluation of academic pensions and more about its effect on students, the first two quotations, in the seventh and eighth paragraphs respectively, are from students. 'Geography student Nick Sundin' is seemingly unable to reconcile a pension dispute with industrial action, stating that lecturers 'seem selfish'. Lexical cohesion is achieved by the selection of another quotation, from Chris Price, which defines the strike as a 'selfish action' and goes further in categorically stating that 'striking is not the answer'. These quotations, although we concede that they may be only a snippet of what the two students said, offer the same narrow view of the strike as pursued by the *Daily Mail*, and they are given priority over the statements from Sally Hunt, General Secretary of the UCU in 2018, and a 'spokesman' from Universities UK. Sally Hunt offers a defence of the UCU's position, stating that she is 'devastated that students will be affected by this'. This quotation does allow the union to offer some explanation for the action and casts blame squarely on an 'imposition' rather than a 'negotiation'. Universities UK is also permitted a counter, which essentially ends the article as it began, with unreasonable academics. UUK make a categorical assertion that 'changes are necessary to put the scheme on a secure footing' and reassert that the strike is an action against students. The *Mail* acknowledges that the proposed changes are 'riskier' but also offers mitigation in acknowledging the 'rising costs' of the pension scheme.

What unifies the content of both the text dimension and the discursive practice section of this article, and what is representative of many ideological pieces of news discourse especially, is the very limited context which is included in the text. This permits the construction of this industrial dispute in a very specific ideological way in this article and brings us to the third stage of the CDA model, social practice.

Social Practice

Social practice is about social context. At this third stage of the analysis we consider the social context of the discourse and ask about the wider societal effects of its linguistic structures. We have analysed these structures in the first dimension of the model and thought about how they operate intertextually and interdiscursively in the second stage. The third stage is where we tie together these findings, where we consider how what this article says about higher education will inform the principles and practices of its readers.

As has been pointed out already, this article reinforces the prominent neo-liberal view of higher education as a commodity. From this perspective, higher education is something which students pay for as consumers and which academics should therefore deliver as service providers. A failure to provide this service would result in a refund, just like how you might seek a refund for a faulty product. This view is clearly identifiable in the position of the government, UUK and students, according to this article. Whilst on the surface the article is solely about the pensions dispute, the position adopted by the *Mail* and reinforced at the text and discursive practice dimension of the discourse contributes to the consistent strengthening of an ideological position which continuously portrays higher education as being about earning over learning. At the social practice stage of the model of CDA, we can also extend specific conclusions to consider how they relate to general ideologies in society at large. The construction of higher education in this article contributes to an overall vindication of capitalism, where individuals are responsible for their own progression, where employees do not possess inherent value beyond their primary tasks within an institution and where institutions, including those in the education or health services, view achievement in monetary terms.

These principles are distributed and strengthened through language in the social world on an almost daily basis. It is important that, when you consider the examples offered throughout this book, you do not view them in isolation, rather the discourse examples should be thought of as representative of the institutional language which is consistently at work in society. This article, for example, is representative of many articles which appeared in the right wing press in Britain throughout this dispute. Prominent broadsheets the *Daily Telegraph* and *The Times* alongside the *Daily Mail* covered this strike in detail, and the language of their articles consistently reinforced a dominant view of higher education as a commodity.

If you are a student in UK higher education today, you will be painfully aware that student fees are at their highest and government financial aid has been significantly curtailed. You may also have noticed a narrative which 'sells' the 'university experience' to students which is constantly reinforced in discourse through references to employability, entrepreneurship and earning power (see further Chapter 5). Students are cast as consumers who are 'investing' in their financial futures. The 'university experience' sales pitch prominent in the UK is used to justify massive fees which lead to students graduating with huge debt, and it is legitimised in articles like this one. If you are an international reader, you will be able to compare these narratives to those which are prominent in your own higher education environments.

When considering the social context of a piece of discourse at the social practice stage of this model, it is a useful exercise to investigate that context a bit further. This is particularly important because, as noted in the discussion of discursive practice, the ideological positions disseminated and reinforced by the language of the media achieve their goal through a somewhat limited or selective provision of context in the text. For example, the position of students in this article is represented solely by the two quotations from Nick Sundin and Chris Price, both of whom appear to have a very negative view of the dispute and whose position will help to persuade the article's readers that students view lecturers as 'selfish'. These quotations have been selected specifically for this purpose; however, they are not in fact representative of student opinion overall. An independent poll, i.e. not commissioned by either the UCU or UUK, conducted by YouGov on 22nd February 2018, only three days after this article was published and on the eve of the first day of industrial action, found that only two percent of students blamed lecturers for the disruption, whilst three-fifths of students (61%) indicated support for the strikes. The National Union of Students (NUS) stated their unequivocal support for lecturers. The article constructs the perception of facticity through its consistent use of certain statistics, as discussed in the text dimension above; however, other seemingly relevant statistics have been omitted. Of course, other discourse examples relevant to this dispute, such as the publicity material produced by UCU or NUS, which includes these statistics but perhaps omits dissenting voices amongst a minority of students, is no less an ideological publication than the *Daily Mail*. Neither are neutral and both push political agendas. It is perhaps likely that most students of CDA would adopt a position closer to that of the NUS or UCU than that of the *Mail*, and CDA recognises the inevitability of such positioning; however, it is erroneous to claim that even this position is neutral. We will consider the marketisation of higher education more specifically in Chapter 5 by conducting an analysis of the type of discourse produced by institutions themselves to reinforce the new capitalist reality in the higher education sector internationally. It is relevant to note here that other contextualising information is omitted from this article, including reference to the massive salaries of university managers, usually justified by the apparent necessity to compete with private sector salaries. Reference to the decades-long devaluation of lecturers' salaries is also omitted. Overall, the social practice stage of this analysis finds that this article reinforces for readers the new capitalist perspective of higher education as a commodity which is measurable by examinations and fees rather than the acquisition of knowledge. As we move through this book other models of analysis will be applied to various examples of institutional discourse. In each discussion we will consider the wider context by thinking about the ideological role of language both in terms of what is included in a text and also what might have been omitted.

Summary of Chapter 2

Fairclough's three-dimensional model demonstrates how to analyse institutional discourse through description, interpretation and explanation. Chapter 2 illustrates how this model provides a very in-depth examination of, in this case, discourse from the news media. By approaching language in the all-encompassing way proposed by this model, an analysis transcends the merely descriptive. We can see that the analysis of the first stage of this article certainly yields insights as to its motivation, but it is also clearly important to take these descriptions further. By treating the language as ideologically loaded discourse we have been able to extend our conclusions at the discursive practice and social practice stages of the model by paying close attention to features of production and consumption and to appropriate elements of social context.

Further Reading

Fairclough, N. (2015) *Language and Power*, 3rd edition. London and New York: Routledge.

3 Beginning Analysis
Critical Discourse Analysis and Systemic Functional Linguistics

KEY TERMS IN CHAPTER 3: Systemic Functional Linguistics, *understanding*, *explanation*, experiential function, interpersonal function, textual function, processes, participants, circumstances, passivisation, nominalisation

MODELS OF ANALYSIS IN CHAPTER 3: transitivity

3.1 Introduction

In Chapter 1 we established that Critical Discourse Analysis takes a social constructionist view of language which stresses the interconnectedness of language, power and ideology. We demonstrated that CDA recognises that language is multifunctional. For example, a piece of discourse in the news does not just describe an event or incident but contributes to a perception and an interpretation of that event for society. Chapter 2 applies an important model in CDA to a piece of institutional discourse and demonstrates that discourse in society operates with an ideological agenda. In the next three chapters we will build upon these fundamentals by exploring the connection between CDA and **Systemic Functional Linguistics** (SFL) (or Systemic Functional Grammar, SFG), a functional-semantic approach to language which is concerned with the relationship between language and social structure. This chapter will explore the SFL framework of **transitivity**. First, we will consider the main theoretical underpinnings of SFL and how these link to CDA.

3.1.1 CDA and SFL

Fairclough (1995:6) describes CDA's view of language as multifunctional, reminding us that it 'incorporates an orientation to mapping relations between language (texts), and social structures and relations'. The view in CDA of language as inevitably connected to social structures is strongly linked to MAK Halliday's view of language as a 'social semiotic'. The social semiotic view of communication views language as a set of resources which can be used by speakers or writers to realise their interests or goals, a view which is prominent in SFL and CDA.

In his highly influential text *Introduction to Functional Grammar* (1994), Halliday states that the linguistic analysis of discourse pursues two possible levels of achievement. What he deems the 'lower of the two levels' is the ***understanding*** of the text:

> The linguistic analysis enables one to show how, and why, the text means what it does. In the process, there are likely to be revealed multiple meanings, alternatives, ambiguities, metaphors and so on. [This level] should always be attainable provided the analysis is such as to relate the text to general features of the language – provided it is based on a grammar, in other words.
>
> (Halliday, 1994:xv)

The second level is what Halliday terms the pursuit of ***explanation***:

> The linguistic analysis may enable one to say why the text is, or is not, an effective text for its own purposes – in what respect it succeeds and in what respects it fails, or is less successful [...] It requires an interpretation not only of the text itself but also of its context (context of situation, context of culture), and of the systematic relationship between context and text.
>
> (Halliday 1994:xv)

Halliday is clear that the analysis of discourse must transcend the descriptive aspects of language (understanding) and also consider the operation of a text in context (explanation). This view is at the heart of SFL. From this perspective, the system of language is intimately connected to the function it serves, and this links SFL intimately to CDA, wherein we also must interpret and explain how a text operates in its social context. SFL provides models and terminology to evaluate discourse at several levels. For Halliday, language represents a series of grammatical options which are chosen according to social circumstances.

> It is not only the text (what people mean) but also the semantic system (what they can mean) that embodies the ambiguity, antagonism, imperfection, inequality and change that characterise the social system and the social structure.
>
> Halliday (1978:114)

With this assertion in mind, consider again for a moment the analysis of the *Daily Mail* article in the last chapter and the student task where you thought about alternative constructions of the sentence 'Students at almost every mainstream university could have their final exams cancelled or disrupted this year because of striking lecturers' (see Chapter 2.3).

This discussion suggested three alternative constructions for this sentence, each one a linguistic representation of the lecturers' pension strike. The sentence which actually appears in the article serves the purposes of the newspaper, which are to represent structural oppositions and a fractured relationship between academics and students. The newspaper has available to it all of the options suggested in Chapter 2 as well as the sentences with which you may have answered the student task. But in order to serve the ideological function of the article, the sentence used and those which accompany it in making up the article are all 'chosen' from the system of language available. The choice of linguistic forms in discourse therefore always has significance. For Halliday, this significance is not just about the technical structure of the sentence, the words used and how they are combined (i.e. the lexicon and the syntax), but also if this use of the system of language, in Halliday's terms, 'succeeds' in achieving its function.

The success of linguistic choices in achieving the function of a text is also at the heart of CDA, and CDA develops the SFL notion of 'success' to also consider ideological motivation. That is, CDA analyses the significance of linguistic choices and assesses their effectiveness in context whilst also asking why these linguistic choices are made. If we consider again the sentence from the *Daily Mail*, for example, exposing the intention to construct an opposition between students and lecturers in the sentence and to contribute to the perspective of higher education as a commodity throughout the article is also fundamental to the analysis. CDA therefore pursues a fully contextualised interpretation and explanation of a piece of discourse. The models, terminology and fundamental recognition of the connection between language and its social context in SFL make this approach very useful for critical discourse analysts. Young, Fitzgerald and Fitzgerald (2018:26) suggest that SFL and CDA can be 'joined in a continuum relationship because the focus on issues such as power and ideology begins with SFL and is extended by CDA'.

> SFL [...] provides you with the methodological tools to answer questions which provide a *description* of a discourse. You can then take the description supplied by SFL and answer CDA questions that provide an *explanation* and *interpretation* of a discourse in terms of the relationships between language, power and ideology.
>
> (Young, Fitzgerald and Fitzgerald, 2018:26)

The discussion of the *Daily Mail* article in Chapter 2 essentially encompasses a general lexico-grammatical analysis at the text stage of the three-dimensional model. To be sure, this analysis provides ideological insight and contributes significantly to the discussion of the other two dimensions of the discourse, but we have not used any specific model to analyse the text at this stage. SFL provides a number of models which can be integrated into the three-dimensional model, essentially using Fairclough's structured approach as a type of umbrella or organising model. SFL models can also be used independently of Fairclough's model so long as the analysis attends appropriately to the ideological motivations of the discourse being examined. Using specific models of analysis enhances the rigour, replicability and scholarly credibility of an analysis.

Whilst the three-dimensional model is one very successful way of pursuing the principles of CDA, this approach can also be enhanced by utilising the models which encompass SFL.

Having established the link between SFL and CDA, the next section will introduce key terms in SFL and give an account of the first of the important analytical frameworks we will consider in the next three chapters, the transitivity model.

3.2 The Functions of Language

In Systemic Functional Linguistics, Halliday seeks to describe three functions of language which are simultaneously fulfilled by texts. These functions are known as the **experiential** (or the **ideational**), the **interpersonal** and the **textual** functions of language, and we can identify a range of linguistic choices that can be taken for each function. In CDA 'researchers seek to interpret the ideological functions of these choices' (Hart, 2014: 20). We recognise that by making particular choices in how to linguistically (re)construct an event, writers or speakers are exploiting the 'meaning potential' of language. A summary of each function is provided in the box.

The Functions of Language in SFL

- The **experiential** function encodes patterns of experience in a written or spoken text and is primarily relayed through transitivity, which can be analysed by a model which significantly surpasses traditional lexico-grammatical examinations.
- The **interpersonal** function refers to how language operates as an interactive event, between a reader and a writer as well as between a speaker and a listener. The interpersonal function is often analysed through choices made in the mood system in English, between imperative, declarative or interrogative forms, and through modality and polarity, i.e. the level of commitment to a proposition undertaken by a writer or speaker.
- The **textual** function is about how writers or speakers connect parts of discourse. It is examined by considering cohesion and coherence in text, the former referring to the internal connection between clauses in a text and the latter to how external connections are built between the text and its context.

The remainder of this chapter will be dedicated to demonstrating an analysis focussed on the experiential function by explaining and applying the transitivity framework to a number of institutional discourse examples. Chapter 4 will address the interpersonal function and introduce an important model for the analysis of Appraisal in English (Martin, 2000; Martin and White, 2005).

Chapter 5 will conclude the focus on SFL by analysing the textual function through examining discourse in higher education in the Middle East.

3.3 The Experiential Function: Transitivity

As indicated by its name, the experiential function refers to how experience, the various 'goings-on' in the world, as Halliday has it, are represented in language. The experiential function refers to the transitivity of clauses in a text. In SFL the term 'transitivity' is used in a different, more expansive sense than in traditional grammar. Traditional grammatical analysis of transitivity essentially refers to whether or not a verb takes a direct object, i.e. whether it is transitive or intransitive. For our purposes in this book, where we recognise the importance of contextual meaning, this traditional view of the transitivity of a verb is not sufficient. However, by examining the experiential function in SFL through the transitivity framework proposed by Halliday, we can go far beyond the limits of traditional grammar. Transitivity in SFL categorises verbs into different meaningful types and explores their participants and accompanying circumstances. In CDA this system enables us to consider much more expansively the lexical and grammatical choices made in the production of a piece of discourse. If you are a student encountering the transitivity framework for the first time in this book, it might seem like there are quite a lot of technical terms, but each will be fully explained so that by the end of this chapter you will be able to replicate the analysis included here in your own investigations of choices made in language.

Fowler (1991:71) states that 'transitivity is the foundation of representation: it is the way the clause is used to analyse events and situations as being of certain types'. In order to fully appreciate the range of 'types' there might be for a situation or event in SFL, transitivity expresses a range of **processes**. Each process carries with it specific terminology which relates to accompanying **participants**, which carry out or are affected by a process. The third component refers to any accompanying **circumstances**. Simpson (1993:88) outlines these key components:

1. The *process* itself, which will be expressed by a verb phrase in a clause.
2. The *participants* involved in the process. These roles are typically realised by noun phrases in the clause.
3. The *circumstances* associated with the process, normally expressed by adverbial and prepositional phrases.

There are six types of process which are defined according to whether they refer to actions, feelings, speech, states of mind or states of being:

- Material
- Mental

- Behavioural
- Verbal
- Relational
- Existential

The processes will be fully considered in the rest of this chapter. In order to briefly expand upon participants and particularly circumstances, consider the following sentence: 'Paul read the book in the library'. The process is the verb 'read', in this case a Material process. The participants are 'Paul' and 'the book', known as the subject and the direct object in traditional grammar, and 'in the library' refers to the circumstances, which in this case express location. Circumstances can also express manner, such as 'Paul read the book intently'; time, as in 'Paul read the book in the morning'; and reason, such as 'Paul read the book for pleasure'. These are known as the 'core' circumstantial elements of a clause and answer the questions where?, why?, how? and when?

There are also a number of 'non-core' circumstantial elements which you need to be aware of in carrying out a thorough analysis. These elements answer the following questions in a sentence:

Accompaniment: with whom? – 'Paul read the book with his daughter'
Contingency: under what circumstances? – 'Paul read the book despite it being difficult'
Role: as/into what? – 'As a lover of literature, Paul read the book'
Extent: at what interval? – 'Paul read the book from afternoon until evening'
Angle: whose/which perspective? – 'Paul read the book according to the librarian'
Matter: about what? – 'Paul told everyone about the book he had read'

These 'non-core' circumstantial processes add to the core circumstances to recognise the many different possibilities in a clause.

We will now look at each of the six different types of process in turn before carrying out a transitivity analysis of a text which will demonstrate the clear contribution of the framework to CDA.

3.3.1 Material Processes

Process: Material **Sub-processes:** event, action, intention, supervention
Participant(s): Actor, Goal, Recipient, Client, Range (Scope)

Material processes are processes of *doing*. Usually these refer to some concrete action with a discernible result or consequence, such as in a sentence like 'Soldiers shot insurgents'. The participant components are known as the Actor and the Goal, the person or entity who does the act and the person or entity to whom/which it is done respectively. In this case 'Soldiers' fulfil the Actor participant, and 'insurgents' the Goal participant. These processes can be non-Goal directed, such as 'Soldiers <u>fired</u> when they arrived in the village' where there is only an Actor and a circumstantial element accompanying the Material process but no Goal participant. As we will see below, the omission of clear participants can be particularly ideological. Material processes can also be non-Goal directed when they refer to abstract and metaphorical processes like 'After Johnson's elevation the value of sterling <u>fell</u>'.

Material processes can be further divided into several sub-processes, distinctions which can be useful in an analysis. For example, if the Material process is carried out by an inanimate Actor, it is known as an 'event process', in a sentence like 'The tank fired several rounds at the village', whereas it is known as an 'action process' when carried out by an animate Actor, e.g. a person, like in the sentence 'The soldier fired several rounds at the village'. If a news report chose to represent this incident as an event process instead of an action process, there is an element of mitigation offered to the soldier here, because an object rather than a person attacks the village. An action process like this one is tellingly called an 'intention process', when an Actor acts voluntarily. When an action is involuntary, such as 'The soldier slipped and fell', the action process is referred to as a 'supervention process'.

Material processes can also have beneficiaries known as Recipient and Client. These roles refer to someone for whom the action occurs. In the sentence 'The doctor gave medication to Helen', Helen is the Recipient; and in 'He bought the teddy bear for Ella', Ella is the Client. Material processes can also be linked to a participant known as the Range, which is a participant which is unaffected by the process. In the sentence 'I carried out research', research is closely connected to the process; it is not the Goal in itself. The Range is also known as the Scope of a Material process.

Often noteworthy in critical language analysis are sentences which include a Material process but where the Actor element is not expressed. In most declarative sentences some entity in a sentence must occupy the subject position so that grammaticality is retained; for example, *'shot several rounds at the village' is not a grammatical sentence. However, the entity which occupies this position does not necessarily have to be the Actor, the doer of the process. Try the student task before reading on.

Student Task

The six sentences below are different ways of representing the same event. For each sentence try to decide: to which participant in the sentence is responsibility attributed? Also, think about the representation of participants. How are different impressions created?

a. Allied soldiers kill fourteen innocent civilians in Basra.
b. Fourteen innocent civilians were killed by soldiers in Basra.
c. Fourteen innocent civilians were killed in Basra.
d. Fourteen innocent civilians die in Basra.
e. Fourteen civilians die in Basra.
f. Fourteen die in Basra.

In completing the student task, for how many of the sentences were you able to offer a clear answer to the questions? Remember that these sentences are different ways of representing the same event. So, if we accept that sentence a. is true, then all of the others are true also. However, as you will have discovered when thinking about the attribution of responsibility and the representation of participants in these sentences, the encoding of ideology in discourse is not a simple matter of truthfulness or falsehood but rather something more complex. In the box below we offer a commentary on these eight sentences which will extend some of the answers you may have offered to the student task and which will introduce some important key terms.

In sentence a. all the core elements in a transitivity analysis are clearly identifiable: 'Allied soldiers' fulfil the Actor role and 'fourteen innocent civilians' the Goal, 'kill' is a Material process and 'in Basra' provides circumstantial information of location. The verb is in the simple present tense and has an active voice, therefore the Actor is placed first and the Goal, the entity affected by the process, comes afterwards. For Simpson (1993:86), this sentence is an example of the 'up-front approach' to representing an event.

Sentence b. refers to the same event but in this case the sentence is in the passive voice. Rather than the Actor taking up the subject position at the beginning of the sentence, this is filled by the Goal, and therefore the reader encounters the entity affected by the Material process before the agent of the process. Whilst the Actor is still identifiable, agency in sentence b. is syntactically backgrounded. **Passivisation** refers to the representation of an event in the passive voice. SFL recognises that language is a system of options, and in CDA we are interested in the ideological motivation of representing an event through passivisation as opposed to the 'up-front approach' of the active voice.

The ideological potential of passivisation is demonstrated by sentence c. In this representation of the event the Actor has been omitted. The reader knows that 'fourteen innocent civilians were killed' but is not able to discern by whom or by what from this sentence. The writer obscures syntactic agency in this sentence by using the Goal in the subject-initial position of the sentence and deleting or omitting the Actor of the Material process, so we do not know who did the killing. An institutional discourse representation of an event like this which deletes the Actor of the Material process is highly ideological; for example, this type of representation might be proffered by a media organisation which is in favour of whatever conflict is being referred to. It could also be given by official government or military organisations that might wish to background the role of soldiers in the killing of civilians.

Sentence d. represents the incident through a different Material process, using 'die' instead of 'kill'. By representing the incident in this way, the discourse decreases the expectation of the reader that an additional agent might be present. A reader of sentence c. might still ask the question 'By whom?'; after all, someone must have done the killing, even if s/he is omitted from the sentence. However, in sentence d. we know who has done the dying, as it were. 'Die' is usually a supervention process in that it is not done deliberately but it does not necessarily require the involvement of another Actor. Sentence d. shifts the participant roles of the original sentence. The 'fourteen innocent civilians' who were the Goal of 'kill' in sentence a. are now the Actor of 'die' in sentence d. 'Die' is a non-Goal directed process and is often thought of as self-engendered in that the Actor is the only participant that can be directly affected by the process. Sentence d. is still a 'true representation' of this event; what a writer is doing here is exploiting the linguistic options available to present the event in a heavily obscured way.

In sentence e. the writer can go one step further and remove the adjective 'innocent' as a modifier of the noun 'civilians'. Of course, there are still some connotations of innocence which are carried by 'civilians' in the context of a war or conflict; they are non-combatants. These connotations can be eliminated by choosing to represent the event through sentence f.

The account of these examples demonstrates the view in SFL that language offers a series of options for the representation of 'goings-on' in the world. In CDA this analysis would pay close attention to the context of these sentences and ask about the position of the newspaper, its owners and advertisers on this conflict, for example. A publication which condemns the action might print sentence a. and one which endorses it might run sentence f. In both cases an accurate account of the event has been given but the difference in the linguistic articulation tells the analyst something about the ideology encoded in the discourse. Each sentence offers a different interpretation of the event. CDA applies the transitivity framework to explain this interpretation. We will now consider Mental processes.

3.3.2 Mental Processes

> **Process:** Mental **Sub-processes:** Cognition, Affection (Reaction), Perception
> **Participant(s):** Senser, Phenomenon

Mental processes are processes of *sensing*. The participant roles are Senser, the entity which thinks or feels or perceives, and Phenomenon, that which is thought or felt or perceived. There are three different types of Mental processes, known as cognition, affection (or reaction) and perception. In most cases, the Senser is a person, but not always; for example, in literary contexts we might imagine feelings being ascribed to an inanimate object. The Phenomenon can be a person, a thing or indeed an abstract notion such as an idea or a concept. Unlike Material processes, which are inherently external in that they refer to an action in the world, Mental processes are internal; they are something possessed by the Senser.

Mental processes of cognition refer to thinking and can be identified by various synonyms or near synonyms of the verb 'think', such as 'understand' or 'know' or 'consider'. Mental processes of affection basically refer to an expression of liking or disliking, and Mental processes of perception refer to the senses, and include verbs of seeing or hearing, for example.

> g. Johnson (Senser) does not understand (Process: cognition) progressive politicians (Phenomenon).
> h. Trump (Senser) approves of (Process: affection) unchecked capitalism (Phenomenon).
> i. Wilder (Senser) heard (Process: perception) angry exchanges (Phenomenon) in the crowd (Circumstances: location).

It can be of particular significance in a piece of discourse if Mental processes are attributed to one participant or type of participant whilst Material processes only are attributed elsewhere. Imagine that in a news report about an industrial action the only participants to whom Mental processes, say of worry or concern or a lack of understanding, are attributed are affected consumers, or to patients in a health service strike or to students in an education strike. In a report like this the reader can only empathise with this select group of 'feeling' participants. If the doctors or the lecturers in the same report are primarily represented through Material actions, then they are literally 'unfeeling' in the discourse.

3.3.3 Behavioural Processes

Process: Behavioural
Participant(s): Behaver

Behavioural processes refer to psychological or physical behaviour. They have a number of aspects in common with both Material and Mental processes but also possess important unique characteristics. Behavioural processes have one participant known as Behaver. Processes such as 'laugh', 'smile', 'frown', 'watch', 'stare', 'ogle', 'dream' and 'breathe' are all examples of Behavioural processes. Behavioural processes can be viewed as a sort of 'halfway house between Material and Mental processes in that they represent both the activities of sensing and doing' (Simpson, 2014:25). Behavioural processes in this way might be seen as the physiological articulation of feeling. For example, 'like' is a Mental process whereas 'smile' and 'laugh' are Behavioural, 'hear' is Mental whilst 'listen' is Behavioural and 'see' is Mental and 'watch' is Behavioural.

Whilst there can clearly be a Material aspect to Behavioural processes, the choice to use a Behavioural process in a discourse representation of certain actions can be ideologically significant because, unlike Material processes, a sole entity – the Behaver – experiences the action in a Behavioural process. Machin and Mayr (2012:109) offer the clause 'The soldier watched' as an example which shows that the Behaver does not demonstrate 'particularly strong agency'. As this is a Behavioural process rather than a Material one, such as the 'The soldier reconnoitred', for example, there is no discernible affected participant. If this clause formed part of the sentence 'The soldier watched the village', the 'village' is unaffected and undisturbed by the soldier's behaviour, whereas 'reconnoitred' might suggest the village is in somewhat more peril.

3.3.4 Verbal Processes

Process: Verbal
Participant(s): Sayer, Receiver, Verbiage (speech act, content)

Verbal processes (or processes of Verbalisation) refer to the process of saying and are represented by the verb 'say' and its synonyms. The participant roles are Sayer, the person or occasionally the thing which does the saying, Receiver, the person or thing that the Verbal process is directed at, and Verbiage, that which is said.

j. Theresa May (Sayer) says (Process: Verbal) EU will not negotiate (Verbiage).

> k. Boris Johnson (Sayer) tells (Process: Verbal) EU (Receiver) they must negotiate (Verbiage).
> l. EU (Sayer) claims (Process: Verbal) British government is deluded (Verbiage).
> m. British government (Sayer) lambasts (Process: Verbal) EU (Receiver).

As you can see from sentences j.–m., the Receiver participant is not always explicitly stated. In sentence j. we can assume that Theresa May's audience is the public at large, but of course public statements from politicians are often targeted at multiple audiences: they are intended to be heard by voters, supporters, detractors, allies and enemies. The Verbiage element is also not always stated. From sentence m. we can extrapolate from the choice of 'lambasts' as the verb to represent the process that the content of the British government's words is fairly angry but we are not offered any direct or descriptive rendering of the words themselves.

This highlights an important distinction in the Verbiage element that can be seen in the sentences n. and o.

> n. Donald Trump (Sayer) tells (Process: Verbal) Democratic congresswomen (Receiver) to 'Go back' where they came from (Verbiage: content).
> o. Donald Trump (Sayer) calls (Process: Verbal) for changes in Democratic immigration policies (Verbiage: speech act).

In sentence n. the reader is informed of the words spoken by Trump through direct speech in an example of a 'content-type Verbiage'. In sentence o. we are given a description of what Trump 'calls for' without any direct speech, so this is known as a 'speech act–type Verbiage'. The choice in discourse to describe Verbal processes through these different types of Verbiage can be ideologically significant. Depending on the context, a media organisation, for example, can use direct speech to endorse or to condemn what has been said. As noted in Chapter 2, we also know that often direct quotations are highly selective and may be edited at several stages of the media production process so that they best represent the ideological position of the institution.

An additional point of potential ideological importance when representing Verbal processes is the verb which is chosen to represent the act of speech itself. In sentences j. to m. we have 'say', 'tell', 'claim' and 'lambast'. 'Say' and 'tell' do not possess the explicit evaluation of verbs like 'claim' and 'lambast'. Caldas-Coulthard (1997) defines these verb types as 'neutral structuring verbs' and 'metapropositional verbs' respectively, where the latter carry with them an author's interpretation of the speech act. When speech is represented as a 'claim', some doubt may be cast on its validity. Therefore, the Verbiage is not being represented to the reader as necessarily true but instead it is only representative of the interested position of the speaker. In sentence l. the delusion of the British government is attributed only to the opinion of the EU. The effect would be somewhat different if a Verbal process like 'explains' or 'accepts' had been used. We will consider the full model of verbs of saying (Caldas-Coulthard, 1994, 1997) in Chapter 6, but this short account demonstrates that this model can be used to fine-tune and expand the transitivity framework in terms of Verbal processes.

3.3.5 Relational Processes

> **Process:** Relational **Sub-processes:** Intensive, Possessive, Circumstantial
> **Modes:** Attributive, Identifying
> **Participant(s):** Carrier, Attribute, Identifier/Token, Identified/Value

Relational processes is a rather complex category that refers to a particular type of states of being and encodes meanings where things are stated to exist in relation to other things. There are three different types of Relational processes which come in two different modes, resulting in six categories.

The three types of Relational processes are intensive, possessive and circumstantial. Intensive Relational processes denote a relationship of equivalence 'x=y' and usually can be identified through the verb 'to be', usually with an adjective, adverb or noun phrase. Possessive Relational processes refer to an 'x has y' relationship and are identified by the verb 'to have' or indicated by a possessive apostrophe. Circumstantial Relational process denote an 'x is at/on/in/with y' type relationship, usually marked by the verb 'to be' alongside a prepositional phrase.

These three types are subdivided into two modes. Attributive Relational processes have the participants Attribute and Carrier, and Identifying Relational processes have the participants Identifier/Token and Identified/Value. In the Attributive mode the Carrier is a noun or noun phrase whilst the Attribute expresses a quality or description.

> p. EU negotiator Michel Barnier (Carrier) is (Process: Attributive Intensive) apprehensive (Attribute).
> q. EU President Donald Tusk (Carrier) has (Process: Attributive Possessive) a plan (Attribute).
> r. The negotiations (Carrier) are on (Process: Attributive Circumstantial) all day (Attribute).

Identifying Relational processes differ grammatically and semantically from Attributive processes. Rather than ascribe or classify, Relational processes in the Identifying mode operate to identify or define.

s. EU negotiator Michel Barnier (Token) is (Process: Identifying Intensive) one of many leaders present (Value).
t. The house (Value) is (Process: Identifying Possessive + 's) EU President Donald Tusk's (Token).
u. The EU representatives (Token) are with (Process: Identifying Circumstantial) the British delegation (Value).

A method which will help you to correctly identify Attributive and Identifying modes is reversibility. In most cases Identifying clauses can be reversed whereas Attributive ones cannot. So we can have 'One of many leaders present is EU negotiator Michel Barnier', 'EU President Donald Tusk's is the house' and 'The British delegation are with EU representatives'. When Identifying clauses are reversed, grammatical function is also changed. In the first sentence, for example, 'EU negotiator Michel Barnier' is the subject but in the reversed clause this noun phrase is the complement.

In most cases Attributive processes cannot be reversed, and therefore we would not usually have sentences like 'Apprehensive is EU negotiator Michel Barnier', 'A plan has EU President Donald Tusk' or 'All day lasted the negotiations'. It is not necessarily the case that reversed Attributive processes are ungrammatical, but certainly they are non-standard sentences. These examples all express what is known as a 'marked theme', when an element other than the subject is foregrounded in the clause. These are usually quite deliberate in contemporary grammar when a writer wishes to make some feature of the clause particularly prominent, in these examples the fact that apprehension rather than some other emotion, such as hope perhaps, is present, a 'plan' exists and that negotiations have been lengthy. Sometimes marked theme structures can sound quite archaic. A crucial point is that even if Attributive processes have been reversed, there is no change in grammatical function like we have with Identifying processes. In these examples 'EU negotiator Michel Barnier', 'EU President Donald Tusk' and 'the negotiations' remain the subject in the respective sentences.

All types of Relational processes are potentially significant in discourse because these are the processes through which the very 'being' of participants is expressed. You can see from the examples here that a vast array of options exists through which a writer or speaker can classify, define, describe and symbolise a person or a thing through language. The preference of a speaker or writer for Relational processes as opposed to other processes in certain contexts might also be significant. For example, Simpson and Mayr (2010) discuss gendered representations of participants in lifestyle magazines wherein men are represented primarily through Material processes, reinforcing masculine traits of physical competitiveness, whereas women are often more so represented through Relational processes, as being rather than doing in often highly sexualised contexts.

3.3.6 Existential Processes

> **Process:** Existential
> **Participant(s):** Existent

Existential processes are used to encode in language that something exists or happens. These process types have just one participant, known as the Existent. In sentences such as 'There has been <u>an assault</u>' or 'There was <u>a decrease in economic activity</u>' the underlined phrases represent the Existent, which can be any kind of physical or conceptual phenomenon. The verb 'to be' and synonyms such as 'occur', 'exist' or 'arise' express Existential processes. In these sentences 'there' operates as what is known as a 'dummy subject', because it does not possess any function other than to make the sentence grammatical. Sometimes students express confusion in differentiating between Existential processes and Relational processes given that both express a form of being or existing. However, any confusion is easily resolved by noting that Relational processes must have two participants – Carrier/Attribute or Token/Value – because these processes are about one thing existing in 'relation' to something else. On the other hand, Existential processes can only have one participant; the clause is about the existence of the Existent, as it were, not its relationship with another entity.

> v. There (Dummy subject) was (Process: Existential) a killing in Basra (Existent).

Sentence v. returns us to the list of sentences through which Material processes were discussed. Sentence v. is an equally truthful representation of the event as sentence a., but obviously the information is much more limited. By representing an action like 'killing' through a noun phrase, sentence v. is an example of **nominalisation**. Nominalisations are frequently present in institutional discourse examples, particularly media headlines. In sentence v. the Existential process only expresses the existence of a 'killing', a choice of representation which makes no statement about responsibility, causality or culpability.

Both sentence a. and sentence v. offer a potential answer to the question 'What happened?', and both are true representations of the event *per se*, but they carry different ideological connotations. Existential processes therefore bring us back to the Material processes with which we began our review of the transitivity framework; the expressions of the event using both of these processes are part of the 'world of physical existence', as Simpson (2014) has it. Figure 3.1 illustrates the connection between processes in the transitivity framework and demonstrates that a range of grammatical options can be taken when representing an event in discourse.

CDA AND SYSTEMIC FUNCTIONAL LINGUISTICS

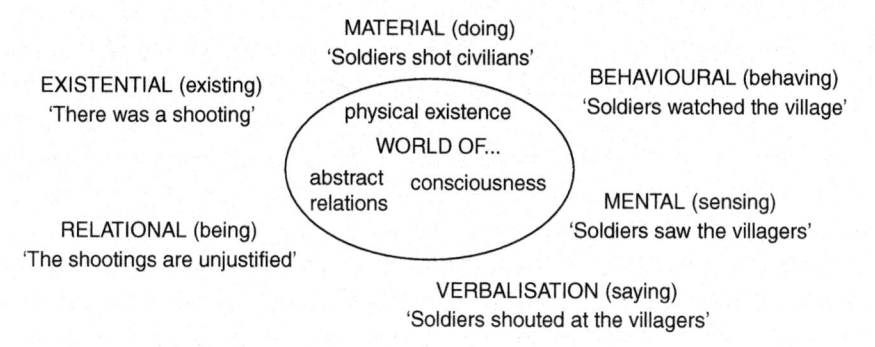

```
                        MATERIAL (doing)
                       'Soldiers shot civilians'
   EXISTENTIAL (existing)                    BEHAVIOURAL (behaving)
   'There was a shooting'    physical existence   'Soldiers watched the village'
                             WORLD OF...
                          abstract   consciousness
                          relations                MENTAL (sensing)
   RELATIONAL (being)                              'Soldiers saw the villagers'
   'The shootings are unjustified'
                        VERBALISATION (saying)
                       'Soldiers shouted at the villagers'
```

Figure 3.1 Transitivity processes

Source: After Simpson (2014)

3.4 Transitivity in Action

What remains for this chapter is to apply a transitivity analysis to a real discourse example. The article below was published in *The Sun* newspaper on 11th December 2011 and relates an account of a British military operation in Helmand Province, Afghanistan.

Example 3.1 Firefight as 90 Brits smash Taliban base

Afghan cop is saved in bomb factory raid
 MORE than 90 daring British troops stormed a Taliban bomb factory at dawn — and rescued a cop due to be executed within HOURS.
 As comrades surrounded the base in Afghanistan, the soldiers landed in helicopters and forced back terrorist gunmen during two monster gun battles.
 They then picked their way through a ring of hidden bombs before finding the captured Afghan policeman, who had been tied up and told he was about to be shot.
 The elite soldiers from the Brigade Reconnaissance Force had swooped with Afghan commandos after a local tip-off that Taliban killers were making explosives.
 They discovered that the bomb factory had been abandoned.
 But as they moved out, they spotted suspicious activity at a separate compound close by — and after another gun battle unearthed 30kgs of opium, an AK-47 sub-machine gun and bundles of cash.

> Last night the man in overall charge of last week's 12-hour mission paid tribute to his soldiers, saying it was a classic example of Our Boys working with the local security forces.
>
> Lieutenant Colonel Jasper de Quincey Adams, the commanding officer of 1st The Queen's Dragoon Guards, said: "All of the soldiers and airmen involved in the operation worked together to deliver a high-impact effect that demonstrates the reach of the Afghan government.
>
> "This will send out a clear message to our Afghan partners that we will continue to offer our support however dangerous or complex the mission."
>
> The operation — dubbed Eagle's Shadow — was launched at first light in Nahr-e Saraj district, Helmand Province. Scimitar tanks first surrounded the target and trained their 30mm cannons on the enemy base.
>
> Warthog all-terrain troop carriers, armed with heavy machine-guns, reinforced the cordon before two Chinook choppers and a US Sikorsky troop carrier swept in.
>
> An Apache attack helicopter also joined the fight.
>
> Intelligence officer 2nd Lieutenant Barnaby Smith said: "This Afghan-led operation not only recovered a member of the Afghan uniformed police but disrupted the insurgents in their backyard."
>
> The BRF consists of soldiers of 1st The Queen's Dragoon Guards and 1st Battalion the Yorkshire Regiment, while the Warthog Group is manned by soldiers from the Queen's Royal Hussars.
>
> (*The Sun*, 11th December 2011)

A transitivity analysis is focussed on identifying patterns of processes, participants and circumstances in the article. In terms of carrying out this analysis as an example of Critical Discourse Analysis, we must also consider potential ideological motivations for the options which have been chosen to represent this event. We ask why the event is linguistically constructed in this way and consider what this construction can tell us about the persuasive work being done by this publication in society at large.

There are forty processes over the thirty lines of the article, of which all but ten are Material. We can state categorically that processes of doing dominate the article, which is unsurprising given that this is a piece about a military operation. When we look more closely at these Material processes, other aspects of meaning are clear. Firstly, only five Material processes – 'executed', 'tied up', 'shot', 'making' and 'abandoned' – are carried out by the Taliban insurgents. Indeed, for three of these processes, and an accompanying Verbal process, the reader has to assume that the Taliban is the Actor. For example, we are told that the British Army finds an Afghan policeman 'who had been tied up and told he was about to be shot'. Because this clause has been passivised, the Actor or Sayer – who did the tying and the telling, as it were – are not explicitly stated. Therefore, the British military are almost the exclusive Actor in the article, making the focus very much the actions of British troops.

A consideration of the Material processes carried out by the British troops and equipment is also ideologically informative. They are: smash, saved, stormed, rescued, surrounded, landed in, forced back, picked, finding, swooped, discovered, moved out, unearthed, worked, deliver, demonstrate, continued, launched, surrounded, trained, reinforced, swept in, joined, recovered. The Actors in the article are both soldiers and inanimate military equipment, so there are both event and action Material processes. The processes are all deliberate rather than involuntary actions, so they are intention rather than supervention processes. Whilst the British military is very materially active, there is a particular interpretation of these activities offered by *The Sun* in this article. This is a report about a military operation against enemy personnel in a warzone, yet there is no verb to 'kill', 'attack' or 'assault', for example. Indeed, the single occurrence of the verb to 'shoot' is not attributed to British troops despite the fact that the article focusses heavily on the military hardware which is in the field: Scimitar tanks, Warthog all-terrain troop carriers, Chinook choppers, a US Sikorsky troop carrier and an Apache attack helicopter all play some part in the operation. The Material event processes of which these vehicles are the Actors are: surrounded, trained, reinforced, swept in and joined. Seemingly none of these heavily armed vehicles have fired a shot but rather have asserted only a threatening presence. In this vein, the sentence 'Scimitar tanks first surrounded the target and trained their 30mm cannons on the enemy base' is indicative of the narrative reconstructed by *The Sun* in this article. The weapons are targeted but not fired; the base and the village are unaffected. Neither the soldiers nor the military equipment, which are the Actors of this list of intention Material processes, partake of violent actions. The perception of the military which is constructed via processes like 'stormed', 'smash' and 'swept in' is one of dramatic daring, but this is also tempered with a vigilant professionalism through the processes 'picked their way' and 'unearthed 30kgs of opium'.

This construction of professionalism is reinforced by the naming practices in the article, which include the names of military equipment, the full names and ranks of soldiers and their regiments, and the name of the operation, 'dubbed Eagle's Shadow'. Naming practices cohere in the article to construct a clear sense of legitimate armed forces engaging in a legitimate, brave, ultimately non-violent military action.

The Goals of these Material processes also play a role in the legitimisation constructed by *The Sun*. Where Goals for the Material processes carried out by the military are stated in the article they are: Taliban base, Afghan cop, Taliban bomb factory, a cop, the base in Afghanistan, terrorist gunmen, captured Afghan policeman, 30kgs of opium, an AK-47 sub-machine gun, bundles of cash, high-impact effect, the reach of the Afghan government, our support, the target, the enemy base, the cordon, the fight, a member of the Afghan uniformed police, the insurgents. In most cases the Goals are inanimate, where the military act against buildings or objects rather than people. The 'Afghan cop' is a notable exception. In this case the human Goal is an obvious beneficiary of the operation rather than a casualty. On only two occasions are 'terrorist gunmen' and 'the insurgents' the Goal of the processes, 'forced back' and 'disrupted' respectively. Again there would seem to be no casualties.

Material processes like 'forced back' and 'disrupted' are examples of euphemism: the use of words or phrases which make something seem 'more positive than it might otherwise appear' (Thomas et al., 2004:48). The representation of violent actions through processes that, whilst Material, are somewhat semantically downgraded or made obscure is particularly ideological. There are only two references to fighting in this article: 'two monster gun attacks' and 'another gun battle'. Both of these occurrences form part of the circumstances in their respective sentences, comprising part of circumstantial adjuncts of time preceded by the prepositions 'during' and 'after', and both are examples of nominalisation. The materiality of the only references to violence and direct engagement between the British military and the Taliban has been represented through noun phrases. As noted above, when the British Army are Actors, the Goals are mostly inanimate objects.

An application of the transitivity framework to this article reveals much about the ideological position of *The Sun* in terms of this operation. CDA charges us to look beyond the detailed SFL-based description above to consider interpretation and explanation. In terms of intertextuality, an important aspect in the discursive practice section of Fairclough's three-dimensional model, we note that the only sources in this text are official British military sources, an intelligence officer and the commanding officer of 1st The Queen's Dragoon Guards. There is no accommodation of other voices or perspectives. The content of these quotations is an example of formal and euphemistic military language, such as 'worked together to deliver a high-impact effect that demonstrates the reach of the Afghan government'. Descriptions like this are good examples of how official sources use language to obfuscate the unpalatable realities and horrors of war. The real meaning of 'high-impact effect' in the context of war is likely to be measured in death and destruction. Interpretation of this event is given through official military sources.

It is important in CDA that more than just how a piece of discourse constructs a single event in a single conflict is considered. Critical interpretations must view discourse as working consistently and continuously to legitimise general concepts for society, such as the right to intervene militarily in other countries, and must further consider how discourse contributes to views of things like national superiority and how these views might be manifested at the ballot box and through other, more potentially malignant social actions. Fowler (1996:10) notes that whilst it is not necessarily its main intention, critical linguistic analysis provides very useful insights for historians.

The persuasive effect of this article in society as a whole is to legitimise the war in Afghanistan and by extension subsequent military operations and invasions which proceeded under the auspices of the 'Global War on Terror'. The most recent conflict in Afghanistan began with the US-led invasion in October

2001 and followed the 9/11 attacks on the World Trade Center in New York. Given the explicit connection between these two events, the initial invasion to overthrow the Taliban regime in Afghanistan received fairly widespread Western support, although this gradually diminished as the conflict lengthened. British troops fought in Afghanistan until 2014, and by 2011 calls for the withdrawal of the British armed forces, and indeed US and other NATO troops, had increased significantly. *The Sun* is fairly representative of the position taken by most right wing media in Britain, that the conflict was legitimate and of continued importance, and through articles like this reinforced this ideological position in the social world. The legitimisation work done through the institutional discourse of the media was not exclusive to the invasion of Afghanistan but rather formed part of a larger narrative which sought to legitimise the notion that Western governments, particularly Great Britain and the United States, retained a perpetual right to undertake military action against what they viewed as enemy states. The discourse construction of conflict abroad as aid missions in articles like this provides a strong counter-voice to opposition positions on military intervention ostensibly under the flag of humanitarianism.

Perhaps the most controversial military operation which took place during this period of the 'Global War on Terror' was the US and UK invasion of Iraq in March 2003. Unsurprisingly, given our analysis of this article, *The Sun* newspaper was a staunch supporter of a military campaign which divided both the country and the ruling Labour Party. The House of Commons vote to invade only passed owing to support from the Tories. Rupert Murdoch, then owner of *The Sun*, was an unequivocal supporter of conflict. In 2012 erstwhile editor of the *Daily Mail* Paul Dacre gave the following evidence to the Levinson Inquiry, which investigated the false intelligence which was used to justify the invasion of Iraq:

> I don't think there's any doubt he had strong views which he communicated to his editors and expected them to be followed. The classic case is the Iraq War. I am not sure that the Blair government or Tony Blair would have been able to take the British people to war if it hadn't been for the implacable support provided by the Murdoch papers. There's no doubt that came from Mr Murdoch himself.
> (Mr Paul Dacre, Levinson Inquiry, 6th February 2012)

A document declassified by the Chilcot Inquiry in 2016 entitled 'Media Strategy' and prepared by the Blair government made, amongst others, the following recommendations:

> The outlets for this information [on Saddam Hussein] should cross the spectrum so that we can encourage support from sympathetic newspapers and carry the argument to those likely to criticise our policy. It is as important to force the reality of Saddam's Iraq on papers like *The Guardian*, as it is to give papers like *The Sun* the chance to popularise our case.

> We should produce a list of ten facts about Saddam for *The Sun* based on our assessments of Saddam's attempts to equip himself with weaponry and abuse the sanctions regime.
>
> (UK Government 'Media Strategy', 11th March 2002)

Documents like this, tellingly written an entire year before the invasion of Iraq, illustrate the network of power relations which prevails between important institutions such as government and media, in this case very explicitly between the Blair government and the Murdoch press. It is clear that powerful groups are acutely aware of the persuasive capacity of media discourse. There is a clear link between the legitimising work done by transitivity processes, in articles like Example 3.1, and the political alliances of media owners. By using SFL to carry out an in-depth CDA into institutional discourse we are able to expose the political positions of media owners, amongst others, by analysing the implicit and explicit ideological messages of media language.

Summary of Chapter 3

In this chapter you have been introduced to a major framework within the study of language – Systemic Functional Linguistics (SFL) – and have explored the relationship between CDA and SFL. In particular, SFL focusses on how the system of language is affected by the function it is intended to serve. This recognition that language is more than just a descriptive system but that it also operates within social contexts aligns SFL with the concerns of critical discourse analysts who examine the ideological motivations and effects of this operation. The transitivity framework has been described in detail as a model of analysis for exploring the experiential function of language. Chapters 4 and 5 will explore the interpersonal and the textual function respectively. Chapter 3 has demonstrated how to analyse an example of media discourse using the transitivity model. From this example we have learned that the linguistic structure of discourse can indicate the ideological position of a publication and potentially of its owners. We have also discussed how these institutions exist within a network of powerful groups, such as government, who can work to consciously exploit the potential of discourse to legitimise and persuade. We have seen that by applying transitivity we can expose how institutions which produce discourse do so in ideological ways, such as endorsing or resisting the validity of military campaigns. In CDA we consider the effects of the ideological construction of discourse within society; we acknowledge that discourse has a social function which is manifested in acceptance of, support for or resistance to principles and events in society.

Further Reading

Halliday, M.A.K. (1994) *An Introduction to Functional Grammar*, 2nd edition. London: Arnold.

Simpson, P. (1993) *Language, Ideology and Point of View*. London and New York: Routledge.

4 Developing Analysis
Evaluation in Text

> **KEY TERMS IN CHAPTER 4**: interpersonal function, mood, modality, Appraisal, affect, judgement, appreciation, inscribed appraisal, invoked appraisal
>
> **MODELS OF ANALYSIS IN CHAPTER 4**: Appraisal

4.1 Introduction

This chapter will focus on the second function of language in SFL, the **interpersonal function**. The interpersonal function refers to how language is organised as an interactive event. When considering the interpersonal function of language we are looking at the way language is used to exchange information between various discourse participants and what the content of this exchange tells us about the stance of a speaker or writer. Analysis of the interpersonal function focusses on the level of commitment a speaker or writer has to a proposition in language, expressed by different types of modality, as well as on the feelings or assessments which are expressed by speakers or writers when negotiating social relations. In this chapter we will explore each of these elements of the interpersonal function. Halliday (1979:66) has referred to the interpersonal function as the 'speaker's ongoing intrusion into the speech situation'. Through examining language on an interpersonal plane we therefore consider how an event or occurrence is being interpreted by a text encoder, primarily a speaker or writer but also potentially by a web designer, a graphic artist or a film maker, given the inevitable multimodal nature of contemporary institutional discourse. This interpretation by a text encoder is communicated through discourse to the text decoder.

Young, Fitzgerald and Fitzgerald (2018:98) say that 'when people exchange information, they introduce attitudes and stances into their discourse. This includes both attitudes and stances (1) toward their topic and (2) toward their listeners/readers.' Broadly speaking, these attitudes and stances are expressed through **mood** and **modality**. Mood refers to whether information is being given or asked for, or whether an order is being issued. The three moods in English are known as the declarative, interrogative and imperative. Modality expresses a speaker or writer's attitude, opinion or position on what is being said or written, and is marked in four different ways: probability, frequency, obligation and inclination. These are all important terms which are related to the fact that in the interpersonal function language is viewed as an interactive process. As analysts we can tell much about the position of a speaker or writer through how interactions are structured. These terms and how we analyse them will be explored and explained as we move through this chapter.

Firstly an overview of mood and modality will be offered before we embark on a thorough description and demonstration of the Appraisal system. This is a lexical-semantic model developed by Martin (2000) and Martin and White (2005) to specifically examine the stance of a speaker or writer. In terms of mood and modality, we are most interested in how these systems can aid a Critical Discourse Analysis focussed on the communication and reinforcement of ideologies through discourse.

4.2 Mood

Martin, Matthiessen and Painter (1997:57) define the system of mood as 'the grammatical resource for realizing an interactive move' in language. Information can be exchanged through a number of possible 'moves'; it can come as a statement, a question or an order. Take a few minutes to complete the task before reading the account of mood.

Student Task

Think about the four sentences below. Are they statements, questions or orders? Depending on this, what type of 'move' is the speaker making? Is s/he declaring something or perhaps demanding it instead?

a. The British people voted for Brexit in June.
b. Did the British people vote for Brexit in June 2016?
c. Who voted for Brexit in June?
d. Vote for Brexit!

You have probably been able to conclude that information has been given in sentence a. but asked for in sentences b. and c., whilst sentence d. is demanding an action instead. Sentence a. is an example of the declarative, sentences b. and c. are interrogatives and sentence d. is an imperative. Let's think a bit more about each of these, particularly in terms of how they are important in CDA and how they can be linked to the models we have examined so far.

In a declarative, information is given in the form of a statement. Young, Fitzgerald and Fitzgerald (2018:81) state that the choice to offer information in the form of a declarative sentence indicates two things: that the speaker/writer adopts the speech role of being provider of a viewpoint on a subject, and that the listener/reader is cast as the receiver of that viewpoint. In CDA analysts will appropriately focus on the context in which declarative clauses are given and will often question whether the power possessed by both parties, i.e. the provider and receiver of the statement, is equal or divergent.

Sentence a., for example, might be made in an educational context, given by a teacher and received by a pupil. Like many institutional speech scenarios, this is an unequal encounter in which teachers possess more power than students. The interpersonal element of sentence a. might not seem very significant yet, but, as we will see below, this sentence is presented as a statement of fact, so it could be said to reduce the scope of dissenting voices or opinion. The sentence can also be considered experientially: 'vote' is a Material process with a clearly identified Actor in 'the British people'. Again, this might not seem immediately significant out of context. Remember, though, that the speaker or writer here could have chosen to represent this statement differently, such as through a Mental process of cognition, for example 'The British people decided on Brexit in June 2016'. This would have implied that the outcome of the election was considered by the electorate. If the choice were made to represent the Actor or Senser as the 'British electorate' or something like a 'small majority of the British people', this would also be significant. In each case the interpersonal rendering of the sentence would still be declarative, so information is being given as a statement to one party by another, but the experiential meaning of the statement would be quite different. Of course, in order to carry out a complete CDA of any of these exemplar sentences, we would need to know much more about their situational context.

Sentences b. and c. are interrogatives, where rather than being imparted, information is being requested via a question. There are two main types of interrogative. Sentence b. is a 'polar interrogative': essentially a confirmation or denial in some form of a yes/no response is requested. Sentence c. is an example of a 'wh- interrogative', in which additional information about who, what, where, when, why or how is required. A polar interrogative restricts the scope for information which an interactant might give in response, whilst a wh- interrogative invites more information. In terms of power relations, some power is ceded by the questioner to the answerer in sentence c. The question is basically open-ended, and a response can contain information in mood and content of the responder's choosing. Of course, and as always in CDA, context is crucial. If, for example, a polar interrogative is asked in a scenario where the questioner typically possesses less institutional power than her/his interlocutor, the respondent could simply choose to ignore the polar element of the question. To apply an educational scenario again, a teacher asked the question in sentence b. by a pupil might be ideologically motivated to take issue with elements of this sentence, and s/he might decide to expand upon the meaning of the 'British people' or the difference between 'vote' and 'decide', as we have speculated above. This sort of an answer would be, strictly speaking, more appropriate as a response to sentence c.

One institutional context where the distinction between polar and wh-interrogatives is often very significant is in the courtroom, especially during the evidence phase of a trial when a witness is being questioned by legal professionals on opposing sides. During examination-in-chief (or direct examination), when a witness is being questioned by 'friendly counsel', i.e. by the attorney or barrister who has called the witness, wh- interrogatives are more common than in cross-examination, where 'unfriendly counsel' will attempt to exert as much control as possible over testimony through polar interrogatives. In cross-examination, lengthy evaluative statements may be given by a barrister with the witness only required to confirm or deny. As legal professionals are not allowed to offer their own testimony in the courtroom, they rely on their institutional experience to decide how lengthy or evaluative a question like this will be. We might encounter combinations of declaratives and interrogatives in such a scenario. Consider a question like 'The defendant is an evil man and he has the capacity to commit this crime, does he not?'. This sentence contains two declarative clauses and a final polar interrogative, so the barrister is able to 'smuggle' (Aldridge and Luchjenbroers, 2007) information and evaluation into the courtroom through declaratives. This can be said to reduce the pragmatic force of the interrogative, because even if the polar interrogative is answered with a denial, the evaluation has still been presented to the jury. Negative question forms, such as 'does he not?', have also been shown to be disorientating for witnesses given their syntactic unconventionality. A question like this may of course lead to an objection from opposing counsel.

Another form of interrogative which is important in a legal context concerns presupposed elements which can be contained in the question. Simpson, Mayr and Statham (2018:88–89) consider examples of these 'leading questions' in the 2014 trial of Oscar Pistorius for the murder of Reeva Steenkamp. One example from the evidence stage of the trial is 'Why would she stand right up at the door, looking at you, at the danger?'. This is a wh-interrogative in which the cross examiner is asking Pistorius for an explanation of Reeva Steenkamp's actions at a certain stage of the event being examined, the 'Why' element of the question. However, the question presupposes two additional elements: that Steenkamp stood at the door and that she looked at Pistorius. Regardless of his response to the question, even if it is 'I don't know', these presupposed elements are retained. A polar interrogative like 'Did she stand at the door and look at you?' permits the defendant to deny these propositions. Therefore focussing on grammatical mood can prove fruitful for CDA of language in institutional contexts. Gibbons (2003) and Coulthard, Johnson and Wright (2016) outline the different questioning strategies of legal professionals at trial, and Ehrlich (2001) and Statham (2016) examine question sequences in the more specialised context of sexual assault trials.

Declaratives and interrogatives are both classified in English as being 'indicative' clauses. Sentence d., on the other hand, expresses the imperative, whereby information is exchanged in the form of a command. Usually those in positions of power issue commands to subordinates, say in the workplace or the classroom. Imperatives like those in sentence d. can be found quite habitually in a political context where you are commanded to 'Vote for' a person or a party or both. In Northern Ireland, where party tends to trump personality in politics, voters are urged on countless lamppost election posters to 'Vótáil Sinn Féin' or 'Vote DUP' by the poster's main message whilst the candidate's name appears in smaller text in a sort of mock ballot paper at the bottom of the placard. Donald Trump's 2016 election catchphrase, which also encodes a presupposed element, 'Make America Great Again', is an example of an imperative being used by a powerful figure and being widely adopted by voters at rallies and meetings. Trump's phrase differs in terms of mood therefore from Barack Obama's more inclusive declarative 'Yes We Can' from the 2008 presidential campaign. In a controversial tweet in July 2019, Trump used the imperative mood to suggest that four Democratic Members of Congress who had been critical of his rhetoric and regime 'go back and help fix the totally broken and crime infested places from which they came'. In response, Trump loyalists at a rally in Cincinnati, Ohio adopted the imperative chant 'Send Her Back' as Trump criticised the four women known as 'the Squad' from the podium. Three of the four were born in the United States. Chapter 8 will look in more detail at the effect of racialised rhetoric in politics.

Young, Fitzgerald and Fitzgerald (2018:83) remind us that orders can be issued by forms other than imperative commands, such as through questions and statements. If a teacher asks a pupil, 'Would you explain Brexit?', this is clearly a command given the context despite its grammatical realisation as a question. Equally, the same teacher could say to a student in the midst of a discussion on the subject, 'It would now be a good idea for you to explain Brexit'. This essentially operates as a command even though it is grammatically realised as a statement. In these cases we can say that whilst these sentences are semantically an interrogative and a declarative respectively, they have the pragmatic force of an imperative, whereby the speaker intends to issue an order. Such choices can be explained by politeness, and each of these sentences are examples of 'negative politeness' (Brown and Levinson, 1987). The speaker mitigates against the potential impoliteness of issuing a direct command by using a different grammatical mode. As always in CDA, we come back to context. In certain scenarios such as the workplace or indeed in a classroom, and certainly somewhere with a recognisable hierarchical command structure like the military, superiors do not necessarily have to mitigate against potential impoliteness and will often simply issue orders through sentences in the imperative mood. In other contexts, such as when power relations are fairly equal or when speakers are unfamiliar with one another, commands might be couched in politeness. In order to carry out a precise analysis, knowledge of the social context of the utterance and the status of the speakers will be crucial. For more detailed discussions of politeness, see Brown and Levinson (1987) and the very accessible overview in Cutting (2014).

4.3 Modality

Simpson (2014:131) defines modality as 'that part of the language which allows us to attach expressions of belief, attitude and obligation to what we say and write'. In short, modality is the system which accommodates expressions of varying levels of certainty to spoken or written utterances. Young, Fitzgerald and Fitzgerald (2018:95) refer to modality as an 'in-between area' to describe the fact that modal statements differ from polar ones, i.e. the speaker or writer is not expressing 'yes' or 'no', but rather is indicating a level of certainty which lies between these two opposites. There are four different stances which speakers or writers can adopt when expressing this 'in-betweenness': probability, frequency, obligation and inclination.

Probability refers to how likely you are to believe that something may occur. Probability can be expressed by the nine modal auxiliary verbs in English: 'shall', 'should', 'can', 'could', 'will', 'would', 'may', 'must', 'might'; or by the quasi-modal auxiliaries 'ought to', 'need to', 'has to'. Modal adverbs such as 'probably', 'possibly', 'certainly' or 'maybe' can also express probability. Frequency, on the other hand, is about how often you feel something may occur and is expressed through the use of similar modal verbs and adverbs like 'usually', 'sometimes', 'always', 'never', 'seldom' and 'rarely'. Halliday refers to these types of modality as 'modalisation' and associates them with propositions that are realised as statements and questions.

Obligation and inclination are referred to as 'modulation' and are realised through proposals, offers and commands. Obligation is used to express the extent to which you believe something has to be done. Modal adverbs like 'definitely', 'absolutely' and 'possibly' are noteworthy in a speaker or writer's expression of obligation. Inclination is how you assess the tendency of an occurrence, 'willingly', 'readily', 'gladly' or 'easily', for example. Modulation is realised through a similar set of modal verbs to those which express modalisation. Like so many areas of critical linguistic insight, the specific type of modality being expressed through modal verbs is often determined by the context of an utterance.

4.3.1 Sample Analysis: Modality of Political Speeches

A potent site for modality in institutional discourse is in political language, where politicians and political parties make promises to the electorate, evaluate their achievements against the apparent failings of their opponents and make predictions for the future. Consider these excerpts from the second inaugural address of US President Barack Obama.

i. But we have **always** understood that when times change, so **must** we; that fidelity to our founding principles requires new responses to new challenges; that preserving our individual freedoms ultimately requires collective action. For the American people **can** no more meet the demands of today's world by acting alone than American soldiers **could** have met the forces of fascism or communism with muskets and militias. No single person **can** train all the math and science teachers we'll need to equip our children for the future, or build the roads and networks and research labs that **will** bring new jobs and businesses to our shores. Now, more than ever, we **must** do these things together, as one nation and one people.

ii. We, the people, still believe that our obligations as Americans are not just to ourselves, but to all posterity. We **will** respond to the threat of climate change, knowing that the failure to do so **would** betray our children and future generations. Some **may** still deny the overwhelming judgment of science, but none **can** avoid the devastating impact of raging fires and crippling drought and more powerful storms.

iii. We **cannot** cede to other nations the technology that **will** power new jobs and new industries, we **must** claim its promise. That's how we **will** maintain our economic vitality and our national treasure – our forests and waterways, our crop lands and snow-capped peaks. That is how we **will** preserve our planet, commanded to our care by God. That's what **will** lend meaning to the creed our fathers once declared.

Many political speeches, particularly American inaugurals, are noteworthy for selective idealism and for focussing on broad themes like sacrifice, God and freedom. Modality in these three passages has been marked in bold, and we can identify elements of the types of modality discussed in Obama's level of certainty and commitment to his propositions here.

The first passage is essentially about constructing a sense of obligation. In juxtaposing conflicts against fascism and communism – heavily skewed championing of free market capitalism is another prominent theme in this speech – with aspirations in education, Obama refers to things which 'must' be done. A prominent tactic in political language known as 'abstraction' is easily identifiable in the obligation acknowledged in this passage. Obama offers no specifics about how these somewhat abstract and disconnected ideals can be achieved but simply affirms that they 'must' be done. This necessity to secure the preservation of largely uncontextualised ideals through a commitment to change has 'always' been understood, according to Obama. Frequency is anchored in this speech by the marrying of past, present and future; references to the past deeds of American soldiers are linked to the 'demands of today's world' and to features of an idealised future. Structural oppositions, between change and preservation or individuality and collective action, are notable in this passage and occur frequently in the speech as a whole.

The second passage, with its explicit intertextual reference to the United States Constitution in 'We the people', refers to obligation directly in the first line ('our obligations as Americans'). As is often the case with showcase speeches in American politics in particular, this is an obligation to 'posterity'. This section of the speech addresses climate change, a deeply divisive issue in the United States, and Obama acknowledges the probability that certain political figures 'may' refuse to acknowledge the reality of climate change. 'Can' is a modal verb of obligation in this passage. While 'can' might be used to acknowledge probability in a different context, 'none can avoid the devastating impact' of climate change gives a clear sense of obligation. In June 2017 Donald Trump, Obama's successor to the presidency, announced his intention to withdraw the United States from the Paris Agreement on climate change. After replacing Trump in 2021, President Joe Biden recommitted America to the treaty. These facts remind us that political speeches and the modal verbs and adverbs through which commitments are made are all too often highly idealistic. Powerful imagery of 'raging fires and crippling drought and more powerful storms' might have little effect on politicians with vastly different priorities. For Obama, the 'betrayal' of inaction is improbable, and this interpretation is supported by the clause 'we will respond to the threat of climate change'.

Categorical assertions, which represent states or actions as certain facts, are also important in this speech. Often the highest modal assertion, i.e. the most certain expression of something, is one which does not utilise a modal adverb at all but which simply states that something 'is' or that some action 'will' occur. Consider for example the different effects of a statement like 'it is true' versus one such as 'it is definitely true' or 'it is certainty true'. In most contexts the simple statement of fact carries a stronger sense of definitiveness or certainty without the specific use of these adverbs.

Passage iii is replete with categorical assertions ('technology that will power new jobs', 'we will maintain our economic vitality', 'we will preserve our planet', 'what will lend meaning to the creed'). Obama asserts obligation in stating that America 'must' appropriate the 'promise' of technology, as a result of which these apparently definite outcomes 'will' follow. It is perhaps only through this type of unspecific abstraction that one could present as a certainty the preservation of the environment through 'economic vitality'. It was in apparent concern for the health of the economy that Donald Trump reneged on the US commitment to climate change when he ceded from the Paris Agreement. To Trump, the environment and the economy were exclusive rather than co-existing, and his primary concern was apparently for the latter. In reality, therefore, certainty ebbs and flows with context. The passage concludes in the symbolic language of religious obligation. In America, the 'Founding Fathers' are accorded a significant level of reverence. However, the 'creed our fathers once declared' remains, like most political promises made in founding documents, somewhat less certain than the modality of these passages would have us believe. Barack Obama is a gifted public speaker, certainly more gifted than his successor, and he constructs

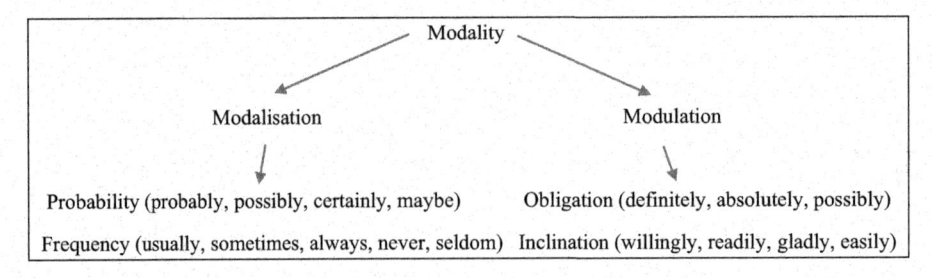

```
                            Modality
                 ↙                        ↘
          Modalisation                Modulation
              ↓                            ↘
Probability (probably, possibly, certainly, maybe)    Obligation (definitely, absolutely, possibly)
Frequency (usually, sometimes, always, never, seldom) Inclination (willingly, readily, gladly, easily)
```

Figure 4.1 Modality

obligation and probability in this speech through modality which has been carefully crafted by his speechwriters. In Chapter 8 we will examine political speeches for coercion, representation and legitimation.

The system of modality in English expresses the interpersonal function of language because a speaker or writer communicates her/his level of certainty to readers and listeners; an interpersonal relationship is therefore constructed through language. In political speeches levels of certainty are often made to appear somewhat more secure than may actually be the case. Politicians use modality often with a high sense of probability to make promises and commitments or to communicate messages to their supporters.

Modality exemplifies Halliday's (1994:179) description of the interpersonal function as 'the clause as exchange' as it provides language users with the resource to modify their commitment to a proposition, thereby indicating something about their stance or attitude towards a specific topic or towards hearers and readers. Figure 4.1 offers a short summary of modality.

The next section will examine a specific model for the analysis of stance in English, the Appraisal framework.

4.4 Evaluation and Appraisal

Seminal and often trailblazing works in CDA (Fairclough, 1989; Fowler, 1991) have traditionally attended to the interpersonal function of language and to its evaluative capacities through the analysis of mood and modality, and we can see from the overviews in this chapter that many valuable insights about a language user's intentions and positions can be drawn from these types of investigations. More recent studies (Hart, 2014; Statham, 2016) have analysed other ways through which a speaker or writer can encode their evaluation of a topic, recognising other language resources for expressing opinion, such as adjective and adverb phrases. As critical discourse analysts, we are interested in how language is used to communicate ideological opinions to listeners and readers, and in turn, therefore, to contribute to widespread and conventionally accepted evaluative positions on important aspects of society.

There is a range of models of analysis to investigate how evaluation is communicated in language. An important text which brings together several central approaches to the language of evaluation is the collection by Hunston and Thompson (2000), who state that one of the main functions of evaluation is to 'express the speaker's or writer's opinion, and in so doing reflect the value system of that person and their community' (Hunston and Thompson, 2000:6).

The model for analysing evaluation in text which we will introduce in this chapter is the **Appraisal** system (Martin, 2000; Martin and White, 2005), which is a systemic-functional lexical-semantic framework for analysing how a speaker or writer can express stance through language. Martin and White (2005:1) offer an introductory description of the Appraisal framework which, whilst fairly extensive, is very useful for newcomers to the model:

> [Appraisal] is concerned with the interpersonal in language, with the subjective presence of speakers/writers in texts as they adopt stances towards both the material they present and those with whom they communicate. It is concerned with how speakers/writers approve and disapprove, enthuse and abhor, applaud and criticise, and with how they position their readers/listeners to do likewise. It is concerned with the construction by texts of communities of shared feelings and values, and with the linguistic mechanisms for the sharing of emotions, tastes, and normative assessments. It is concerned with how speakers/writers construe for themselves particular authorial identities or personae, with how they align or disalign themselves with actual or potential respondents, and with how they construct for their text an intended or ideal audience.
>
> (Martin and White, 2005:1)

As noted previously, Halliday (1979:66) has referred to the interpersonal function as the 'speaker's ongoing intrusion into the speech situation', and he describes this component of meaning in terms of the 'clause as exchange'. By offering, either explicitly or implicitly, an opinion or stance on a person or an event in one or more of the ways described by Martin and White in this introduction to Appraisal – approving or disapproving, or applauding or criticising, for example – a speaker or writer is exchanging this opinion in a conscious process of persuasion with a listener or reader. We can see from Martin and White's introduction that evaluation can be expressed in a multitude of ways, and the Appraisal framework offers a model which organises these different types of evaluations into a system which can be applied to multiple discourse situations. The Appraisal system also acknowledges that, by making linguistic choices to evaluate events or people, language users are also addressing 'actual or potential respondents'; speakers or writers are using evaluation to persuade listeners and readers of the legitimacy of their opinion. This process of persuasion aligns evaluation with the interpersonal function of language, which attends to how language users interact. The Appraisal system enables the critical discourse

Ethics/morality (rules and regulations)

Feelings institutionalised as proposals

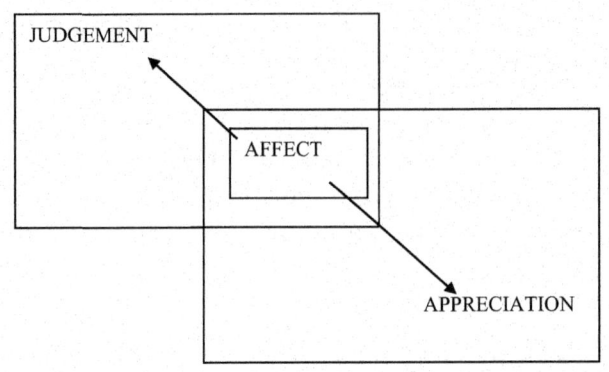

```
JUDGEMENT

        AFFECT

                    APPRECIATION
```

Feeling institutionalised as propositions

Aesthetics/value (criteria and assessment)

Figure 4.2 Appraisal

Source: After Martin (2000:147) and Martin and White (2005:45)

analyst to investigate the expression of emotional, ethical and aesthetic evaluation in interactions. The three main types of evaluation are known as **affect**, **judgement** and **appreciation**. Affect encodes emotions, the 'expressive resource we are born with', as Martin and White (2005:42) have it, whilst judgement and appreciation recontextualise these emotional feelings to specifically address judgements about behaviour and appreciation of aesthetic value. Figure 4.2 outlines the connection between these types of evaluation.

4.4.1 Affect

Affect is positioned at the centre of the evaluative capacity of language and broadly refers to how good or bad on a positive/negative spectrum a speaker or writer thinks something is. There is a potentially limitless set of lexical and grammatical expressions for the realisations of affect in language, although these can be grouped together into sets of general categories which will help you in carrying out an analysis of affect.

Categories in the system of affect address happiness and sadness (un/happiness), expressions of peace and anxiety (in/security) and feelings of achievement and frustration (dis/satisfaction). As demonstrated by the representative, although certainly not exhaustive, examples in Table 4.1, how good or bad a speaker believes a person or an event is can be wholly positive (jubilant) or wholly negative (heartbroken) and a range of circumstances in between. We often find positive

Table 4.1 Affect

Affect	Positive	Negative
Un/happiness	Cheerful, buoyant, jubilant, like, love, adore	Sad, melancholy, despondent, sorrowful, heartbroken
In/security	Together, confident, assured, comfortable, confident	Uneasy, anxious, freaked out, startled, surprised
Dis/satisfaction	Involved, absorbed, engrossed, satisfied, pleased	Flat, stale, jaded, cross, angry, furious, bored with

Source: After Martin and White (2005:51)

expressions of affect present when victory is being declared or celebrated. The statements below are from the speech of British Prime Minister Boris Johnson following the Conservative Party's election victory in December 2019:

> In this **glorious, glorious** pre-breakfast moment, before a new dawn rises [...]
> This election means that getting Brexit done is now the **irrefutable, irresistible, unarguable** position of the British people.

Johnson repeats the positive statement of happiness in 'glorious' and inscribes three positive expressions of his security ('irrefutable', 'unarguable') and satisfaction ('irresistible') that he could now 'Get Brexit Done', which was a major Tory slogan in this election campaign. Conversely and unsurprisingly, we tend to encounter statements of negative affect in moments when sorrow rather than jubilation is in the ascendency. The following statements are from the concession speech of Jeremy Corbyn, leader of the heavily defeated Labour Party in this election:

> This is obviously a very **disappointing** night for the Labour Party.
> The attacks [from the media] that take place on loved ones continue, and they're **disgraceful** and frankly they're **disgusting**.

Corbyn expresses his unhappiness ('disappointing') at what was the worst Labour Party performance at the national polls since the 1930s and also takes the opportunity to express his dissatisfaction ('disgraceful', 'disgusting') at the aggressive actions of the pro-Conservative media in this election.

Key Distinction: Inscribed and Invoked Appraisal

Lists of lexical items, such as those which compose Tables 4.1, 4.2 and 4.3, are very useful for setting out examples of evaluation and demonstrating the parameters of each evaluative type. However, these representative lists do not fully capture the fact that all three types of evaluation can also be rendered by more indirect strategies. The words in Table 4.1 and the examples in the utterances of Boris Johnson and Jeremy Corbyn are examples of affect which 'has been directly inscribed in discourse through the use of attitudinal lexis' (Martin and White, 2005:61). This type of direct evaluation is said to be **inscribed**. The Appraisal framework acknowledges, however, that evaluation in language can also be achieved by what are called ideational 'tokens'. These are words or clauses that do not directly construe evaluation but rather imply the emotional response of the speaker or reader and potentially the listener or reader with whom s/he is exchanging opinions. This is known as **invoked** evaluation. Let's look at an example. The following excerpt is from an article in the sports section of *The Scotsman* newspaper which is reviewing the rise and fall of tennis player Naomi Osaka after her defeat at Wimbledon in 2019:

> Her rise to the summit of the rankings mountain was **swift** and it was **spectacular**. She has only won three titles in her short career and two <u>of them have been grand slams</u>. When she won the second of those at the Australian Open, <u>she also became the world No.1</u>, a position she held until two weeks ago. In theory, <u>all her Christmases had come at once</u>.
>
> (*The Scotsman*, 1st July 2019)

In bold are two instances of directly inscribed evaluation where the reporter describes Osaka's success as 'swift' and 'spectacular', both positive judgements (when 'swift' is coupled with 'decline' rather than 'rise' it would, of course, be a negative evaluation). However, the extract is additionally evaluative beyond these direct construals. The underlined phrases are examples of invoked evaluation; 'two of them have been grand slams' and 'she also became the world No.1' are positive judgements of Naomi Osaka's success. These are statements of fact which the writer has chosen to include, and they operate to strengthen the positive portrayal of Osaka. 'All her Christmases had come at once' is suggestive of Osaka's happiness and satisfaction with this success. These underlined phrases do not directly construe judgement and affect but instead they imply the emotional response of the reporter.

4.4.2 Judgement

Judgement refers to evaluation about how people should behave, and therefore codifies ethical or moral reactions. The Appraisal framework recognises that evaluations of morality, ethics, behaviour and ultimately the character of a person have different levels of seriousness and so proposes two main types of judgement: social esteem and social sanction. Judgements of social sanction tend to be somewhat more serious than those of social esteem, as Martin (2000) explains:

> Social esteem involves admiration and criticism, typically without legal implications; if you have difficulties in this area you may need a therapist. Social sanction on the other hand involves praise and condemnation, often with legal implications; if you have problems in this area you may need a lawyer.
>
> (Martin, 2000:156)

Judgements of social sanction are more approving or condemning than those of social esteem. Social sanction is further subdivided into evaluations of propriety (how un/ethical someone is) and veracity (how un/truthful someone is). There are three subdivisions of social esteem: capacity (how in/capable someone is), normality (how un/usual someone is) and tenacity (how ir/resolute someone is). In some cases it is possible to chart a progression of judgement, an elevation of indicators of social esteem towards greater expressions of social sanction, for example, the difference between being naïve or foolish, which are negative judgements of capacity, and being dishonest or deceptive, which inscribe negative judgements of veracity. Indeed Martin and White (2005:52) offer the useful comparison of venial and mortal sins to refer to these different types of seriousness in terms of evaluative judgement. Table 4.2 offers a range of representative examples of how judgement can be inscribed.

These exemplar tables are useful starting points in an analysis, and we should remember that all types of evaluation can be invoked as well as inscribed. The tips offered in the box below will help you to carry out an analysis which is focussed on all three or just one type of evaluation. Have a look at the suggestions before reading the analysis of Example 4.1, which concentrates on the construal of judgement in a newspaper opinion piece.

Table 4.2 Judgement

Social Esteem	Positive (Admire)	Negative (Criticise)
Normality	Normal, natural, familiar, lucky	Odd, peculiar, erratic, obscure
Capacity	Powerful, sound, balanced	Slow, stupid, naïve, foolish
Tenacity	Cautious, careful, thorough	Timid, hasty, capricious
Social Sanction	Positive (Praise)	Negative (Condemn)
Veracity	Truthful, honest, candid	Dishonest, deceptive, lying, liar
Propriety	Good, moral, ethical, just, fair	Bad, immoral, corrupt, unfair

Source: After Martin (2000:156) and Martin and White (2005:53)

Tips for Applying the Appraisal Framework

- Consider the type of Appraisal to analyse. Are you interested in how the speaker or writer is offering judgement on the ethics of an event? Perhaps a consideration of aesthetic beauty is more apposite for your purposes.
- If you do not have a predetermined focus like this, you should carry out a twofold process. First, identify what type of evaluation is present in a text. Then think about the patterns that have emerged. Is one type of Appraisal more prominent than others? Is there a discernible pattern here? For example, is social esteem more prominent than social sanction in texts with a lot of judgement? Is in/security prominent but dis/satisfaction absent in texts marked for affect?
- Note instances of invoked evaluation as well as inscribed evaluation. Inscribed evaluation is often grammatically realised as adjectives, although – as you can see from the tables in this chapter – this is not always the case. For invoked evaluation, look out for descriptions of events or people which have an evaluative meaning. Often, invoked Appraisal will be represented by lengthier phrases or clauses but, again, not always. You will have to use your judgement as an analyst and your knowledge of language in an application of Appraisal.
- Appraisal of an event or people can be positive or negative. Mark positive Appraisal with [+ve] and negative Appraisal with [-ve].
- Practically speaking, a good but simple key is very useful. Mark one type of Appraisal or identify inscribed versus invoked Appraisal by using bold and italics, for example, or employ a colour code.
- The distribution of different types of Appraisal will tell you a lot about the stance of the speaker or writer. Remember that in CDA we are interested in the ideological implications of discourse. For example, if you find more social esteem than social sanction in a text which is focussed on the perpetrator of a murder, you might consider why this would be the case. After all, this is possibly the most heinous of all deviant acts. So, ask yourself about what factors might have prompted a less condemning representation.
- Also remember that in CDA we recognise the social power of discourse. If your Appraisal analysis of a text identifies a harsh evaluation of a minority group, for example, you should consider the effect of texts like this on how the group in question might be considered by society.

Example 4.1 is from the Comment section of *The Sun* newspaper, a British tabloid usually noted for social and political conservativism. The opinion piece is written by television personality Jeremy Clarkson, who is known for, amongst other populist opinions, a scepticism of the effects of climate change and global warming. Positive and negative judgement is marked here by the convention

[-ve] for negative and [+ve] for positive; instances of inscribed judgement are in bold whilst invoked judgement is underlined, judgements of social esteem are in italics, and other judgements indicate social sanction.

Example 4.1 Just leave *Greta Thunberg's Extinction Rebellion groupies* [-ve] glued to the railings to cause a real stink

Today, thousands of mums and dads will climb into their Volvos and drive to London to pick up their Extinction Rebellion kids, who've <u>spent the past two weeks at a fancy dress street party</u> [-ve].

I was in the centre of the capital last night and God, it was *annoying* [-ve]. [...]

Like almost all *sensible* [+ve] adults, I'll be glad to see the back of them, but I fear our relief will be short lived. Because <u>when the weather improves, we can be certain they'll be back</u> [-ve]. Only next time, I have devised a plan...

As we know, the police are so hamstrung by <u>human rights red tape</u> [-ve], they can't simply pick up these **halfwits** [-ve] by the ears and <u>lob them in the river</u> [+ve]. <u>Each one must be carried, gently, by five trained officers to a comfortable van and then driven off for a nice cup of tea</u> [-ve]. [...]

So, how's this for an idea. As these *fancy dress enthusiasts* [-ve] are largely middle-class kids, <u>they really don't want to throw a plant pot through a shop window</u> [-ve]. <u>They don't want to riot</u> [-ve]. <u>They just want to sit about humming</u> [-ve]. So, let's not waste a single minute of police time on them.

We therefore let plod get on with the problem of knife crime while we handle the eco protesters ourselves. We saw that happen this week. Early-morning commuters got to the Tube station for the cramped journey to work to find that one of the **eco loonies** [-ve] had <u>climbed on to the roof of the train</u> [-ve].

Did they call for the police? Did they <u>entice him down with celery</u> [-ve]? No. <u>They threw stuff at him</u> [+ve], and when that didn't work, <u>they climbed up there themselves and threw him very roughly to the ground</u> [+ve]. **Excellent** [+ve].

(Jeremy Clarkson, *The Sun*, 19th October 2019)

It is clear from this article that Jeremy Clarkson is no friend of climate change activists Extinction Rebellion, the group which has staged demonstrations globally since its founding in 2018, and their members are judged negatively throughout. Most of these negative judgements are expressions of the commentator's belief that these protestors are privileged youths with neither the ability nor the genuine will to effect any sort of change. In the headline they are described in terms of negative social esteem as nothing more than 'Greta Thunberg's Extinction Rebellion groupies', referring to the Swedish environmental activist who has publicly challenged governments and global institutions on climate change. The behaviour of these 'groupies' is repeatedly judged negatively by Clarkson, particularly in terms of social esteem: tenacity. By describing the demonstrators as having 'spent the past two weeks at a fancy dress street party' and 'fancy dress enthusiasts' who will return 'when the weather improves' and whose dedication to their cause is limited to 'sitting about humming', Clarkson is judging Extinction Rebellion as undedicated and uncourageous. Whilst these evaluations are invoked rather than explicitly inscribed, their force is not diminished. Clarkson does not use the words 'undedicated' and 'uncourageous' but instead offers several scenarios which leave the reader in no doubt about his evaluative opinion of these protestors.

This article also demonstrates how consistent use of negative or positive judgement can create a sort of crescendo effect in discourse through which the type of judgement used is elevated or increased. The constant lambasting of Extinction Rebellion right from the headline of the piece enhances the reader's negative impression of the group. The consistent inscriptions and invocations of negative social esteem cumulate so that by the fifth paragraph of the article – where the group's apparent lack of conviction is laid bare – the judgement has reached the level of social sanction: propriety. The overlexicalised portrayal of the demonstrators culminates so that the consistent negativity constructs an impression whereby they are not only to be criticised, but they should also be condemned. Negative social esteem piles up so that it eventually reaches the height of social sanction.

Clarkson also negatively judges certain social conditions in this article, proffering the notion that legislation which regulates police actions is too restrictive. It might seem anomalous for some to refer to human rights as unnecessarily obstructive, as is clearly implied by the phrase 'human rights red tape'. This negative judgement of social sanction: propriety is emphasised by the sarcastic scenario in which protestors must be 'carried, gently, by five trained officers to a comfortable van and then driven off for a nice cup of tea'. For Clarkson, the preferred scenario would be to 'lob them in the river'. In many contexts this action might invoke a negative judgement of social sanction, it usually being somewhat improper to throw a protestor into a river, but in this case the judgement invokes a positive alternative solution. Clarkson's opinions here are representative of a section of the Right in Britain which is generally hostile to human rights legislation, seeing it as overly restrictive and generally lacking common sense. This sort of 'common-sense defence' is often used to naturalise and legitimise certain unpalatable political or social positions. Part of the diatribe against the influence of the European Union in Britain has been to utilise anti-human rights arguments, and consecutive Conservative governments have promised to replace the Human Rights Act (which legislates for the European Convention on Human Rights in Britain) after Brexit.

It is not surprising that the positive judgements offered in this article are reserved for direct action, 'common sense' type responses to the apparently ineffectual and 'annoying' 'groupies' of Extinction Rebellion. 'They threw stuff at him' and 'they climbed up there themselves and threw him very roughly to the ground' both invoke positive social sanction: propriety. In Clarkson's opinion, this is the proper way to deal with 'middle-class kids' who do not really have the courage of their convictions in any case. The relatively informal language of this piece is called 'conversationalisation', and it helps to reduce the distance and build allegiances between writer and reader. Informal language is reminiscent of many opinion columns, particularly in the tabloid press. Clarkson's statement that a more sensible type of direct action would 'let plod get on with the problem of knife crime' is a good example of conversationalisation. The use of informal language in discourse contributes to interdiscursivity and would be addressed in the discursive practice dimension of Fairclough's model of CDA.

4.4.3 Appreciation

The third type of evaluation in the Appraisal framework is appreciation. This refers to expressions of how things are valued. Appreciation is comprised of the important subsections reaction, composition and valuation. Table 4.3 contains some representative examples to help explain appreciation.

Reaction describes impact (did it grab me?) and quality (did I like it?), composition refers to balance (did it hang together?) and complexity (was it hard to follow?), and valuation addresses questions like 'did I find it meaningful?'. You might notice a certain overlap between the types of appreciation and the three types of Mental process in the transitivity framework. There is an alignment between reaction and Mental processes of affection, composition and Mental processes of perception, and valuation and Mental processes of cognition. In

Table 4.3 Appreciation

Appreciation	Positive	Negative
Reaction: impact	Captivating, arresting...	Dull, boring, tedious, flat...
Reaction: quality	Good, beautiful, splendid...	Bad, ugly, repulsive, plain...
Composition: balance	Harmonious, symmetrical...	Unbalanced, contradictory...
Composition: complexity	Simple, pure, intricate, clear...	Ornate, extravagant, unclear...
Valuation	Profound, original, creative...	Shallow, derivative, dated...

Source: After Martin (2000:160) and Martin and White (2005:56)

Chapter 5 we will see how discourse can be analysed with the three functions of language in SFL simultaneously.

As part of a reshuffle of the UK Cabinet in July 2014, the then British Prime Minister, David Cameron, promoted eight female MPs to senior positions in government. One headline in the *Daily Mail* reported the arrival of the new members of the Cabinet to Downing Street with the headline 'Thigh-flashing Esther and the battle of the Downing St catwalk' in reference to the dress worn by new employment minister Esther McVey. Another article in the *Mail* (15th July 2014) was headlined '"Cameron's Cuties" make their presence felt as they march into Downing Street following dramatic Cabinet reshuffle' and was accompanied by several photographs of the new ministers. Despite this article being ostensibly about political manoeuvring at the highest level of government, the focus was on the fashion sense and physical appearance of the new ministers. Positive appreciation featured heavily in the article. In a positive expression of reaction, the reader is told that the new ministers will 'bring a touch of style to Number 10', and one of the ministers is described through inscribed positive reaction as 'glamorous' and 'looking good'; she also 'looked chic' and is 'leading the style set' with her 'long blonde hair perfectly coiffed'. 'Cameron's Cuties' in the headline is also an example of positive reaction.

There was very little reference to the political prowess of the new ministers. The appreciation was exclusively positive, but the focus of the article was aesthetic instead of judgemental, and the article came in for quite a lot of criticism. Writing in *The Guardian*, Hannah Marriot calls it an example of 'bleak predictability'. As critical discourse analysts, we are continuously focussed on the social work being done by discourse and must consider media language beyond the level of the text. Textually speaking, the Appraisal framework tells us that this article is replete with inscribed and invoked positive appreciation, but a consideration of the social impact of the piece recontextualises somewhat this ostensible positivity. These women have just been appointed to senior political roles, and yet this profile, heavy in aesthetic evaluation, does not include judgements of their capacity or tenacity for government. The article states that Esther McVey 'boasts a CV just as impressive as her wardrobe' and then proceeds in the remainder of the article to say nothing whatsoever about this CV. Ms McVey's qualifications for her new job would seem to be therefore that she has an admirable sense of style. This type of coverage is reminiscent of media pieces which focus overmuch on the dress sense of female politicians all the while addressing only in a limited way their professional status. Discourse which adopts a textual focus like this therefore furthers patriarchal agendas and undermines gender equality in professional life. If you were writing an essay or extended analysis on this article you might consider as part of its social practice how the article contributes to societal impressions of female professionals being somehow of less value than their male counterparts. Such impressions are manifested in the ongoing gender pay gap and in the requirement for ongoing schemes and projects to redress inequalities in workplace practices.

Summary of Chapter 4

This chapter has offered a comprehensive account of the interpersonal function of language within SFL by presenting overviews of mood, modality and the Appraisal framework. In each case the usefulness for CDA of viewing language as an interpersonal exchange has been explored. Through framing a proposition as a declaration, an order or a request, and by indicating probability, frequency, inclination or obligation through expressions of modality, a great deal can be communicated about the feelings of a speaker or writer to a listener or a reader. By considering certain institutional exchanges and a political speech, this chapter has illustrated the ideological significance of the 'clause as exchange'. This exchange between text encoder and text decoder is also at the heart of the expression of stance in language. The Appraisal framework is a model which you can apply to a whole range of texts and at varying levels of language to examine attitude to a person or event, how good or bad it is and how it is judged or valued by examining affect, judgement and appreciation. In the examples analysed in this chapter, the role of critical discourse analysts to pay close attention to the ideological operation of language has been central. So much of the power of language is contained within communicative exchanges. When we analyse the feelings which mark these exchanges with an appropriate focus on ideology, CDA can reveal a significant amount about the operation of discoursal exchanges in the social world: how a political audience is persuaded, how a newspaper commentator can celebrate or malign a protest movement or even only seemingly celebrate the advancement of women in politics. In Chapter 5 we will examine the third function of language in SFL, the textual function, and we will also demonstrate how all three functions can be applied in a single analysis.

Further Reading

Eggins, S. and Slade, D. (1997) *Analysing Casual Conversation*. London: Continuum.
Halliday, M.A.K. and Matthiessen, G. (2014) *An Introduction to Functional Grammar*, 4th edition. London and New York: Routledge.
Martin J.R., Matthiessen, G. and Painter, C. (1997) *Working with Functional Grammar*. London: Hodder Arnold.
Martin, J.R. and White, P.R.R. (2005) *The Language of Evaluation: Appraisal in English*. Basingstoke: Palgrave Macmillan.
Simpson, P. (1993) *Language, Ideology and Point of View*. London and New York: Routledge.
Thompson, G. (1996) *Introducing Functional Grammar*. London: Arnold.
Young, L., Fitzgerald, M. and Fitzgerald, S. (2018) *The Power of Language: How Discourse Influences Society*, 2nd edition. Sheffield: Equinox.

5 Strengthening Analysis
Cohesion and Coherence in Text

KEY TERMS IN CHAPTER 5: textual function, cohesion, coherence, chains, Themes, repetition, ellipsis, anaphora, cataphora, demand image, offer image, Given, New

MODELS OF ANALYSIS IN CHAPTER 5: cohesive devices, SFL

5.1 Introduction

Chapters 3 and 4 have explored the experiential and interpersonal functions of language in Systemic Functional Linguistics and demonstrated how the main models associated with these functions can reveal for critical discourse analysts much about the ideological operation of discourse. In this chapter we will examine the third function of language in SFL, known as the **textual function**, and will also consider how an analysis can pay attention to all three functions simultaneously. For students in particular, analysing the three SFL functions in a CDA-based essay or project can allow you to produce in-depth and revealing examinations of language. The analysis of a public information leaflet (Figure 5.2) will also be used to expand upon the discourse construction of the crime of sexual assault at the end of the chapter, demonstrating again the twin motivations of CDA to carry out close technical analysis of language and to explicate how this language operates ideologically in real-world scenarios.

The textual function is about how writers or speakers connect parts of discourse, and it is usually analysed by paying attention to **cohesion** and **coherence** in text. Cohesion refers to the internal connection between clauses in a text and coherence to how external connections are built between a text and its context. Essentially, the textual function is about how speakers or writers build connections with discourse; analysis is focussed on the organisation of text within a piece of spoken, written and indeed visual language. Young and Fitzgerald (2006:20) state that the textual function of language attends to questions like 'What holds the discourse together?' and consider cohesion initially in terms of **chains** and **Themes**. Chains are words which refer to a given topic and Themes are the 'starting point' for each 'message' in the discourse' (Young and Fitzgerald 2006:20).

5.2 Cohesion and Coherence in 'Innovative' Education

Example 5.1 is from the website of Zayed University in Abu Dhabi, an excerpt from the 'About ZU' section of the homepage where the institution offers academics and students a definition of its core values.

Example 5.1 Zayed University website

About the University

<u>Zayed University</u> is a national and regional leader in educational **innovation**. <u>Founded in 1998</u> and proudly bearing the name of the Founder of the Nation – the late Sheikh Zayed bin Sultan Al Nahyan, this flagship institution has met the President's high expectations. <u>Zayed University</u> has two **modern** campuses in Dubai and Abu Dhabi that welcome both national and international students.

Vision Statement

<u>Globally recognized</u> as the **leading** university in the region for **excellence** in educational **innovation**, research, and student **leadership** development that serves the changing needs of the nation in **economic**, social and cultural **advancements**.

University Values

<u>Zayed University</u> is committed to:

- Professional Ethics
- Leadership
- Excellence
- Collaboration
- Innovation
- Civic Responsibility
- Respect for Diversity
- Positive Educational Environment

> **Strategic Objectives**
>
> - <u>Prepare</u> qualified graduates in an **innovative** and supportive educational environment who demonstrate academic excellence and **leadership** skills
> - <u>Enhance</u> the **leadership** role of the University in scientific research and development in ways that contribute to a **knowledge-based economy**
> - <u>Demonstrate</u> institutional and academic **excellence** through national and international accreditation programs
> - <u>Ensure</u> provision of all administrative services in compliance with quality, efficiency and transparency
> - <u>Enhance</u> the culture of **innovation** and creativity (within institutional environment)
>
> (www.zu.ac.ae/main/en/explore_zu/index.aspx)

Vocabulary chains are constructed by considering the words and phrases which refer to dominant topics in a text. In this text 'innovation' and 'leadership' are main topics, and lexical items which construct vocabulary chains on these topics are in bold in this example. We can see that references to 'innovation' and 'leadership' permeate the discourse, feature prominently in each of these short subsections and are one way that cohesion is constructed across the text by the repetition of synonymous terms. By constantly referencing how 'innovative' the institution is, this text constructs a perception of Zayed University as 'modern' and forward-looking. The text is cohesively held together by the consistent restatement of associated words and phrases. Phrases like 'educational innovation' and 'knowledge-based economy' are representative of the recasting of higher education institutions throughout the world as commercial companies and contribute to the marketisation of education referred to in Chapter 2. You may be aware of the prominence of phrases with similar meanings in the publicity material of your own institutions; websites and brochures of UK universities for example are replete with phrases like 'enterprise' and 'entrepreneurial university', a phrase that Mautner (2005:96) has called a 'previously unthinkable adjective-noun combination'.

It is also important to note the fact that many words and phrases in this context are abstract and unspecific. It is frequently the case in higher education, particularly but by no means exclusively in the United States and Britain, that 'innovation' is achieved by large-scale expenditure on campus building projects and capital investments whilst other areas of higher education such as permanent staff appointments and research in the Arts and Humanities are heavily divested. A report from the Higher Education Statistics Agency (HESA) which assessed UK university expenditure between 2015 and 2017 found that institutions had increased capital spending on building projects by 34.9% whilst spending on staff had reduced by 3.35%. In the same period institutional income and the value of university assets increased. The report found that combined UK universities reserves had almost quadrupled since 2010 and stood at £44.27bn. Institutions which peddle the 'innovative' model of higher education can then be seen to hoard huge reserves whilst decreasing commitments to teaching and learning. Utilising words and phrases such as 'innovation', 'leadership' and 'excellence' is one way that institutions use language to obfuscate the insidiousness of their operations; these words are all semantically positive but the discourse in which they appear rarely provides specific information about how these strategies will be pursued. Phrases like 'development that serves the changing needs of the nation' and 'scientific research and development in ways that contribute to a knowledge-based economy' are equally euphemistic. We know that CDA also addresses what is not present in discourse, and Mayr (2008:44) reminds us that 'what is completely omitted from governmental and university management discourse is the question of whether or not it is morally right to promote consumerism and managerialism as the only viable model in academia'. In the case of this example, references to teaching and learning are also notably absent.

By considering vocabulary chains alone in terms of lexical cohesion, we have been able to carry out a compelling, if fairly short, Critical Discourse Analysis of this section of text from a university website. Beginning with a focus on the text, the discussion can be broadened to consider ideological motivations and implications of the discourse. There are, however, several other important features of cohesion which should also be addressed by an analysis focussed on the textual function of language which will be outlined below.

You are probably very familiar with the term 'theme' in a general sense. For example, students will usually have attended to major themes when writing essays about literary works. The textual content makes it clear that the main theme of the university website example here is the description of the various ways in which the institution is a 'leader in educational innovation', although we have noted that it is not necessarily clear how this leadership is achieved. 'Theme' also has a more specific function in SFL, where it is used to refer to the word or phrase at the beginning of a clause. Each clause must have a 'Topical Theme', what Martin, Matthiessen and Painter (1997:24) describe as 'the first element in the clause that expresses some kind of "representational" meaning'.

The Themes in Example 5.1 have been underlined and are as follows: Zayed University, Founded in 1998, Zayed University, Globally recognized, Zayed University, Prepare, Enhance, Demonstrate, Ensure, Enhance. An important part of cohesion relates to how text encoders order the message they wish to communicate to text decoders, and a focus on Theme reveals to the analyst how these messages are begun. We can see from this list that the major Themes in the text correlate very much with the message which has emerged from our previous discussion on vocabulary chains. 'Zayed University' itself is the element which expresses 'representational meaning' in three of the clauses, importantly those at the beginning of the discourse, whilst 'prepare', 'enhance', 'demonstrate' and 'ensure' identify Material actions which the institution will undertake. A clear impression of activity and improvement is recognisable here. Owing to the repeated reference to Material actions and the prominent presence of the university itself, these Themes operate strongly to hold the discourse together. They are words which are intended to represent or stand for the institution. When Theme refers to the beginning of a clause and indicates what it will be about, the remainder of the clause, the part which realises the message indicated by the Theme, if you like, is known as the Rheme. So in the sentence 'Zayed University *is a national and regional leader in educational innovation*' the Rheme is in italics and provides the reader with additional information. Again, we can demonstrate through this commentary the complementary relationship between SFL and CDA. Where SFL focusses on the organisation of the discourse through identifying the Theme and Rheme of a text, CDA expands upon this identification to tell us about the motivations and the ideological positioning of the producer of that text.

Topical Themes, the elements underlined in the university text for example, are made up of participants, processes or circumstances, which you will remember as the core elements of a clause when discussing the experiential function of language and which we used in the transitivity analysis in Chapter 3. This is why Topical Themes are sometimes referred to as Ideational, another word for Experiential in SFL. There are two other types of Theme which can occur in discourse which can be significant. Interpersonal Themes reveal a speaker or writer's position towards the content of a clause. Given the information-giving nature of the Zayed University text which we have focussed on so far, none of the clauses which make up this discourse have an Interpersonal Theme, which is usually indicated by adverbs such as 'fortunately', 'happily', 'honestly' or 'correctly', for example. This is not at all surprising in this sort of text, but Interpersonal Themes may often be indicated in different types of discourse arenas, such as in commentary pieces in newspapers. Obviously, these types of words indicate something about the feelings of a speaker or writer and so are identified as Interpersonal. The third type of Theme is known as the Textual Theme, which contains conjunctions such as 'and', 'but' or 'therefore'. Conjunctions connect clauses together and contribute to the organisation of discourse. You will notice that these three types of Theme correspond with the three functions of language in SFL, a reminder that discourse can be examined with all three functions in mind simultaneously. Before turning to an example of this type of analysis, we must first outline some of the other devices in language which are used to construct cohesion.

Alongside Theme and vocabulary chains, there are a number of other related **cohesive devices** which can be significant in discourse. The most obvious of these is probably **repetition** of the same lexical item or phrase throughout a piece of text. Repetition is clearly related to other cohesive devices, and there are several instances of repetition in Example 5.1, most notably 'leadership' and 'innovation'. Repetition enables the consistent restatement of important aspects of a discourse. In advertisements, for example, the name of a product or one of its key features is likely to be repeated, whilst in the media repetition is used to construct overlexicalisation, which was introduced in Chapter 2. In an article in the right wing press, which is anti-immigration, for example, we might expect the repetition of words like 'illegal'. This in turn leads to the construction of an ill-informed 'moral panic' (the representation in discourse of an issue in society as more threatening than it may be in reality) around immigrant communities, which are then the victims of racist and xenophobic behaviour. This is an example of what critical discourse analysts recognise as the social consequences of ideological language.

Ellipsis is another important feature of cohesion and occurs when speakers or writers omit certain words or phrases in a message, safe in the knowledge that listeners or readers will be able to decode the textual meaning from the surrounding text. The 'Vision Statement' section of the Zayed text begins 'Globally recognised as the leading university in the region for excellence…' and continues in the same innovation-establishing vein without actually stating the name of the institution, which is easily retrievable from the rest of text. Advertising language is often replete with ellipsis, the easy retrievability meaning that the text encoder can be comprehensive and concise.

Anaphoric reference is a cohesive device through which speakers or writers connect words in a text to ones that come later. For example, if we consider the two opening sentences of the Zayed University text, there are two examples of anaphora. These are underlined below:

> Zayed University is a national and regional leader in educational innovation. Founded in 1998 and proudly bearing the name of the Founder of the Nation – the late Sheikh Zayed bin Sultan Al Nahyan, this flagship institution has met the President's high expectations.

In this example 'this flagship institution' and 'the President' are examples of referents which connect back to 'Zayed University' and 'the late Sheikh Zayed bin Sultan Al Nahyan' respectively. Often anaphoric references are used in discourse to enhance the readability of a text. If the initial noun phrases were simply repeated here, the text would not be very concise. Using noun phrases as referents also enables text encoders to make additional or emphatic points; in this case defining the university as a 'flagship institution' contributes further to the overall message of this discourse. Many examples of anaphora are realised through the use of pronouns. Have a look at the interaction below, which might occur in a workplace scenario:

> MANAGER: I would like you to ensure that Paul carries out the review.
> ASSISTANT MANAGER: I have spoken to him but he has spoken to his union and they insist it is voluntary.

There are several instances of anaphora underlined here. the pronouns 'him', 'he' and 'his' all refer to Paul; 'they' refers to Paul's union; and 'it' is the review which

Paul may or may not have to carry out. We are able to understand the Assistant Manager's words because they link back to the Manager's utterance. Consider how unwieldy this utterance would be without the use of anaphora:

ASSISTANT MANAGER: I have spoken to Paul but Paul has spoken to Paul's union and Paul's union insist that the review is voluntary.

Anaphoric references in texts are complemented by **cataphoric references**. These are references which refer to words in the following text, essentially operating in the opposite way.

ASSISTANT MANAGER: Our position is that you have to complete it.
PAUL: My union does not agree with the company's position that the review has to be completed.

In this case the pronoun 'our' links forward to 'the company', and 'it' links forward to 'the review'.

Anaphora and cataphora both comprise the broader category of **endophora**, which simply refers to linguistic items which are connected to other linguistic items in the same text. Both anaphora and cataphora are examples of endophoric references. Endophoric references are contrasted by exophoric references, which are those that occur outside of the text in the broader external context.

PAUL: You think you're so important, you're only the Assistant Manager.
ASSISTANT MANAGER: Excuse me?
PAUL: You're only from the Old Mill Road.
ASSISTANT MANAGER: How dare you?

In this additional element to the invented narrative above, Paul invokes background knowledge which is shared by the Assistant Manager to make a point, in this case geographical awareness of the local area. This exophoric referent is obviously external to the previous interactions. Depending on your own experiences, you might consider these sorts of workplace interactions as fairly representative despite the invention here.

A consideration of exophoric alongside endophoric references brings us to the topic of **coherence**. Coherence often forms part of the phrase 'cohesion and coherence' in a general sense, which can give the somewhat misleading impression that the two terms are interchangeable. However, there is an important difference. Cohesion refers to the internal connections in a text – which can be realised by combinations of the cohesive devices discussed here – whilst coherence refers to the connection of a text with its wider context. In the exophoric example above, coherence relies on the pragmatic principle of cooperation (Grice, 1975). Paul's second turn 'You're only from the Old Mill Road' is an example of conversational implicature. Essentially, he is implying that the Assistant Manager should not consider herself so important because she is from a fairly conventional social background. We know that the Assistant Manager

COHESION AND COHERENCE IN TEXT

has successfully inferred what has been implied through her response 'How dare you?', which of course pragmatically operates as a rebuke despite its semantic appearance as an interrogative.

So whilst textual cohesion can be taken as a component of coherence, much broader considerations are necessary to evaluate the coherence of a text. Young, Fitzgerald and Fitzgerald (2018:129) state that coherence is an 'aspect of the textual metafunction that refers to the connection between the discourse and the immediate and broader situation outside the discourse'. Coherence is the external connection between the text and the situation in which it occurs. In order to analyse coherence you should refer to the immediate situational context of a text and to its wider cultural context. Use the task to think about the coherence of the Zayed text before reading on.

Student Task

Example 5.1 is from a university website. Think about the homepage of institutional websites with which you might be familiar, perhaps a local council or your own educational institution. What provides the situational context of the main text? Are there other sections such as menus or sidebars? What about images?

Given the commentary in this chapter and in Chapter 2, what aspects do you think are important for the wider cultural context of this example? What does the text and image say about the world beyond the website? How does this discourse envisage higher education?

In this text the immediate situational context refers to the accompanying text and image on the website. Example 5.1 comprises the 'About ZU' part of the homepage; additional text comprises tabs titled 'Colleges', 'Admissions', 'Student Affairs', 'Library', 'Research', 'Alumni', 'Media Center', 'Employment' and 'e-Participation'. There is also a sidebar menu with links to 'Accreditation', 'President's Message' and 'Strategic Partnerships'. The text is accompanied by a prominent image of the university's futuristic campus. There are no images of students or specific facilities on the homepage, although they do appear in other sections of the website.

The context of this example is created by this text and image and by the wider cultural context in which the website takes on meaning. References on the website to 'strategic partnerships' and the almost *ad nauseum* references to 'innovation' and 'leadership' alongside the image of a state-of-the-art building reinforce certain values in higher education in general. Viewers of this webpage can connect this text to texts produced by other institutions which advertise and define themselves through very similar language. This business-based language links education to commercialism. This text assumes the societal importance of certain principles and it is using this webpage to demonstrate the university's embodiment of these principles, that there is value in modern campuses, that higher education is served by 'innovation' and 'leadership', and that international connections are desirable, for example. This website is representative of the content and focus of university websites throughout the developed world and particularly in Britain, the United States, the Middle East and China. Whilst Anglo-American examples do not always appear as patriotic as their international counterparts, their discourse does refer frequently to concepts like 'civic responsibility' and 'cultural heritage'.

By analysing the textual function of language in this text through focussing on cohesion and coherence, we have been able to say a great deal about how linguistic connections are developed and how this discourse is organised. As critical discourse analysts we have paid attention throughout the analysis to the operation of this text as a piece of discourse in the social world, constructing, disseminating and reinforcing ideologies in society. Like the examples offered in Chapters 3 and 4 on the experiential and interpersonal functions, this examination of the textual function makes clear the important link between Systemic Functional Linguistics and Critical Discourse Analysis. SFL encompasses models and approaches to discourse which facilitate CDA in exposing ideologies and principles operative in discourse, and we must always be strident in pointing out that discourse has a crucial role in naturalising and legitimising the seemingly 'common sense' organisation of the social world.

5.3 SFL in CDA

The experiential, interpersonal and textual functions of language have been comprehensively explored and applied in the last three chapters, and you should by now have a keen appreciation of the usefulness of a systemic functional perspective when undertaking a critical analysis of language. The analyses so far have occasionally made links between the three functions of language, noting for example the fact that a commentator's judgement in the Appraisal system is also an example of an Interpersonal Theme when addressing the textual function; or when we assess words like 'prepare', 'enhance', 'demonstrate' as a vocabulary chain, they can also be defined experientially as Material processes which reinforce the activities of an institution. Generally, however, we have treated the functions of language and their major models and approaches separately in order to ensure that they are well understood. It is therefore important that we also make clear that these functions work together and simultaneously when constructing the meanings of text and, as such, all three can be utilised in an analysis. A student essay or a similar investigatory writing task which can demonstrate an ability to apply analysis of the three functions of language and which articulates the links between these functions and attends to the overall operation of the data being examined in society will usually be a very successful piece of work.

5.3.1 Political Leaflets

You will also have developed an appreciation by now of the close connection between language and politics, and an awareness of CDA as itself a political exercise. We have examined the representations of a few political situations already, such as industrial disputes and a climate change demonstration, and in Chapter 8 we will think specifically about critical language models for the analysis of political speeches. Alongside being reported and through giving speeches, politics is also done, perhaps much more fundamentally, through the process of campaigning. Recent decades have also seen the increased 'mediatisation' of politics, which refers to a dialogical relationship between the political and media spheres in our contemporary context. Media now plays an essential role in politics. It is a vehicle through which political messages are communicated, and also a site for the assessment and analysis of those messages. This reality in turn shapes how politicians use language such as in speeches or political advertisements. In the twenty-first century, politicians conduct themselves in unprecedented ways through social media. For example, former US President Donald Trump has been particularly noteworthy for his unfiltered and frequently undignified Twitter presence – although he is now banned from the platform – and Montgomery (2017) has pointed out that rather than be condemned for the frequent inappropriateness of his discourse, Trump's supporters often view this as a sign of his authenticity.

Despite the importance of new discourse arenas like social media (see further Chapter 11), traditional methods of campaigning such as leaflets and placards continue to be central to the political process. The utilisation of text and image and the necessity to focus on core messages in a fairly limited space make political leaflets a type of discourse particularly amenable to critical analysis, and they can be examined using the three functions of SFL. Figure 5.1 is a political leaflet from the Irish Green Party's campaign for local government elections in 2019.

Experiential Function

The transitivity processes in this leaflet are almost exclusively Material; it is important that politicians are seen to be 'doing' rather than, say, only 'thinking' about the actions they will take. The three sections labelled as 'Priorities' are replete with Material processes which establish this candidate as a proactive politician. Given that the Green Party, an environmentally aware and ostensibly left wing party, is often characterised as a movement which is against what might be termed industrial progress – think of their well-established commitment to processes like recycling and opposition to building schemes and transport initiatives which are not environmentally friendly or have high 'carbon footprints' – the semantics of these processes are also important. The Material processes are not about stereotypical 'Green' actions like reducing or reusing but are 'build' and 'strengthen' whilst also acknowledging the importance to 'repair' and 'improve' rather than just replace. The environmental agenda is retained by

COHESION AND COHERENCE IN TEXT

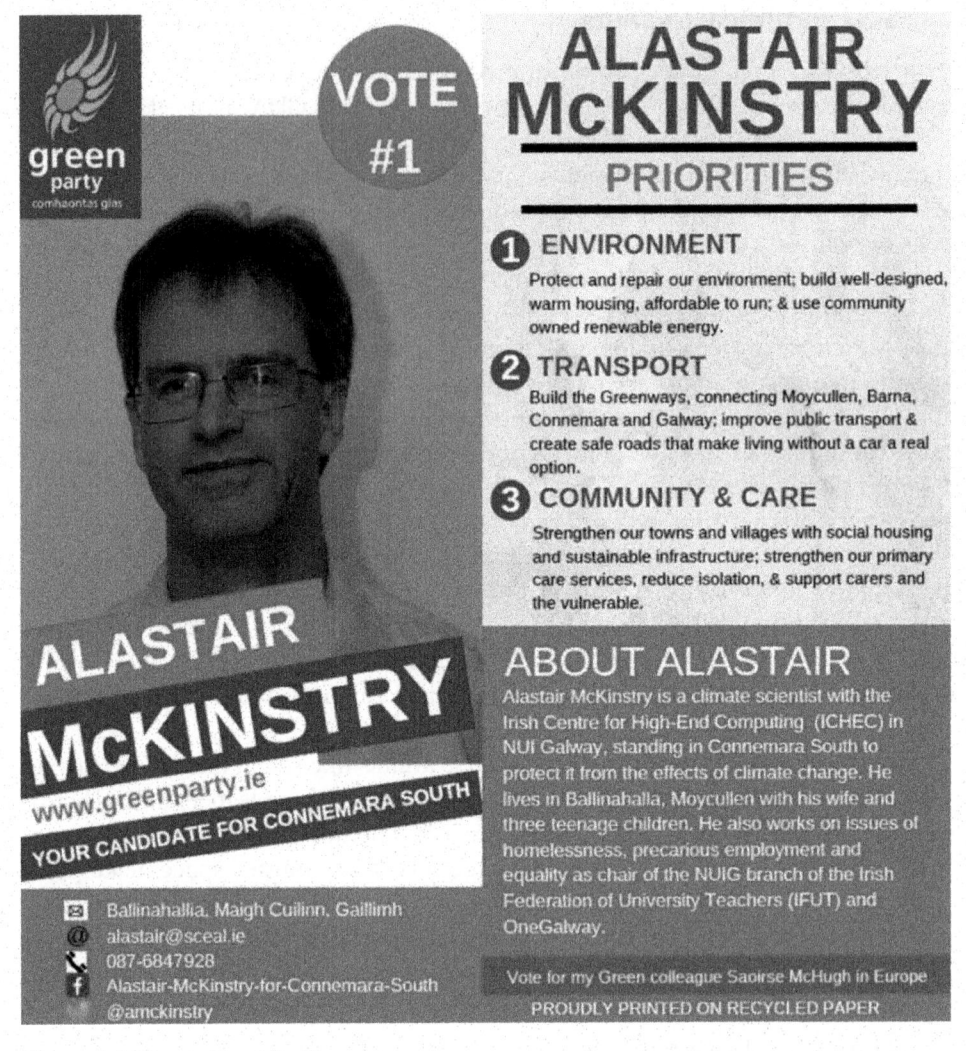

Figure 5.1 Green Party leaflet

the other elements of these clauses, Goals such as 'well-designed, warm housing' and Circumstances like 'with social housing and sustainable infrastructure'. The section about the candidate himself opens with a fairly conventional Relational clause telling the voter what he 'is'; in this case, being a climate scientist at a reputable Irish university adds status to the candidate. This status is enhanced by a statement on the other socially important issues on which he 'works'; this candidate is welded tightly to community actions.

Interpersonal Function

The leaflet contains the most prominent imperative mood in any political campaign document, telling the reader to 'vote', but in general the mood of the leaflet is almost entirely declarative, and information is given in the form of statements. The clauses in the 'Priorities' section might initially appear as imperatives, but these do not command the voter to 'protect', 'build' or 'strengthen' but rather they are an expression that these are the intentions of the candidate. The clauses could be envisaged as 'Alastair McKinstry will protect/build/strengthen…' or 'Alastair McKinstry's priorities are to protect/build/strengthen…', but sometimes full sentences can be deemed too unwieldy in advertising language. When words are omitted from a clause like this, it is an example of ellipsis or elliptical constructions, which are common in many information-giving texts. There are no interrogative clauses in this leaflet, so any questioning or equivocation is not present, although you may have seen other political campaign material which makes use of the interrogative mood in question-and-answer sequences. In such cases the answer to negatively focussed questions – 'Which party failed to improve healthcare?', for example – will be inevitably a candidate's political opponents, whilst positively focussed questions – 'Who will improve healthcare?' – will be the candidate her/himself. Wh- questions – such as 'What will you do to improve healthcare?' – can also be used to set up a list of declarative answers which contain a candidate's policies. In this leaflet these are offered in the 'Priorities' section. The leaflet also does not use modal verbs and adverbs. Clauses with high modal statements of inclination and obligation – such as 'I will definitely improve healthcare' – might seem potentially useful in this context but, as acknowledged in Chapter 3, often categorical assertions – 'I will improve healthcare' for example – are actually more effective. Political language often employs modality in statements like 'I am committed to improving healthcare', but again these are somewhat less effective than the categorical assertion, even if in many cases neither the commitment nor the assertion will actually be realised. In this example the Green Party chooses to declare what their priorities are with a list of statements which gives the impression that they are all achievable. If we follow the tips for applying the Appraisal framework (see Section 4.4.2) and focus on the lexical semantics of this discourse, each of these priorities can be said to invoke positive judgements of the candidate. Having these policies and this status implies capability and tenacity.

We will outline specific models for multimodal analysis in Chapter 10, but obviously the visual elements of political leaflets are also significant. In terms of the interpersonal function, the main interaction between viewers and represented participant in this leaflet is through the gaze of the candidate. Kress and van Leeuwen (2006:59) define an image where there is eye contact between a represented participant and viewers as a **demand image**, whilst an **offer image** refers to an image where this direct gaze is not present. In demand images direct interaction operates to build some sort of psychological relationship, often of affinity, between represented participant and viewers, whilst in an offer image viewers look at the image and evaluate the participant. Obviously other elements of an image like additional props and settings are also important, although in this case the setting is decontextualised so that the viewer's attention is exclusively on the candidate. Other candidates might choose to be photographed with a crowd of supporters, with another party member such as the leader or an elite party elder, or in a setting relevant to a specific campaign such as in a hospital or a local factory. The photograph here is a demand image. There is direct interaction between candidate and viewer so that there is no sense that he might have anything to hide. The candidate literally looks potential voters in the eye and stands alongside his policies. This leaflet also adheres to Kress and van Leeuwen's **Given** and **New** compositional structure, in which the Given information on the left-hand side of a text refers to knowledge a viewer already knows or recognises whilst special attention is paid to New information on the right. Machin (2007) connects this type of structure to the cognitive processes involved in reading from left to right in many Western cultures. In this leaflet the recognisable candidate (probably even more recognisable as this is an election for local government rather than national parliament) comprises the Given whilst the New is composed of the policies of candidate and party. It is also noteworthy that many of the visual aspects of this leaflet in particular are reminiscent of the analysis carried out by critical discourse analysts when considering advertising language (Simpson, Mayr and Statham, 2018:97). After all, election leaflets are advertisements of a specific type. Whilst it is unlikely that there has been no technological enhancement to the photograph – as we will see in Chapter 10 airbrushing and colour manipulation are very common in visual discourse – this has been kept to a minimum here. The light of the camera flash is visible on the candidate's spectacles, for example, where this could have been airbrushed out, and this retains the sense of trustworthiness and authenticity in the image. The visual modality of this discourse is somewhat higher therefore than the very low modal worlds which are presented in a discourse arena like women's lifestyle magazines, for example (Machin and Thornborrow, 2003). Simpson, Mayr and Statham (2018:97) state that 'high modality in visuals means that things or people look "realistic" – the way they would look if we saw them in real life (e.g. in a family photograph)'. This is exactly the authentic and approachable impression the Green Party would like the electorate to have of this candidate through the retention of aspects of 'reality' in the image.

Textual Function

Visual aspects of discourse are also important when assessing the leaflet in terms of the textual function. Machin (2007) explores the importance of colour when considering visual semiotics. The reproduction in Figure 5.1 is in black and white, but the original leaflet, unsurprisingly, makes significant use of the colour green. The prominence of green is an obvious choice and constructs cohesive connections in the original leaflet linking party, candidate and polices. There is also coherence with political contexts outside the text through image. The Green Party emblem connects this leaflet to the party organisation nationally (and indeed internationally in terms of the wider 'green movement').

Most of the cohesion in the leaflet is achieved at the verbal level, and several of the cohesive devices overviewed earlier in this chapter are identifiable here. Repetition is evident in some of the candidate's key policies; 'build', 'strengthen' and 'protect' are repeated to emphasise their importance. As this is a very short text, repetition is particularly noticeable and, as noted in the experiential discussion above, these are all Material processes which elevate the sense of proactivity in this campaign. Perhaps unsurprisingly, 'environment' is also repeated. The text producer emphasises certain words through grammatical structuring. 'Build' and 'strengthen' both form the Topical Theme in two clauses, and 'protect' is the first Theme identified in the 'Priorities' section. These repeated Topical Themes also form vocabulary chains with words with similar meanings in the surrounding text, such as build-repair-connect, improve-create-support. Thematically important vocabulary chains operate throughout the discourse, safe-sustainable-well-designed-renewable-environment-reduce, for example. It is clear that very strong cohesive links are constructed throughout the discourse. The name of the party is repeated on three occasions and the candidate's name four times, seven when you consider the names of the social media accounts given underneath the main image. We are reminded of the observations above on the importance of media and social media in particular in contemporary politics. This aspect is just as significant in a local election as at a national level. The name of the Connemara South constituency (a region in the west of Ireland) is also repeated on three occasions. The extent of the repetition of key aspects provides a conceptual link between Green Party-Alastair McKinstry-Connemara South. There is further lexical cohesion constructed through reference to places within this locale (Moycullen-Barna-Connemara-Galway-NUI Galway-Ballinahalla). These references to external contexts are exophoric and therefore construct coherence between the immediate context of the leaflet and the outside world. The text is therefore internally cohesive and externally connects through coherence to the areas which will benefit if this candidate is elected. The Galway element (Galway is the largest urban centre in the region) is repeated on several occasions, also referring to OneGalway, a social aid initiative which joins student unions and trade unions in the area, and NUIG (National University of Ireland Galway), where the candidate works as a climate scientist. It is very clear that this candidate is connected to this area and to the policies which will affect it.

There are clear connections between the aspects of the discourse which are examined by each of the functions of language within SFL. Some of the repeated elements above are Material processes at the experiential level and invoke positive judgements of capacity and tenacity at the interpersonal level. The main image is a visual Relational process which identifies Alastair McKinstry as the Green Party candidate for Connemara South, and it can also be examined interpersonally in terms of being a demand image. 'Vote' is a Material process rendered here in the imperative mood and surrounded by a colour which textually links it to candidate, policies and party. Again, all three functions are relevant to the analysis. The Facebook page for the candidate operates similarly.

'Alastair-McKinstry-for-Connemara-South' is Relational in identifying the candidate, interpersonal in declaring this information and cohesive within the text through repetition of the constituency's name and through vocabulary chains which connect it to areas in the locality mentioned in the text. That this is a social media page lifts the campaign out of the local context of the leaflet into the wider context of the campaign online, which we can assume will itself have links to other candidates and the party organisation nationally, as well as to election information and voter registration instructions.

Students who produce an analysis which utilises knowledge across the three functions of SFL not only demonstrate awareness of this fundamental approach to critical language studies but will also be able to construct an extremely thorough examination of the data. As critical discourse analysts you must of course consider the discourse within wider societal contexts. In terms of this example, the context can be both specific and more general. Specifically, the effectiveness of the language here potentially affects the make-up of local government (and this candidate was elected); an environmental voice may be in a position to further the many policies referred to here, for example. The lexico-grammatical structure of the leaflet which has been analysed through the three functions of language in this chapter legitimises environmentally focussed actions; the promises and priorities of the candidate are assumed to be positive and desired. The general election in 2020 was the best-ever result for the Green Party in Ireland, which is reflective of an increased electoral success for the green movement throughout Europe in an age when progressive voices are attempting to establish the importance of the climate emergency for society. Whether the decision of the Green Party to support the formation of a much less progressive government following the 2020 election comes back to haunt the party at the ballot box remains to be seen. Students of modern British politics will know that the decision of the Liberal Democrats to form a coalition with the Tories in 2010 has almost eradicated the electability of the party amongst its traditional voter base. In Chapter 4 we saw an example of powerful discourse in the right wing media which is resistant to the contemporary upsurge in environmental activism. At a more general and perhaps more subtle level, political leaflets like this operate to legitimise the political process overall. They further strengthen the notion that elections and democracy are the so-called 'natural order of things', which in turn legitimises the power of parliaments constructed in this way. It is important to remember that, regardless of whether or not you might have an affinity with the democratic process, democracy is no more organic or inherent than any other system. It too is constructed, and this construction is manifested in many ways. It is likely that many people hold a somewhat idealistic view of dominant political processes, assuming that they ensure that the 'will of the people' is properly represented, for example, but of course we know that the people's consent is actively fought for and that discourse plays a crucial role in this hegemonic process.

5.3.2 Public Service Leaflets: Victim Blaming

We will conclude this chapter by examining another leaflet. This flyer is not for a political campaign but instead formed part of a public awareness campaign administered by the Northern Ireland Office (NIO), the Department of Health, Social Services and Public Safety (DHSSPS) and the Police Service of Northern Ireland (PSNI). The leaflet shown in Figure 5.2, originally commissioned in 2013, was redistributed at an event for young people in Belfast in February 2020.

Experiential Function

This leaflet addresses the very traumatic issue of sexual assault and ostensibly operates as a safety warning to potential victims. In terms of transitivity, both Relational and Material processes dominate the discourse. The headline is clear that 'alcohol is the number one date rape drug', and this campaign is focussed on persuading potential victims of sexual assault to therefore control consumption and regulate associated behaviours. The Material focus of the text is therefore on things which people should not do, 'get so drunk', 'go alone', 'accept drink' or 'walk home alone'. We will pick up on the ideological significance of how this discourse is constructed in the discussion below, but it is important to note at this stage the prominence of 'you' as the sole participant of these processes. This is an example of what Fairclough (1989:62) calls 'synthetic personalization'. Given the high value placed upon individuality in Western cultures in particular, readers may have an aversion to being addressed as part of a mass audience, so messages in advertising language are considered more effective when they

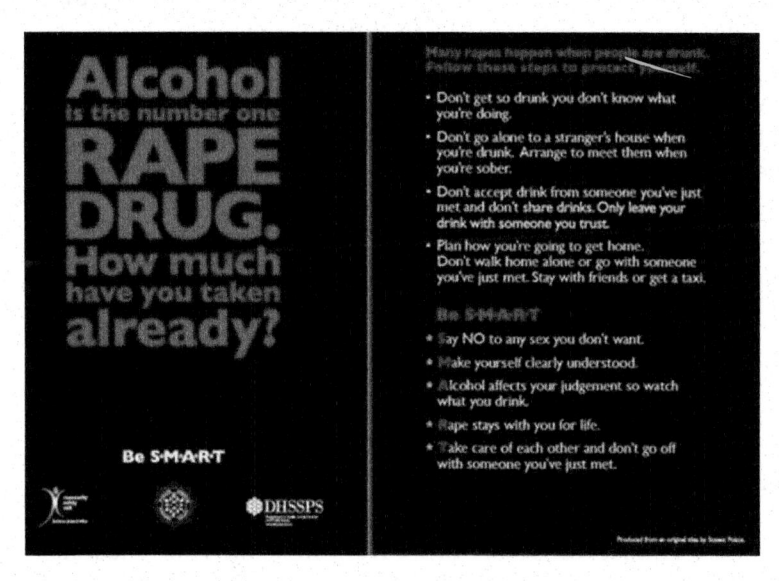

Figure 5.2 PSNI leaflet

are aimed apparently at an individual reader. The prominent use of the 'you' pronoun is an example of direct address, which clearly places the responsibility for the careful behaviour this leaflet is promoting on potential sexual assault victims. The second person pronoun is present in the following clauses: How much have you taken already; protect yourself; you don't know what you're doing; when you're drunk; when you're sober; someone you've just met; leave your drink with someone you trust; how you're going to get home; you've just met; sex you don't want; make yourself clearly understood; alcohol affects your judgement; watch what you drink; rape stays with you; someone you've just met. 'Alcohol' is the Identifier in the headline of the leaflet and the Actor in the clause 'Alcohol affects your judgement'; rape is the Sensor in 'rape stays with you' (whilst 'stay' might usually be a Material process, in this case it is a Mental process of cognition in that it is a metaphorical reference to the process of remembering) and the Existent in 'Many rapes happen', where the process of rape has been nominalised, but otherwise 'you' is the main participant in all of the processes in this discourse.

Interpersonal Function

As an example of direct address, as well as being the main Carrier and Actor of Relational and Material processes, the 'you' pronoun is also important for the interpersonal function. As noted, 'you' is a major feature of how the writer is interacting with the reader. Direct address is also present in the interrogative mood of the second sentence in the leaflet's headline, 'How much have you taken already?'. The dominant mood of this discourse is the imperative, whilst a number of important clauses, including the first part of the headline, are declaratives. The reader is commanded to 'follow' four steps for protection: 'Don't get so drunk...'; 'Don't go alone...'; 'Don't accept drink...' and 'Plan how...' The first three of these instructions are given by the contraction 'don't' instead of the more formal 'do not', an example of conversationalisation which contributes further to the impression of reduced social distance between writer and reader established by the almost ubiquitous direct address in this text. The mnemonic S-M-A-R-T is also composed of a number of imperative commands: 'Say no...; Make yourself...'; '...watch what you drink; 'Take care...' and '...don't go off...'. A consideration of the interpersonal function reaffirms the conclusions reached through the application of transitivity; responsibility for care and protection in the face of the danger of sexual assault is attributed strongly to potential victims through the dominance of imperative clauses and the level of direct address. Imperatives which instruct the reader how to behave operate alongside declaratives which establish the danger of alcohol to invoke strong negative evaluation in this text. In Appraisal terms, to 'get so drunk' or 'go alone to a stranger's house' or 'accept drink from someone you've just met' are negative judgements of propriety, given the context that these behaviours will put the transgressor in significant danger.

Textual Function

In a similar manner to the political campaign leaflet in Figure 5.1, colour operates cohesively in this example. Whist Figure 5.2 has been printed in black and white, the original version of this leaflet prominently featured fluorescent pink. This colour connects the headline to the S-M-A-R-T mnemonic (which is also repeated three times) and to the subheading, which instructs potential victims on protection. This colour also connects intertextually to the situational contexts called to mind in this leaflet. In short, the leaflet uses similar colours to those which advertise nightclubs in a conscious attempt to emulate this discourse for readers. The instructions are also connected by colour; in the original leaflet the text is in white font and stands out against the leaflet's black background. The three official logos at the bottom of the page, for the Community Safety Unit of the NIO, the PSNI and DHSSPS, are also connected in this way. These public bodies connect the discourse through coherence to the wider socio-political context of safety initiatives undertaken by public bodies and by the police. Cohesive devices are widespread in this example, important aspects of the message – particularly references to drink and drunkenness and to being or going anywhere alone – are repeated and there are significant vocabulary chains which consistently reinforce the central messages of the leaflet, protect-trust-friends-take care, for example. Through the process of overlexicalisation, a clear rationale for sexual assault being the result of victims putting themselves in vulnerable situations through 'go[ing] off with someone' and 'get[ting] so drunk' is evident in this discourse. We have discussed the prominence of the 'you' pronoun in terms of the experiential function as the dominant participant of transitivity processes and the interpersonal function as an example of direct address. When considering the textual links and connections in the discourse, 'you', through excessive repetition, is an example of overlexicalisation.

Through this analysis we can see clearly the links between the three functions of SFL and we can demonstrate the fact that an analysis which utilises all three functions yields extensive textual insights. A critical discourse analyst considering this leaflet would be expected to comment on the very uncomfortable ideologies perpetrated here, especially given that the ideological view taken by this leaflet is reminiscent of equally uncomfortable positions often adopted in the language of other social institutions which address sexual assault, such as various forms of media.

5.4 Ideological Implications: The Language of Sexual Assault

In this section we offer an extended discussion of the language of sexual assault with references to the findings of our analysis of Figure 5.2 in order to demonstrate that CDA is primarily focussed on the role of language in society. Conclusions from the analysis of individual texts, in this case an application of approaches in SFL to a public information leaflet, are connected to other texts in the public sphere which address similar topics. All of these texts operate as discourse in that they disseminate and reinforce a particular construction of, in this case, the crime of rape. The following discussion places our analysis of this leaflet in context with other critical linguistic research into the language of sexual assault and discusses the real-world effects of how this language is constructed. Well-rounded investigations in CDA should carry out technical linguistic analysis of texts as well as consider how they operate in wider society. It is worth reminding ourselves here of the comments of Fairclough (2010:10 and see Section 1.2) that CDA should be rooted in systematic analysis as well as be 'transdisciplinary' by addressing the social process. So our analysis should be extended to consider how the text operates ideologically by considering how its linguistic construction of sexual assault affects how this crime is viewed and how this in turn affects how it is reported and investigated.

The most obvious of the ideological positions in this leaflet is that blame for sexual assault is attributed to victims. This is established particularly by the focus on the 'you' pronoun and the prominence of the imperative mood. The actions, and indeed the very presence, of any male perpetrator is wholly absent in this leaflet. We are also told that rape 'happens' and it 'stays with you', as if rape itself is a perpetrator who attacks those who have left themselves vulnerable, when of course rape is a violent sexual assault carried out by a rapist. The rapist participant is not present in this discourse but instead the message is that rape is the result of the inappropriate behaviours of victims. This leaflet also reinforces perceptions of rape which are prominent in other victim-blaming texts, such as the role of alcohol and certain actions of the victim.

Alcohol has long been used to denigrate the legitimacy of rape victims. The principle, which is reinforced for society through the use of language in texts like this leaflet, is that if an alleged victim is drunk then inhibitions are lessened and s/he might make decisions otherwise unsafe, such as 'walk[ing] home alone' or 'go[ing] off with someone you've just met'. Mooney (2007:206) states that the 'effect of alcohol on a woman in a rape scenario is to make her culpable' and notes the almost perverse alternative position that when 'an attacker has been drinking, it somehow exculpates him'. Public discourse, particularly the language of the media, connected to traditional and patriarchal stereotypes of female behaviour view excessive alcohol consumption as inappropriate and somehow unfeminine whilst the same behaviour is normalised within traditional views of masculinity. A female rape victim who is drunk is therefore viewed as culpable for the attack upon her, and this view is operable in a range of discourse examples, from so-called 'public awareness' campaign literature like Figure 5.2 and in the press to the discourse of the courtroom where the status of alleged rape victims who were drinking at the time of the attack is adversely affected. Anderson and Beattie (2001:12) state that 'the legitimate victim is someone who was not under the influence of alcohol or drugs at the time of the rape'. In these terms, a victim who ignores the instructions of Figure 5.2 is seen as illegitimate, which can significantly lessen the chances of securing a conviction in these cases, or indeed of them going to trial at all.

Clark (1992), in work which uses naming analysis and transitivity to examine the language of *The Sun* newspaper, establishes that media discourse often constructs dichotomies in sexual assault cases wherein male perpetrators are mitigated and female victims are blamed. Clark proffers a distinction between 'respectable/sexually unavailable' and 'unrespectable/sexually available' to describe the fact that when the victim adheres to characteristics which have been constructed for society as 'respectable', such as being a mother, being married, dressing appropriately, staying sober and behaving in the responsible ways advocated by discourse like this leaflet, then the media will characterise her as 'sexually unavailable' and she will not be the subject of 'victim-blaming'. It should be noted, however, that in these cases rapists are often constructed as 'monsters' rather than 'men' so that the patriarchal organisation of society remains largely unscrutinised. If a victim is viewed as 'unrespectable', such as being a sex worker, being drunk, dressing in a way which is viewed as inappropriate or behaving in a way that could be viewed as flirtatious, or doing the things which Figure 5.2 instructs against, she may be constructed as 'sexually available' and will therefore be viewed as culpable in rape.

This media-constructed distinction can be appropriated by legal participants in the courtroom, and Statham (2016) demonstrates how defence barristers can attempt to cast victims as 'unrespectable' by constructing a number of narratives which can affect the outcome of sexual assault proceedings. Two of these narratives are 'Party Girl' and 'Chose Not to Go Home' and focus on the victim's propensity for alcohol and her accompanying alleged perpetrators to their home. These narratives recall the dominant messages in Figure 5.2 and therefore demonstrate the connection between the ideologies which are naturalised for readers of leaflets like this and the attitudes to behaviour that defence barristers can assume are possessed by members of a criminal jury. Barristers and attorneys know that members of the public who make up a jury will have a number of internalised concepts about what is 'respectable' behaviour and what is not. The chances of an acquittal will increase if they can cast an alleged victim as 'unrespectable'. Temkin (2000) conducted interviews with legal professionals in Britain with widespread experience of sexual assault trials who acknowledged that attacking aspects of an alleged victim's character is a core component of defence strategies in court. One barrister stated:

> There is a difficulty in properly presenting women with a right to decline sexual intercourse despite the fact that they may have been very drunk or have acted in a sexually explicit way towards the man. It goes down to a number of attitudes which are ingrained in people. There is plainly a perception that women should act in a certain way.
>
> (Barrister 5, Temkin, 2000:232)

For critical discourse analysts, 'attitudes which are ingrained in people' are not inherent attitudes which are somehow organically possessed by members of a jury or by society in general. These attitudes are constructed by powerful patriarchal institutions partly through language and are disseminated through media discourse which constructs a hierarchy of legitimacy for victims. This notion of a legitimate victim is reinforced by language like that of Figure 5.2, which places the onus for tackling sexual assault on potential victims rather than on perpetrators.

Another of the 'unrespectable' narratives considered by Statham (2016) and alluded to by the barristers interviewed by Temkin (2000) is 'Offered No Resistance', which is also relevant when carrying out a thorough CDA of Figure 5.2. Part of the S-M-A-R-T mnemonic is to 'Say NO to any sex you don't want' and 'Make yourself clearly understood', which refers to the 'ingrained attitude' which expects victims to offer some form of resistance to the act of rape. Despite the fact that most legal systems do not require this act of resistance, defence barristers operate by the safe assumption that jurors will expect it to be present. Tiersma (2007) reminds us that in many jurisdictions a 'notorious resistance requirement', now dispensed with by the statutes if not by the expectations of the jury, was once the norm. As Larcombe (2002:132) states, 'A case is more likely to have success if it is clearly interpretable as violence: if the assailant is a stranger, if violence is used, if the victim/survivor's resistance is overt and physical injury is sustained and documented'. It might seem therefore important that discourse like this leaflet instructs victims to overtly 'Make yourself clearly understood'. However, this is problematic because such instructions construct a concept of rape for readers and potential jurors which naturalises the notion that resistance should always be present and fails to acknowledge the reality of an act which can be so traumatic that a victim can be paralysed by fear.

Tiersma (2007:95) points out that consent, the key component in distinguishing rape from sex, is a mental state rather than a physical or vocal act, so it is possible for consent not to be present even though a victim does not 'Say NO to any sex you don't want'. Given this fact, some legal jurisdictions have been considering making amendments to the law which would require the defence to prove that consent was present in rape cases. Such moves are however controversial and potentially highly problematic because the burden of proof – the legal concept designed to protect the assumption of innocence and which requires that the prosecution must produce proof to the contrary – would be fundamentally altered in these cases. It would perhaps be preferable if sexual assault trials could instead rely on a jury which is better informed about the crime of rape instead of one which may have internalised the ideologies perpetrated by discourse like Figure 5.2.

In an example of the potential power of resistant voices, many social media users, including a number of academics working in CDA, highlighted and criticised the content of this leaflet to the extent that the PSNI issued an apology which acknowledged the status of victims and the culpability of rapists in these cases. Whilst any critical reader might be able to condemn the representation of rape in this leaflet, a critical discourse analyst who utilises a systemic-functional view of language is able to point specifically to how the lexico-grammar of the text constructs rape and to how this language in turn plays a problematic role in society. There is therefore an important societal role which critical discourse analysts can perform through the forum of social media. Whilst perhaps not necessarily being as emancipatory as it might always appear (see further Chapter 11), social media provides an important platform through which powerful institutions can be held to account.

Summary of Chapter 5

This chapter has examined the third of the functions of language in SFL by analysing cohesion and coherence in a text from a university website. The textual function considers how discourse is organised, how language is constructed to make connections within a text, both verbally and visually, and how the text connects to wider social contexts. In the case of the university text in Example 5.1, this social context is one in which education is increasingly defined as a commodity. The opening chapters of this book provide you with comprehensive insights into the experiential, interpersonal and textual approaches to critical linguistic analysis, and this chapter illustrates how students can produce extensive and insightful analysis of institutional discourse by drawing conclusions based on all three of these functions. All three SFL functions operate simultaneously. In essays and projects where you consider these three functions, this chapter demonstrates how you can produce thorough and in-depth investigations of your data. The link between all of the exemplar analyses in this book is that CDA always goes that one step further and considers how the ideologies uncovered through these analyses can play significant social roles. The two leaflets here are highly ideological. Figure 5.1 prioritises environmental agendas in politics and in so doing legitimises the political process itself. Figure 5.2 operates in a similar public arena as the first example but has very different motivations. The SFL analysis of this piece of discourse leads us to a consideration of the role of the police, the media and the courtroom, and we can explore therefore how language plays an important role in a process so apparently fundamental as the administration of justice. The analysis here can be used to point out to police and legal authorities the problems inherent with constructing the crime of rape through language which blames the victim and omits the perpetrator. This in turn can have a potential effect on how sexual assault is investigated and prosecuted. Fairclough (2010:10) is clear that by being systematic and 'transdisciplinary', CDA should also address 'social wrongs' and 'offer possible ways of righting or mitigating them'. Perhaps the most tangible effect of the discourse of Figure 5.2 in society is the very low conviction rate in sexual assault trials. CDA analysis offers both an explanation and a way to mitigate against this by changing the language through which sexual assault is constructed. So far this book has demonstrated how CDA expands upon the findings of close linguistic analysis to consider the wider social implications of discourse. In Chapter 6 we will focus specifically on the institutional discourse of the media. The chapter will demonstrate how institutional practices, such as the processes of production, play a role in the construction of media language. The chapter will also introduce a new model for the analysis of verbs of speaking.

Further Reading

Cotterill, J. (ed.) (2007) *The Language of Sexual Crime*. Basingstoke: Palgrave Macmillan.
Mayr, A. (2008) *Language and Power: An Introduction to Institutional Discourse*. London: Continuum.
Young, L. and Fitzgerald, B. (2006) *The Power of Language: How Discourse Influences Society*. Sheffield: Equinox.

6 Voices in Discourse
Media Sources and Institutional Practices

KEY TERMS IN CHAPTER 6: institutional practices, newsworthiness, geographical spectrum, political spectrum

MODELS OF ANALYSIS IN CHAPTER 6: verbs of saying

6.1 Introduction

The examples we have analysed over the last four chapters have each demonstrated that CDA builds upon the findings of close linguistic analysis in order to consider the wider social context of discourse. Discourse drives the process through which readers or listeners internalise certain ideologies as common-sense principles which appear natural and legitimate. We have analysed institutional discourse examples, such as election leaflets, speeches and newspaper articles, which play prominent and powerful roles in the social world. These examples, especially those from the news media, often utilise official sources, particularly through quotations, to provide context or give insight into a topic. These voices in the text, in terms of how and why they are selected and presented, often strengthen the ideological agenda of a piece of discourse.

In this chapter we will present a model which analyses the textual representation of those whose voices are present in discourse. We have noted in Chapter 2 the importance of prominent and absent voices in texts (see 'Discursive Practice' in Section 2.3). As well as their presence in a text, sources are also represented through the type of verb which describes how they speak. For example, do they 'describe' a reality or merely 'claim' to represent one? Caldas-Coulthard (1988, 1994, 1997) offers a model for examining verbs of saying which enables the analyst to reach conclusions about the ideological position of a publication. Sometimes merely the inclusion of a quotation from a specific speaker in an article does not necessarily indicate an endorsement of this speaker's position, but rather we have to delve further to consider how a speaker's voice is represented.

The analysis of voices in discourse will form part of a larger focus on the institutional practices of the news media throughout this chapter. The use of sources in media discourse is one of several important **institutional practices** which contribute to the construction of the media examples which are examined by critical discourse analysts. As examples of institutional discourse, the texts we analyse in this book are products of various processes of production which are closely connected to the ideological agendas of speakers, writers and wider organisations. The discourse of the media is a particularly good example of this fact. Newspaper articles are not simply an unedited representation of a journalist's viewpoint, but rather they are the manifestation of established institutional processes. These include criteria about the type of event that gets to be news in the first place, the sources which are selected to be included in a story and how their voices are represented, and the processes of editing and attributing headlines, images and captions in media articles. When we analyse the language of the media, we are engaging with discourse which is not merely the unfiltered view of a journalist but with discourse which is the product of institutional practices which contribute to the language we are investigating. All of these factors come together in a complex network of institutional practices, which in the media includes the role of advertisers and owners, which are relevant to the critical analysis of discourse. In this chapter we will use the media to demonstrate how and why you should examine these practices as part of CDA.

This chapter will provide a unified perspective of the production of news, overviewing institutional practices like the importance of sources, the influence of owners and advertisers and considering at the very beginning what aspects of stories help them to 'make the news' at all. The rationale for focussing on the media in this chapter is that the language of this type of institution is heavily influenced by external factors which will help you to focus on the many relationships which contribute to the production of a text. The media is also very often the medium through which the positions of many other institutions are represented, endorsed, criticised and questioned. In the discussions which follow you should therefore look upon the media as a special kind of institution, one which is comprised of a range of powerful organisations and communicates its messages through several platforms – on paper, online, on television and radio – as well as being the site of evaluation of ideologies of other powerful organisations like government.

6.2 How to 'Make the News'

At the very beginning of the process of the production of news, decisions have to be made about what is included and excluded from a newspaper or from a news broadcast. Some of these decisions might be practical: newspapers and broadcasts are limited by space and time, for example. These limitations are not quite so restrictive online, however, and yet there is no news website which can claim to have covered every event which may have happened everywhere in the world on any given day. Of course, it would also be practically impossible for a reader to fully engage with this level of content in any case. Other decisions might be more philosophical than practical: certain events in very many contexts may be deemed less likely to be engaging for a publication's assumed readership. And into this mix we must add both the **geographical spectrum** and **political spectrum** of the news.

6.2.1 Geographical Spectrum of the News

Geographically there are four broad types of news: local, regional, national and international, and these distinctions are reflected in all of the news media's platforms. For example, Irish readers might be aware of the *Derry Journal* (local), the *Irish News* (regional) and *The Irish Times* (national and international); UK readers with the *Croydon Post* (London, local), *London Evening Standard* (regional) and *The Times* (national and international); and US readers with the *Asbury Park Press* (Asbury, NJ, local), the *Star Ledger* (NJ, regional) and the *New York Times* (national and international). Of course, these boundaries are not always quite so clear-cut, and there may be a fair amount of overlap in terms of content. Local newspapers will not necessarily ignore national or international stories, but the stories may be presented with some aspect of 'local interest', for example. For instance, during the bushfire crisis in Australia in the summer of 2019–2020, my hometown newspaper (a weekly publication serving a town of twenty thousand residents in Ireland) carried interviews with local people living and working in Sydney, Perth and Melbourne; however, the causes of the fires, particularly the arguments around climate change which were raging on international news platforms, were only referred to in one lead sentence. Newspapers with websites, regardless of their position on the geographical spectrum, are all arguably international in terms of accessibility (although those which operate paywalls are not universally accessible for economic reasons), but even in these cases the general readership is broadly in line with these four main types. Readers from China are free to read the website of a local newspaper in Scandinavia, for example, if they possess the requisite language competence, but this is unlikely to occur in large numbers or without a very specific purpose.

Television news is organised along similar lines as newspapers; many major channels cover national and international news for the most part but dedicate a certain amount of daily coverage to news from the viewer's region. Conversely, local television or radio stations will prioritise local events and will cover international incidents from a local perspective, much as local newspapers do. Most national and regional newspapers will have dedicated international news sections, variously labelled as 'World Events' or 'Around the Globe' and suchlike. Despite the seeming geographical diversity here, additional criteria influence the stories which appear in these sections. Stories about conflict in the Middle East and in Africa, which can almost inevitably be linked through history or contemporary economic interests to the activities of Western countries, are given woefully low exposure in the Western press, for example, whilst something like the US presidential election is covered in minute detail across the European media. These factors bring us to political considerations of news content.

6.2.2 Political Spectrum of the News

The perspective offered in the news on socio-political events often depends on the political position of a newspaper or broadcaster on a broad Left–Right spectrum. In Britain, for example, most newspapers occupy the right wing in terms of their political allegiances. The *Daily Telegraph* and *The Times* are largely conservative in their coverage and consistently endorse the Tory Party in elections, whilst the *The Guardian* is considered to be further to the Left and generally adopts a progressive socio-political and economic agenda. There is an additional distinction between the so-called 'quality press', broadsheets like *The Times* and the *Telegraph*, and the tabloid press or 'red tops', like the *The Sun* and the *Daily Mirror*, which generally cover more entertainment-based, sexualised and sensationalist news items. Newspapers like the *Daily Mail* and the *Daily Express* are said to occupy the middle ground in terms of broadsheets and tabloids, although their contemporary outputs are much closer to the tabloid end of this spectrum, and there is nothing middle ground about their hard-right political perspective. Similar distinctions operate in most Western democracies, whilst countries with one-party systems of government, such as the Democratic People's Republic of Korea (North Korea), will usually have state-owned rather than private media organisations. Where the latter exist, they are often subject to strict censorship laws. Nonetheless, you should resist uncomplex generalisations which present Western media as a bastion of liberalism in the face of apparent oppression elsewhere. As we shall see in this chapter, the realities are often more nuanced. Admittedly, the distinctions above are themselves generalisations and are intended only to offer a broad overview. You should recognise similar arrangements in your own contexts, between local and international, between Left and Right, and between broadsheet and tabloid.

6.2.3 Newsworthiness

In the case of all of these publications and associated agencies of broadcast and online news, the practical and political decisions considered here are also taken with concerns of '**newsworthiness**' in mind. News editors consider which characteristics of an event make it worth covering. Most producers of news, journalists, photographers, presenters, anchors and editors will have internalised characteristics known as 'values of newsworthiness' or 'news values' and will consider them when evaluating a story. It is not necessarily that there is a physical checklist which journalists will tick off, but rather through daily practice criteria will have become ingrained. When you hear a journalist described in terms of having a 'good nose for a story', what is really being referred to is the adoption of institutional practice. For critical discourse analysts, recognition of the importance of institutional factors is crucial; they are significant driving forces behind the eventual verbal and visual articulation of news discourse.

The most influential list of 'news values' was developed in a seminal paper by Galtung and Ruge (1965:70–71), who assessed the components of the coverage of three major international events and developed twelve news values:

- Frequency: how close a story happens to the moment of publication.
- Threshold: the level an event must reach to stand out to be 'newsworthy'.
- Unambiguity: a story that is clearly understood rather than uncertain.
- Meaningfulness: relevant to likely readers' frame of reference, have some familiarity.
- Consonance: stories that meet with the media's expectations and cultural norms will receive more coverage.
- Unexpectedness: unpredictable events are particularly attractive.
- Continuity: a 'big story' can be updated as it develops, and hence garner newsworthy longevity.
- Composition: an equilibrium of stories in a publication, 'light' stories to balance more serious ones.
- Reference to elite nations.
- Reference to elite people.
- Reference to persons: the 'human interest' angle constantly peddled by news organisations.
- Reference to something negative: a sort of culmination of the above criteria; bad news almost inevitably contains more newsworthy factors than positive stories.

The first thing that you might notice about a list like this is that it seems rather obvious. Essentially, this is because as readers you have undergone a similar internalisation process as journalists have when they produce the news, so you have a set of expectations based on your interactions with this discourse. Secondly, there are some overlaps and potential contradictions in this list which can only be explained when geographical or political contexts are considered.

Let's think about the second criterion on Galtung and Ruge's list, for example. 'Threshold' suggests that a story must have a certain significance to be sufficiently newsworthy. From January 2020 news agencies have dedicated extensive coverage to the spread of the coronavirus Covid-19, for example (see further Chapter 9), whilst usually less serious winter influenzas receive relatively scarce commentary in the news. They do not reach pandemic proportions or result in so many fatalities, so they are less newsworthy. The biggest health scares or the worst natural disasters or the most violent crimes are reported whilst apparently lesser occurrences are not. However, a marginal rise in occurrences of influenza, the death of fish in a lough caused by agricultural activity and a melee outside a public house will all 'make the local rag'. That is, they will be covered in a local newspaper, which in contrast includes a different sort of local-focussed commentary on a pandemic and usually says comparatively little about oceanic damage from oil tankers and a riot which has occurred somewhere overseas. So Threshold depends on the context of the newspaper or website or broadcast agency from which you are acquiring your data. The well-known mantra 'all politics is local', most commonly associated with American politician Tip O'Neill, could equally be applied to the news.

You might also perceive a clash between 'Unexpectedness' and 'Continuity'. After all, there is nothing new or unexpected about a story which is receiving widespread coverage. However, Continuity here usually refers to the so-called 'big stories', which seem to infinitely appeal to audiences. These are often negative or refer to particularly harrowing events. Fifteen years after her disappearance in Portugal, the case of English toddler Madeleine McCann still appears quite often in the British press, for example, and the ongoing investigation was headline news again in June 2020. Other big stories, the coverage of the spread of Covid-19 again being a good example of this, can be updated as they develop on a daily basis in print, an hourly basis or more often on television, and almost up to the minute on social media and 'live text' on news websites.

Other criteria, particularly those which refer to 'elite people' and 'elite nations', obviously depend both on geographical and political contexts. Members of royal families are covered almost *ad nauseum* in the press of their own countries but might appear comparatively less often elsewhere, for example. What or who is considered 'elite' is obviously dependent on various contexts. The local men's football captain is often an 'elite' in his hometown whilst he is an unknown regionally or nationally; on the other hand, the leader of the government is an 'elite' everywhere and across the political spectrum. Furthermore, you should not assume that 'elite' in this context refers only to people endorsed by a news agency. Often political opponents draw the most attention. In the 2019 general election in Britain, the leader of the Labour Party, Jeremy Corbyn, drew an almost obsessive amount of press attention from right wing newspapers and from the British Broadcasting Corporation (BBC). As critical discourse analysts we know that such coverage, whether it is supporting or criticising, is highly ideological. One of the very first steps of an analysis into politics in the media should be to note a seemingly disproportionate presence of a particular figure.

Lists like the one produced by Galtung and Ruge are necessarily general, and we can obviously say very much more about many of the configurations and contexts which arise from them. This set of criteria, whilst arising from seminal work which is almost ubiquitously present in textbooks like this one on CDA, has also received criticism. Harcup and O'Neill (2001) proffered an alternative list of criteria based on data drawn from three British daily newspapers, stating that because Galtung and Ruge's list is based on international news it 'ignored day-to-day coverage of lesser, domestic and bread-and-butter news' (Harcup and

O'Neill, 2001:276). Their alternative list of ten criteria has similarities to Galtung and Ruge's news values, reference to elites, for example, but also includes factors like Celebrities, Sex and Entertainment, and specifically acknowledges that the political agenda of a publication is a significant value of newsworthiness.

In 'News values for a new millennium', Jewkes (2011), who is specifically interested in media constructions of crime, offers an alternative list of twelve criteria. Alongside factors which are similar to those on Galtung and Ruge's original list, such as Threshold, Predictability and Proximity, Jewkes refers to Sex, Violence, Visual Spectacle and Children. Of course, it is notable if perhaps slightly uncomfortable that these are newsworthy features of criminal stories.

Were we to comprise an even more contemporary set of news values we might consider the role of social media, particularly in terms of the dissemination of news. Certain stories might be covered on television news or in newspapers because they have been 'trending' on Twitter, whilst newsworthy stories on more traditional platforms might also gain additional traction on social media. A sort of dialogical relationship operates here. For example, platforms like Twitter and Instagram have become the first port of call for announcements made by 'elite people' such as the retirement announcement of a politician or a pregnancy announcement from a celebrity couple, which is in turn subsequently covered on television news and in newspapers. The participatory element of many social media platforms, the fact that users can effectively post almost anything, means that specific criteria that refer to the news would be somewhat ineffective for general social media content. We will consider social media in more detail in Chapter 11.

The major point that you should take from this discussion is that the discourse with which media audiences interact is subject to a complex array of institutional arrangements right from the very beginning of the news production process. The media is not some neutral reflection of the world and is constantly doing ideological work through content and the linguistic composition of this content.

As a final introductory example, consider the fact that the on 27th November 2017 more than 50 percent of the coverage on BBC news channels was dedicated to the engagement of Prince Harry to American actress Meghan Markle. This was a typical example of a so-called 'good news story' given the seemingly infinite public interest in the British royal family. This is itself the result of a process which legitimises the concept of monarchy through the language of a powerful institution like the media. Given the blanket coverage of this story, a very pertinent issue for a critical discourse analyst is what was not covered on the British state broadcaster as a result. On 27th November 2017 the BBC did not cover on its main news bulletins the fact that food prices had reached a four-year high and a huge rise of 33 percent was projected post-Brexit, that MP Andrew Mitchell had accused the government of 'shameful complicity' over its actions to support Saudi Arabia's ongoing attacks on Yemen or that the government had announced a one-year freeze on benefits which would cost an average working family £315. Good news stories often detract attention from the very bad actions of powerful institutions.

6.3 Sourcing the News

Now that we have established that the news media as an institution is not simply about reflecting reality but that its composition is driven by institutional practices and ideological agendas, we will engage more closely with the textual manifestation of these arrangements. After all, CDA must be a marriage between socio-political and cultural assessments of the social world and close textual analysis of the role of discourse in shaping this world.

One institutional feature of the media which is closely tied to the content and composition of text is the role of sources in the news, the people or organisations with which news producers interact when composing a story. In some cases sources might bring a story to a media participant, an editor or a journalist; in other cases these participants will garner sources to provide official commentary on or insight into a story. When news agencies present stories, they come with the inclusion of additional voices. Consider the politicians or official figures who are interviewed in a news broadcast or those who are quoted in newspaper articles, such as those we have analysed in this book so far. In these analyses we have noted the importance of the inclusion of additional voices and acknowledged the significance in how these sources are presented. The 'Discursive Practice' section of the *Daily Mail* analysis in Chapter 2 discusses the role of quotations from students, politicians and the trade union leadership.

From the somewhat one-dimensional and uncritical view of the media as simply providing information desired by their audience, sources are viewed in terms of their practical importance. They are seen to lend authority to the information in an article or report. From this somewhat idealistic viewpoint, Machin (2008:62) says that journalism can be viewed as 'bravely finding the facts and delivering them to the public with neutrality' and that journalists 'select the events that are most relevant to people, find ways to investigate them further and identify sources that can shed light on central issues'. But this view of the media neglects to recognise the ideological role of the press. Sources are selected and decisions about how much of what they say is presented in a story are made with the ideological agenda of the news agency in mind. As we have noted in the analysis of Chapter 2 in particular, a sub-editor may choose to include only a portion of the quotations that have been provided in a journalist's copy, for example. Owing to the audience expectation of a 'balanced story', often conflicting voices will be included in an article or a report, but different voices can be presented in different ways. So audience expectation is maintained whilst the composition of the discourse with which they have interacted is still ideologically driven. Section

6.4 on verbs of saying presents the model of linguistic analysis for this chapter and will examine this further.

So we can say that news agencies and journalists rely heavily on official sources. Sources are important for constructing the perception of balance and authority and for pushing ideological agendas forward. When the media reports on civil disobedience, for example, the viewpoint of the police is sought; when the general theme of a story is political, journalists will seek out government or parliamentary sources. Sources are at the core of reporting. In the United States a press presence is maintained almost constantly in the White House, for example, and in Britain the lobby system, twice daily unattributed briefings from political officials, keeps journalists updated on parliamentary and governmental events. In times of crisis – such as during the Covid-19 pandemic – there are almost daily government press briefings. Obviously, information from government is important, and indeed the audience has been constructed through consistent interaction with the news over many decades to expect it, but, as critical discourse analysts, we also know that information provided by official sources such as government or the police is not neutral. It is not necessarily the role of CDA to denigrate the professionalism of journalists by pointing out that the 'nose for a story' concept is about the internalisation of news values or that a reliance on official sources undermines the apparent neutrality of news. Whilst recognising that institutional practices hold sway, we acknowledge for example that official voices are important and that media plays a significant role in distributing, filtering and evaluating these voices. But we also know that these processes and the sources with which they interact can never be neutral. Have a go at the student task before reading the discussion on the example.

Student Task

In May 2015 protests in London and Cardiff followed the election of a Conservative government led by then Prime Minister David Cameron. The *Daily Mail* covered one such event, where police clashed with demonstrators, under the headline 'Hate Mob in No.10 Rampage: Hard Left's Shame as Rioters Attack Police and Deface WWII Memorial as Socialists Lay Siege to Downing Street'. The article is lengthy, so it will not be reproduced here, but is easily retrievable online by typing the headline into a search engine. The online article is the top result.

Make a note of all the sources used in the article. Consider who is quoted, how s/he is named, how much s/he says. If there are two 'sides' to this event, are both sides represented equally through the article's use of sources? What do the sources tell you about the newspaper's interpretation of the event?

It is clear from the overlexicalisation (see 'Text' in Section 2.3) of the headline, in which protestors are a 'Hate Mob', the 'Hard Left', 'Rioters' and 'Socialists', that the *Daily Mail*'s evaluation of this event is wholly negative. The sources you will have noted are: the Royal British Legion, the Metropolitan Police, Scotland Yard, former Speaker of the House of Commons Betty Boothroyd, the left wing writer Laurie Penny via comments they made on Twitter, Conservative MP Sir Peter Bottomley, protestors quoted through comments made on social media and Chief Superintendent Gerry Campbell. Whilst an analysis obviously requires more than simply listing the sources in a text, we are able to make some important observations here. Firstly, there is a heavy reliance on official sources, particularly the police, who are quoted at length in the article, initially through metonymic phrases like 'The Royal British Legion today condemned', 'The Metropolitan Police confirmed' and 'Scotland Yard said', and then through Chief Superintendent Gerry Campbell who 'appealed for information'. Two politicians who squarely condemned the protestors, Betty Boothroyd and Sir Peter Bottomley, are senior Conservatives. The protestors themselves are only quoted once as a source, through 'complaints' about the actions of the police issued on social media, although their voices are also present through processes of Verbalisation in the article when the protest is described: 'The mob chanted "Get the Tories out" as large sections of the city were shut down' and 'Some of the protesters brandished highly offensive home-made banners proclaiming "F*** The Cuts"'. Evaluative words like 'mob' and phrases like 'highly offensive' again leave the reader in little doubt about the *Mail*'s stance on the protest. In the Appraisal system used in Chapter 4, these terms are negative judgements of the protestors.

So as analysts we can show that the condemning position of a news publication is reinforced through the sources which are included in a text. In this example these voices are overwhelmingly those which characterise the protest as a riot and condemn the actions of the protestors. *The Guardian* newspaper covered the same protests under the headline 'Anti-austerity protestors take to UK streets after Tory election victory' – the headline immediately demonstrating the different stance taken by this newspaper – and included a very different array of sources. For example, *The Guardian* includes lengthy quotes from singer Charlotte Church, who 'accused the Conservatives of dismantling the NHS'. The protestors are again quoted through social media, but more extensively in this case, with several quotations from Shelly Asquith, president of the University of the Arts Students' Union. The police are quoted through a 'Met spokesman' who refers to an 'unplanned protest', 'anti-Tory graffiti' and the 'disruption to traffic' in a less sensationalist account of the incident than we find in the *Mail*. *The Guardian* gives a much greater voice to those ideologically aligned with the arguments of the protestors and focusses only tangentially on violence, which is presented as very serious in the *Mail*. As always, we must remember that regardless of which of these representations we might espouse or reject, as critical discourse analysts we recognise that both are ideological.

A great idea for an essay or project would be to compare these two articles, or indeed articles from across the political spectrum of the press which deal with the same event, through a full application of Fairclough's three-dimensional model or one of the SFL approaches from Chapters 3, 4 and 5. The fact that the same event can be represented linguistically in so many different ways itself confirms that none of these representations are neutral reflections of reality but instead they are ideologically driven interpretations which in turn have the potential to influence the ideologies of readers and viewers.

Publications make ideological choices about the inclusion of sources, and they make similar choices about how much of what is said to include. It is possible, for example, that the *Mail* and *The Guardian* in this example have attended the same Metropolitan Police press conference, and certainly both will have been on the distribution list for press releases from the police and the government. Obviously, they will have had equal access to comments on social media. However, what comprises the sources in each article is very different. How much or how little of this discourse to include is decided by news producers. Caldas-Coulthard (1997:62) reminds us that those who 'report speech in factual reports are extremely powerful because they can reproduce what is most convenient for them in terms of their aims and their ideological point of view'.

6.4 Verbs of Saying

The ideological use of sources is not limited to the inclusion or omission of sources. Caldas-Coulthard (1988, 1994, 1997) offers a taxonomy of verbs of saying which enables us to consider how speakers and their words are evaluated. The *Daily Mail* article discussed here reports that the Royal British Legion 'condemned' the violence and that the police 'confirmed' the number of arrests, for example. In Caldas-Coulthard's model 'confirm' is an assertive type and 'condemn' is an expressive type verb. Both of these are more authoritative than the verb 'say', for example. A systematic account of verbs of saying allows the analyst to consider more precisely how a speaker is being evaluated. Whilst the transitivity framework illustrated in Chapter 3 provides a starting point here, allowing us to differentiate between processes of Verbalisation and other types of processes and to account for different types of Verbiage, the model of quoting verbs means that we can drill down further into the evaluative element involved when a speaker or writer selects different types of verbs of saying. The full model is given in Table 6.1.

Neutral structuring verbs, the most prominent of which is 'say', do not include any explicit evaluation of an utterance, so readers are not disproportionately encouraged to agree or disagree with a statement. This is not to say that the choice of a writer to represent the speech of a certain source through a neutral structuring verb is itself a neutral process. By deciding to not explicitly evaluate an utterance, the writer is purposely not prompting a reader to evaluate a source

Table 6.1 Verbs of saying

Speech Reporting Verbs	Types	Examples
Neutral structuring verbs		Say, tell, ask, enquire, reply, answer
Metapropositional verbs	Assertives	Remark, explain, agree, assent, accept, correct, counter
	Directives	Urge, instruct, order
	Expressives	Accuse, grumble, lament, confess, complain, swear
Metalinguistic verbs		Narrate, quote, recount
Stage Direction Verbs		
Prosodic		Cry, intone, shout, yell, scream
Paralinguistic	Voice qualifier (manner)	Sigh, gasp, groan, whisper, murmur, mutter
	Voice qualification (attitude)	Laugh, giggle
Transcript Verbs		
Discourse signalling	Relation to other parts of discourse	Repeat, echo, add, amend
	Discourse progress	Pause, go on, hesitate, continue

Source: Caldas-Coulthard (1997:93)

either, which in itself can make a source seem fairly authoritative and factual. Consider the different effect of 'The President complained that the incident was not as serious as portrayed in the press' versus 'The President said that the incident was not as serious as portrayed in the press'. The latter may not always be the strongest way to support the President's opinion here; however, it is certainly less doubtful than the former. Machin and Mayr (2012:59) suggest that neutral structuring verbs can make a speaker appear 'disengaged or even less personalised' and that a reader may empathise less with a speaker who 'said' something than with one who 'cried' or 'whispered'.

The second type of Speech Reporting Verbs are known as metapropositional, and there are three distinct types: assertives, directives and expressives. These types of verbs all allow the writer to include an interpretation of a speaker. Consider again the example above of the President's denial. 'Complain' is a metapropositional expressive and operates here to cast doubt on the proposition. Use of a metapropositional assertive would be much more endorsing, such as 'The President explained that the incident was not as serious as portrayed in the press'. We have seen above how a neutral structuring verb also does not come with this element of doubt. Usually, you can differentiate between assertives and expressives by thinking about the actions of the speaker. With the former s/he is 'asserting' a position through speaking, whilst through the latter s/he is 'expressing' an evaluation through the accompanying speech. Directives are manifested in verbs of saying which 'direct' that an action should take place, such as 'instruct' or 'order'. Caldas-Coulthard (1997:92) notes that these verbs are 'highly interpretive', and they clearly signal the evaluative presence of the writer or speaker.

Metalinguistic verbs specifically address the type of language used by a speaker, and again there is an interpretive element to the use of a metalinguistic verb over a metapropositional one, for example. If a speaker 'recounts' an event, the reader infers an element of facticity given that it does not appear that the speaker is an interested party. For example, a witness to an event interviewed on a news bulletin may be introduced with 'John Smith, who witnessed what happened at the demonstration, recounts the incident'. This statement makes it sound like John Smith does not have a vested interest in presenting the demonstration either positively or negatively but he is merely recounting what happened. Again you can appreciate the effect of this if you compare this sample introduction with one using a metapropositional expressive like 'claim', such as 'John Smith, who was in the area, claims he saw what happened at the demonstration'. Metalinguistic verbs assess how the act of speaking is performed, whilst neutral structuring verbs report that an act of speaking has occurred. It might seem that metalinguistic verbs are more neutral than some metapropositionals but, of course, it is a choice taken by the speaker to present witnesses in ways that validate their statements, so an interpretive message is still being communicated to the audience.

Stage Direction (or Descriptive) Verbs characterise speech with reference to the physical mode of delivery. Prosodic and paralinguistic verbs can signal evaluations of the manner of speech and the attitude of a speaker. Protestors will often be described through verbs like 'shout' or 'chant', whilst those at a more solemn gathering might 'whisper' or 'sigh'. In another context, like when an employee 'whispers' about unfair working conditions or a prisoner 'whispers' about unfair treatment, this verb could signal powerlessness. In politics 'whisper' could refer to duplicity. We often hear political reporters classify rumours as 'whispers' which may be circulating in the corridors of power. As always with CDA, consideration of meaning in context is crucial. Politicians especially must be careful about what attitude they signal when responding to events: groaning or laughing might not always be viewed as appropriate. The media's scope for manipulation is important when considering all of the verbs of saying. A publication may choose not to mention if a politician has laughed inappropriately, for example, whilst a news bulletin with an opposing political agenda could decide to show only a clip of this in its coverage of the same politician.

Transcript Verbs relate an utterance to another part of discourse or signal discourse progress. At first glance these verbs might appear to be solely organisational, but there are examples where they may be used ideologically. Machin and Mayr (2012:60) offer the example of a press release where the speaker being promoted is said to 'add' to a previous piece of information when actually s/he is really just repeating the same point. If a press conference or a speech is reported in the media through positive discourse signalling verbs such as 'add' or 'continue', the speaker is portrayed as being open and elaborative, whilst quite the reverse interpretation is implied if those verbs are more negative. Consider the effect of 'The President added, "The government is operating at full capacity" and he echoed the reassurances offered earlier by the Vice President' versus that of 'The President claimed, "The government is operating at full capacity", although he hesitated to support the reassurances of the Vice President'. 'Add' and 'echo' strengthen the reliability of the statements.

The following article was published on the website of the staunchly conservative newspaper the *Daily Express* in March 2020 and reports on an interaction in the House of Commons. The processes of Verbalisation are in bold.

Example 6.1 Ian Blackford **slapped down** by Boris Johnson in fiery PMQs clash over coronavirus sick pay

SNP MP Ian Blackford was brilliantly **shut down** by Boris Johnson as he **urged** the Prime Minister to raise the UK's statutory sick pay to the average level of that in other EU countries.

The SNP politician **argued** that with coronavirus spreading across the world, workers in the UK will be more affected than others in the EU as the statutory sick pay in the UK is £94.25 compared to Germany's £287. He **said**: "In Ireland, in response to the coronavirus, the Government has just raised their statutory sick pay to the equivalent of £266 per week. This covers those employed and those self-employed. In Germany and Austria, it is £287. In Sweden, it is £230. In the Netherlands, it is £201 and in Spain, it's £121. In the UK, it's a mere £94.25 per week."

But the Prime Minister was prompt to **point out** the UK offers a free national health service to its citizens and residents, unlike many other countries in the EU.

He **blasted**: "As most members of the House understand, in the UK unlike other countries around the world and certainly in the EU, we have a universal free health system. Free at the point of delivery. We have an extensive welfare system."

The fiery clash comes as coronavirus fears have swept through the Government after health minister Nadine Dorries was diagnosed with coronavirus.

(*Daily Express*, 11 March 2020)

This report is representative of the often-triumphalist tone used by the *Express* when championing Tory Prime Minister Boris Johnson. In the headline and the lead, Johnson's combative response to the parliamentary question from Ian Blackford of the Scottish National Party (SNP), a party which advocates for Scottish independence from the UK, is described through the use of a conceptual metaphor: Blackford is 'slapped down' and 'shut down' by the Prime Minister. 'Blast' is also metaphorical and is a prosodic verb in Caldas-Coulthard's framework which captures the energy of Johnson's response. Interestingly, if a more literal prosodic verb like 'shout' or 'yell' had been used here, the Prime Minister might appear somewhat less parliamentary. 'Point out' is a metapropositional assertive and lends authority to Johnson's response, undermining the metapropositional directive 'urge' of Blackford. Blackford is made to appear underinformed and almost histrionic in 'arguing' for what the Prime Minister and the publication classify as an unnecessary response. Johnson responds 'brilliantly' and 'prompt[ly]' in this report and emerges the clear victor in the 'fiery clash'. This report is very reminiscent of one six weeks earlier in the same newspaper:

> 'Get on with day job!' SNP's Blackford shamed as Boris exposes Scottish education chaos.
>
> The SNP's Ian Blackford was shut down by Prime Minister Boris Johnson during PMQs over the Scottish Government's failure to debate the future of Scotland's underperforming education system in favour of debating whether to "fly the EU flag".
>
> (Daily Express, 29th January 2020)

In this example we are given a content Verbiage in the form of a direct quotation from Boris Johnson, an imperative command in the same combative style as above. He 'shames' Ian Blackford, who is again 'shut down' by the Prime Minister. Also note the presupposition here in 'Scottish education chaos', the 'Scottish Government's failure' and 'Scotland's underperforming education system', which asserts and emphasises the publication's opposition to the SNP. The reader is encouraged to think of the SNP-led government as inept.

Prime Minister's Questions in the House of Commons are obviously newsworthy for many publications; in the case of the *Daily Express*, interactions between Boris Johnson and Ian Blackford are an opportunity to lionise one participant and denigrate the other. We are reminded that the political agenda of a publication is an important news value and that close linguistic analysis is augmented by adding the framework of verbs of saying to CDA's analytical arsenal. The framework allows us to specifically assess how sources are evaluated by the media by looking not just at what they said but also analysing how they say it.

6.4.1 Saying It with Style

The taxonymy of verbs of saying accommodates an additional layer to a transitivity analysis so that we can be more specific about processes of Verbalisation.

When our data for a CDA analysis is a piece of media discourse, this model means that we can analyse the role of sources in news texts more closely. The textual composition of a piece of news discourse, including the level of detail which is included in direct quotations from sources, is also affected by certain institutional norms which prevail in the news industry. Many institutions have 'style guides', for example, and most newspaper style guides are now available online. Many of the instructions in these guides clarify spelling or usage, but they also include potentially ideological 'banned lists'. The style guide of the *Press Gazette* does not allow use of the word 'hack' to describe a journalist, for example. Perhaps this is unsurprising given this newspaper's pledge 'Fighting for Journalism', but perhaps it is also misleading to suggest that there are no 'hacks' in journalism despite the simplicity of the term. A more interesting instruction in this style guide is 'Show Don't Tell':

> Numbers and amounts don't stagger, we don't need to tell readers that things are shocking, stunning, surprising, extraordinary, etc. Speakers in quotes can do that. Otherwise please let the facts and the story speak for itself, certainly in news at any rate.
>
> Don't say "only" six out of ten journalists will keep their jobs, or "just" six out of ten journalists will keep their jobs. Again, let the facts speak for themselves.
>
> (*Press Gazette*, 26 July 2013)

For us as critical discourse analysts, a mantra like 'let the facts speak for themselves' seems highly idealistic; instead we view 'facts', like speakers and their quotations, as often selected and ideologically constructed according to institutional norms and the political allegiance of discourse encoders. Whilst we might agree to an extent that the media does not *need* to 'tell readers that things are shocking, stunning, surprising, extraordinary, etc.', we are also aware that they do so nonetheless, and we apply the models within CDA to analyse the language which is used.

So when considering the importance of sources in the news, we must assess the presence and absence of voices in a text and also analyse how these voices are presented linguistically, whether they 'confirm' a statement or make a 'claim'. Acknowledgement of institutional practices is key. Official sources are sought after in the news industry as credible voices; journalists know that this process is expected and fundamental in producing the news. How these voices are presented, the language through which they are given to the audience, depends on factors such as the political allegiance of a news agency, as we have seen above. In this chapter we have demonstrated that the model for verbs of saying can help the analyst to consider more closely how sources are used by and represented in the media.

6.5 Financing the News: Advertisers and Owners

Perhaps the most obvious institutional factor behind the content and composition of the media is the fact that in Western countries media organisations are private companies with the ultimate aim of being profitable. Even so-called 'state broadcasters' like the BBC in Britain and RTÉ in Ireland must be financially viable, often in these cases through the levying of licence fees.

In Chapter 3 we discussed testimony given to the Levinson Inquiry which suggested that the editorial positions taken by newspapers owned by Rupert Murdoch were directly related to the political allegiances of their owner. Rupert Murdoch provides us with a very good example of the business realities of the news media. Murdoch founded a company known as News Corporation, which in 2013 was divided into two equally well-known brands, News Corp and 21st Century Fox. In 1995 *Vanity Fair* famously described Murdoch as 'arguably the most powerful private citizen in the world'. To give you an idea of the context of this power within the corporate structure of the media, consider the fact that major holdings of News Corporation in 2013 were: News International, now known as News Corp UK and Ireland Limited, which owns *The Sun* and *The Times* in the UK; News Limited, now known as News Corp Australia, which owns approximately 140 newspapers and thirty magazines and has massive interests in digital media and subscription television; Dow Jones & Company, a US-based publishing and information company best known as owners of the *Wall Street Journal*; the publisher HarperCollins, one of the so-called 'Big Five' English language publishing houses; and the Fox Entertainment Group, which was eventually acquired by Disney and restructured significantly in 2019. Now consider how many people could be influenced by the information disseminated by a corporation with this level of media ownership and you will be beginning to get a sense of how important it is that the language of institutions and organisations and its role in society be scrutinised and analysed.

When we carry out a CDA of an isolated example of media discourse in a textbook like this one, it is intended that you view these examples as representative of the much larger structures at work in the media. Media organisations are amongst the largest and most profitable organisations and have one of the loudest voices on the planet. When they operate to ideologically structure events through language, they have the power to influence a great many people.

The Murdoch press is just one example of the corporatism of the press. In Britain, Reach (known until 2018 as Trinity Mirror) publishes 240 regional titles, as well as the *Daily Mirror, Sunday Mirror, Sunday People, Daily Express, Sunday Express, Daily Star, Daily Star Sunday, Daily Record* and the *Sunday Mail*. Most of these titles disseminate news in print and online and post stories through social media platforms. The largest media conglomerate in the United States is the Comcast Corporation. As well as being the parent company of the Sky Group, which reaches a European audience of 53 million people in Britain,

Ireland, Austria, Germany, Switzerland, Italy and Spain, amongst the many holdings of Comcast are MSNBC and CNBC. Again, these examples give a sense of the vast amount of power and profit wielded by media companies, and you should therefore be becoming increasingly less surprised by the prominence of capitalist agendas in the mainstream press. Taking the point a step further, consider again the corporatisation of education which is at the centre of ongoing industrial disputes at British universities and which we discussed in Chapter 2 and used as an example in Chapter 5. The reason that this corporate model of education is endorsed by news groups is because of the economic principles which they have in common. When we are considering the social practice element of CDA, we are considering these types of connections and how they operate not just locally or nationally but across vast ideologically driven systems.

Cole and Harcup (2010:6) note the importance of distinguishing between journalists and the media as a product, and we should remember that in recognising media language as ideological discourse and in critically exposing the connections between corporatism and text, the motivation of CDA is not necessarily to denigrate the integrity of journalism. Journalists are chiefly responsible for the content of stories and have relatively little influence on the financial strategies of media owners. Nonetheless, the discussion in this chapter demonstrates that there are inevitable connections here, particularly in terms of the types of stories targeted for coverage in the first place.

An additional factor that we must mention when considering the context of the media is the role of advertisers. We will demonstrate in Chapter 10 that advertising language can be analysed as institutional discourse and, whilst selling behaviours and policies rather than products, the leaflets in Chapter 5 can also be thought of as specific examples of so-called 'non-product' advertisements (Cook, 2001). The media relies very heavily on advertising. The revenues of the companies and conglomerates offered as examples above are chiefly generated by advertising on their various platforms. In this chapter we have discussed some examples of the *Daily Express*, so, to give you a sense of the importance of advertising for the media, have a look at the website of this publication. The homepage is replete with advertising, both space-based (stationary, in-print advertisements) and time-based (videos and moving images). Machin (2008:86) discusses publications which boasted high readerships but which failed to survive in the media industry owing to left-leaning allegiances which prompted them to rely less on advertising revenues. The *Sunday Citizen*, *News Chronicle* and *Daily Herald* – the *Herald* had a higher readership than the *Financial Times*, *The Times* and *The Guardian* – all ran at a loss as income was derived from the cover price instead of advertisements and all eventually folded.

Almost all media and news organisations are heavily reliant on advertisers. This is the reality across the geographical and political spectrums of the press. Some of the newspapers in your local area or hometown, for example, might be so-called 'freesheets', which are community-based publications funded entirely by advertisers and do not levy a cover price at all. Equally, many television channels are free-to-air but dedicate increasing amounts of time to the advertisements which punctuate their other content. Publications with right or left wing sympathies are unified by their reliance on advertisements. Tabbert (2016:17) notes that *The Guardian* newspaper in the UK is distinct from competing titles such as *The Times* because it has no shareholders or profit distribution. *The Guardian* is owned by the Guardian Media Group (owned in turn by Scott Trust Limited), which secures the financial independence of the organisation. This is potentially one reason why the content of *The Guardian*, whilst not free of ideology, is more liberal than most of the other news organisations in Britain.

If you have already had a look at the website of the *Daily Express*, now look at the website of *The Guardian*. You will notice that the latter is much less burdened by advertising and that many of the articles are accompanied by the 'Since you're here...' section at the end of the piece. This is where *The Guardian* asks readers to 'make a contribution in support of our open, independent journalism'. Obviously, as critical discourse analysts we are aware of the problematic nature of terms like 'independent'. Whilst *The Guardian* states that 'our journalism is free from commercial or political bias – never influenced by billionaire owners or shareholders', we know that these ideals are only achievable up to a point. Although many proponents of CDA are likely to find affinity with the more centre-left outlook of this organisation than the hard-right allegiances of the *Express,* for example, it is nonetheless the case that to be 'free from bias' flies in the face of what we know about language as ideological discourse. To be sure, *The Guardian* may be less in hock to conglomerate owners than other news organisations, but it still has a fairly definite political outlook and economically it still requires advertising revenue to be viable. Statham (2016:35) notes that on 3rd May 2011 – a day when the very newsworthy killing of Osama Bin Laden by American Special Forces in Pakistan dominated the headlines – *The Guardian* print edition carried advertisements from a range of corporate kingpins, including Barclays Bank, Nationwide Building Society, HSBC and a full-page spread from Ryanair. Whilst *The Guardian*'s editors do not have to craft content with the political positions of Murdoch-like owners in mind, they may not have the same freedom to denounce corporate capitalism in its entirety given the publication's reliance on advertisers.

Summary of Chapter 6

The factors we have discussed in this chapter – news values, sources, style guides, owners and advertisers – all form part of the institutional context in which the news media must operate. As critical discourse analysts who carry out close linguistic scrutiny of texts, these factors provide us with necessary insights into our findings and offer answers to questions like, 'Why does the media rarely question the validity of a hierarchically organised society?' Or perhaps more simply, 'Why does one news broadcast define an event as one thing (a "riot" for example) and another as something else (a "demonstration" for example)?' Or even simpler again, 'Why is one thing in the news and another thing not covered at all?' The media is a powerful institution and its discourse shapes the ideologies which are considered legitimate by its audience. This chapter is intended to demonstrate that we must also think about the factors behind the news when talking about context. Remember that CDA is also focussed on the motivations which underpin ideological language. Other organisations which produce institutional discourse, such as governments, legal systems, advertisers and political parties, also influence the audiences of their outputs and have driving institutional factors which organise and motivate them. In many ways, the language of the media is the very embodiment of institutional language because it is also a frequent platform upon which these other organisations are represented. This chapter gives you an insight into the sorts of factors you should consider when using media discourse as your data in an essay or a project. In turn you should therefore consider these factors if you are focussing on discourse from other institutions. Ask yourself why an advertiser advocates particular products and what types of lifestyles these products endorse, why a government policy is sold through the language you are deconstructing in your essay, or what a political party's motivation is for one policy position over another. The text you are using as your data is how these organisations legitimise and naturalise these motivations. Throughout the book so far we have commented on the different ways that participants are represented in discourse. In Chapter 7 we turn to a specific model of analysis, social actor analysis, which is focussed on how people are accounted for in institutional language.

Further Reading

Caldas-Coulthard, C. (1997) *News as Social Practice: A Study in Critical Discourse Analysis*. Florianópolis, Brazil: Federal University of Santa Catarina Press.

Keeble, R. (2006) *The Newspapers Handbook*, 2nd edition. London and New York: Routledge.

Richardson, J. (2007) *Analysing Newspapers: An Approach from Critical Discourse Analysis*. Basingstoke: Palgrave Macmillan.

7 Social Actors
Representing Participants

KEY TERMS IN CHAPTER 7: im/personalisation, individualisation, collectivisation, aggregation, nomination, categorisation, identification, functionalisation

MODELS OF ANALYSIS IN CHAPTER 7: social actor analysis

7.1 Introduction

This chapter will focus on an important critical discourse model for the representation of participants in institutional discourse, social actor analysis (van Leeuwen, 1996, 2008). A range of examples will be presented to explain the different categories in the social actor analysis model, which will then be applied to two examples of media discourse. The first analysis revisits *The Sun* newspaper article from Chapter 3 and illustrates therefore that discourse can be examined by a range of different models in CDA. Chapter 3 notes that, alongside processes and circumstances, participants are a key element in the semantic structure of clauses. The model of social actor analysis can be combined with a transitivity analysis in a specific focus on how participants are represented. One of the intentions of this book has been to demonstrate how one piece of institutional discourse can be analysed by several CDA models simultaneously and hence to illustrate how students can produce very in-depth insights into institutional language. The second analysis applies social actor analysis to an article on immigration. The final section of the chapter will then discuss how ideological constructions of immigration in right wing publications contribute to racialised thinking. Firstly we will outline the model of van Leeuwen (1996, 2008) for the representation of social actors.

7.2 Social Actor Analysis

Through the model of social actor analysis, van Leeuwen (1996:32) states that he is offering answers to two interrelated questions:

1. What are the ways in which social actors can be represented in English discourse?
2. What choices does the English language give us for referring to people?

We have seen already the importance of participants in language. We know that agents of processes can be deleted through passivisation, for example, and we know that the semantic meaning of people in a text – 'rioter' versus 'protestor' for example – can carry very different connotations. To reiterate a message we have consistently highlighted in this book, Machin and Mayr (2012:77) confirm that 'there exists no neutral way to represent a person. And all the choices will serve to draw attention to certain aspects of identity that will be associated with certain kinds of discourses'. By this, we mean that every representation of a person in discourse will have some meaning, and this meaning can be related to the ideologies of writer and reader. We are reminded both here and in van Leeuwen's introductory questions of the importance of Halliday's view of language as a system of options. Text encoders have options in terms of how they represent processes, for example, assessed by transitivity, and they have options in terms of how behaviours are evaluated and analysed through judgement in the Appraisal framework, and likewise they have options for the representation of people, and these representations are not neutral. Social actor analysis allows us to focus specifically on the representation of participants and to connect these representations to the ideological operation of a text. Van Leeuwen (1996:66) offers an extensive system network for the representation of social actors. The discussion here will highlight the main categories in the model and consider how they relate to one another and how they are important indicators of the ideologies being communicated in a text.

7.2.1 Social Actor Categories

Personalisation and Impersonalisation

The first social actor distinction we will address is between **personalisation** and **impersonalisation**. Consider the following statements:

a. Jane Smith, the store manager, requires that all staff attend mandatory additional training.
b. The company requires that all staff attend mandatory additional training.

In sentence b. the requirement is given the weight of an entire company and mitigates Jane Smith somewhat from the ire of her colleagues; after all, this training is a company directive. Impersonalisation can be particularly ideological. Consider a third statement:

c. The company will work together to ensure the best service for our customers.

Sometimes large and powerful organisations will find it beneficial to imply that everyone associated with a company is part of the company, a sort of we-are-all-in-this-together type message which conveniently ignores chasms in things like salaries and responsibilities. After all, shareholders and senior managers are more handsomely rewarded for success than employees and usually feel less of the pain of failure (dividends can be kept high by making staff redundant, for example). At other times, such as in statement b., it suits an organisation to be more exclusionary, to construct a relationship of superiority and subordination.

During industrial action in UK universities in 2020, an escalation of the dispute mentioned in Chapter 2, many trade union banners on picket lines across campuses declared 'We are the University', a statement of defiance against management who employ messages like statement c. when levying employees to, say, volunteer for extra work and those like statement b. when equivocating on granting certain rights to those same employees. Seldom will you encounter statements like a. in universities or other organisations. Vice chancellors and CEOs, even though they are influential figures in the decisions of these organisations, very rarely wish to personalise their role. In a message to students before this industrial dispute, many universities issued statements which said that negotiations about industrial action are 'handled at a national level and individual universities are not involved in the negotiations'. In order to demonstrate the ostensible inability of powerful figures to affect negotiations between the parties, statements like this referred to 'universities' as impersonalised entities. Universities ultimately deferred to Universities UK (UUK), the group which represents university management in this dispute, and their statements impersonally referred to both themselves and to UUK. What those statements did not point out to students is that UUK is coordinated by a board which is comprised of university vice chancellors. The quotation here is from the statement of the University of Liverpool, whose vice chancellor was a member of this board, defined by the UUK itself as its 'main decision-making body'. In examples like this, impersonalisation accommodates a concealment of power and by extension a concealment of responsibility. If unpopular decisions are offered with impersonalisation through the guise of 'companies' or 'universities', then it is very difficult for them to be challenged.

Individualisation and Collectivisation

Social actors can also be represented through **individualisation** and **collectivisation**. These labels are fairly self-explanatory and, as you might have extrapolated, individualisation occurs when a social actor is represented individually and collectivisation when s/he is represented as part of a collective. Collectivisation can be used to represent groups of people as having homogenous characteristics, ignoring therefore the heterogeneity of individuals.

As an example of how collectivisation is ideological, and to continue the industrial disputes theme, trade unions will often try to project a sense of solidarity through collectivisation. Statements will be replete with phrases like 'our workers' and 'our members'. By its very definition, trade union action is known as *collective* action. However, certain political positions are more welded to the notion of individual accomplishment rather than collective responsibility. In a now infamous interview given by former British Prime Minister Margaret Thatcher to *Woman's Own* magazine in 1987, she stated, 'There's no such thing as society. There are individual men and women and there are families. And no government can do anything except through people, and people must look after themselves first'. This sense of ultra-individuality was used by the Thatcher regime to justify smashing a wrecking ball through the welfare state in Britain whilst the privatisation policies and anti-trade union activities of this government set the tone for the free market capitalism which is rampant in contemporary Britain and many other countries. Individuality is knitted into the fabric of the United States, for example, where provisions like healthcare, sick pay and family leave are almost non-existent in comparison with some other countries. Nation states which have universal welfare systems which benefit citizens can be viewed therefore as placing value in constructing a general level of prosperity for larger, collective groups, whilst other countries prioritise the notion that placing responsibility for welfare onto individuals themselves will lead to very prosperous persons who, in principle, will set the benchmark for others to reach.

Like all things in CDA, context is key, and it is not necessarily always the case that expressions of collectivisation champion features like group solidarity over less laudable and more self-interested positions. The issue of language and 'race', which will be the focus of Section 7.3, often demonstrates that collectivisation can signal something much more malignant. Both visually and textually, members of immigrant communities are often represented in collectivised ways in the media. You will be familiar with phrases like 'illegal immigrants', 'undocumented aliens' and 'foreign migrants', which are well established in certain sections of the press and which often accompany images of groups of people from other countries. As we will see later in the chapter, this type of representation often comes within narratives which represent immigrants through certain disaster metaphors, like 'swarms of migrants', and which project a 'problem of numbers' in terms of immigration. News agencies will sometimes foreground the number of illegal immigrants estimated to be in a country but will less often focus on the contribution which immigration makes to society. We might also encounter evidence of **aggregation** in such stories. Aggregation is when participants are quantified as statistics in phrases like 'tens of thousands of immigrants' or 'hundreds of rioters'. In these types of narratives individualisation is usually reserved for those with official status or someone whose ideological position is espoused by the publication or news agency, such as a prime minister, president or leader of a political party or political pressure group.

Categorisation and Nomination

This brings us to another important social actor grouping, that of **categorisation** and its associated function **nomination**. Van Leeuwen (2008:40) states that 'social actors can be represented in terms of their unique identity, by being nominated, or in terms of identities and functions they share with others, categorisation'. Nomination refers to naming and is realised by proper nouns. Social actors can be nominated formally (surname and possibly with honorifics – 'Mr Smith' for example), semi-formally (given name and surname – 'John Smith') or informally (given name only or through a nickname – 'John', 'Johnny' or 'Smithy'). Categorisation without nomination may refer to 'nameless characters [who] only fulfil passing, functional roles and do not become points of identification for the reader or listener' (van Leeuwen, 2008:40). Consider the two sentences below:

d. Jen Psaki, White House Press Secretary, announced the new policy on Monday morning.
e. A government spokesperson announced the new policy on Monday morning.

Statement d. names Jen Psaki, White House Press Secretary from January 2021, through semi-formal nomination. She is a point of identification for an audience who might be somewhat less receptive to the rather non-descript 'government spokesperson' in sentence e. Semi-formal and formal nomination might also be augmented by the use of functional honorifics (known as **honorification**), which refer to an official role or title such as 'President' or 'Lord'. Some honorifics are more elaborate than others, with monarchical or royal titles being very decorative. 'Her Royal Highness Catherine, Duchess of Cambridge, GVCO' is the official title of the future British queen consort, for example (GVCO refers to the Royal Victorian Order, a dynastic order of knighthood). The British aristocracy and honours system is replete with honorifics and official titles. Somewhat more functional honorifics are evident in titles like 'Home Secretary' (the usual representation of 'Secretary of State for the Home Department'). A sentence which includes a functional honorific like this rather than using the more general 'government spokesperson', for example, enhances the status and the importance of the social actor.

Sentence d. also includes an example of **functionalisation**, which occurs when social actors are represented by an activity, occupation or role. Functionalisation and **identification**, when social actors are referred to as 'what they, more or less permanently, or unavoidably, are' (van Leeuwen, 2008:42), are two key types of categorisation. Sentence d. recognises the senior White House position held by Jen Psaki. Functionalisation often indicates a sense of authority or refers to the contribution one is making to society. If a member of the immigrant community who possesses a profession, let's say an accountant, is represented through sentence f., she is presented with professional status intact and without reference to 'race'. Sentence g. is somewhat different.

  f. Amira Singh, an accountant who works locally, challenged the town council's new policy.
  g. Amira Singh, who comes from India, challenged the town council's new policy.

Sentence g. references the social actor's nationality – an expression of what she 'more or less permanently, or unavoidably, is' – rather than her profession. In many instances, reference to the religion, nationality or skin colour of a social actor is an example of 'othering', a concept upon which we will expand below but which in this case essentially operates to highlight difference. Do you think you would be likely to encounter a sentence like statement h. in an Irish newspaper?

  h. Paula Murphy, who comes from Ireland, challenged the town council's new policy.

Identifying an Irish person through nationality in an Irish newspaper seems over-specific if s/he is Irish, but it is quite conventional if the person is from abroad, which in turn serves to 'other' the social actor. A text might highlight the difference of a social actor but will not foreground the nationality of someone who 'comes from here'. When this occurs, it is an example of 'exnomination', the pointing out of some supposed 'other', whilst being local, white and Christian, in many Western countries in any case, is viewed as 'natural' or 'normal' and not pointed out.

Van Leeuwen distinguishes three types of identification: **classification, relational identification** and **physical identification**. Classification occurs when a social actor is categorised 'by means of which a given society or institution differentiates between classes of people' (van Leeuwen, 2008:42). The lines of classification in many Western societies are fairly well established, and we are conditioned, in part by the power of institutional discourse, to classify depending on class, wealth, gender, ethnicity and religion, amongst other things. We should remember that these categories themselves are not fixed and often shift across space and time. Gender in contemporary Western societies is increasingly considered as something which is performed and fluid rather than biologically assigned and fixed, for example. Van Leeuwen (2008:42) notes that, at present, a more important role in classifying social actors is played by 'belonging to a company or organisation' such as 'a student at Queen's' or 'a member of the board of directors'. Perhaps functionalisation possessing value is a sign of the prominence and power of organisations and institutions in late modernity. Relational identification is denoted by nouns such as 'mother', 'father', 'friend' or 'colleague' and refers to social actors in terms of their personal, kinship or work networks. Again the importance of these networks is variable across cultures; family relationships have arguably decreased in importance in many capitalist societies, whereas they remain significant in other more traditional or tribal cultures. Physical identification, as you have probably worked out, refers to physical characteristics. Both literary and factual texts offer readers identifiable physical descriptions of characters and other participants. Again, these characteristics have variable importance across time and space. Long curls once denoted such grace that the male monarchs of Europe appeared in powdered wigs which would seem most unlikely in contemporary society. Certain physical characteristics carry ideological connotations which are reinforced in institutional discourse.

i. The 24-year-old blonde from Essex will give a tell-all interview to the tabloids.

In sentence i. we are conditioned to 'think female' despite the fact that the sex of the social actor has not been stated. Tabloid representations of 'blondes' are ingrained, highly sexualised and carry connotations of titillation, promiscuity and a certain lack of acuity. Men are less often represented through physical identification, although obviously this varies between discourse arenas, and a medium like a lifestyle magazine differs from a newspaper story, where men are more often represented through functionalisation.

Many sentences will display more than one social actor, and obviously there are links between the social actor definitions. For example, a phrase like 'former President Barack Obama, a lawyer by profession' is an example of personalisation, individualisation, semi-formal nomination and honorification, and 'black voters who supported him' is collectivisation, categorisation, identification and classification. Van Leeuwen (1996:32) describes social actor analysis as a 'sociosemantic inventory', and the analyst must decide how general or specific an analysis needs to be. On occasion it might be sufficient to point out when participants have been impersonalised or personalised; at other times it might be necessary to go further and consider, for example, how functionalisation and the range of identification are used in a text. Use Figure 7.1, which illustrates

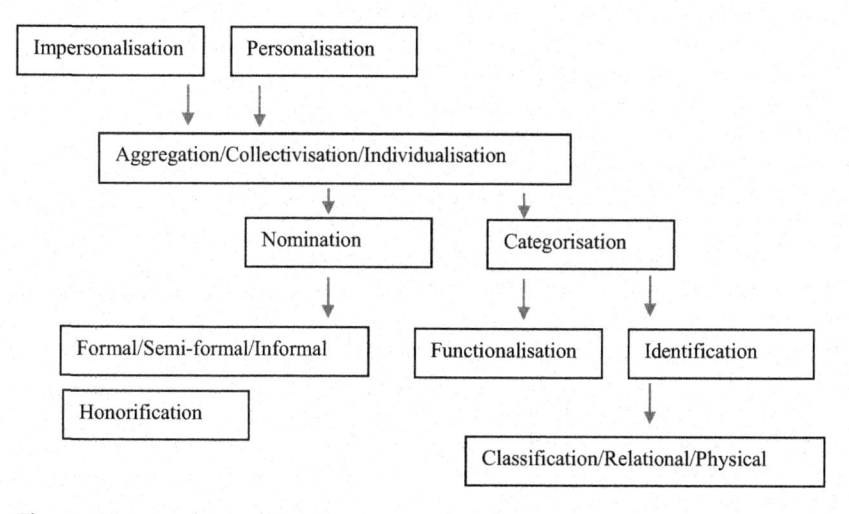

Figure 7.1 Social actor categories

SOCIAL ACTORS: REPRESENTING PARTICIPANTS

the social actor definitions we have outlined here, to help you complete the student task.

Student Task

For sentences a. to i. in our discussion of social actor analysis in this chapter, identify the social actors in each sentence and allocate a social actor label to each participant.

The solution is given after the Further Reading suggestions at the end of the chapter.

7.2.2 Analysis of Social Actors

Before we examine a new textual example using social actor analysis to focus on the issue of 'race', we will first re-examine an earlier example to demonstrate that a range of models in CDA can be applied to the same text to produce very in-depth critical analysis of institutional discourse. Let's look again at the article analysed in Chapter 3, which is reprinted below with social actors underlined.

Example 7.1 Firefight as 90 <u>Brits</u> smash Taliban base

<u>Afghan cop</u> is saved in bomb factory raid

MORE than 90 daring <u>British troops</u> stormed a Taliban bomb factory at dawn — and rescued <u>a cop</u> due to be executed within HOURS.

As <u>comrades</u> surrounded the base in Afghanistan, the <u>soldiers</u> landed in helicopters and forced back <u>terrorist gunmen</u> during two monster gun battles.

<u>They</u> then picked their way through a ring of hidden bombs before finding the captured <u>Afghan policeman</u>, who had been tied up and told <u>he</u> was about to be shot.

The <u>elite soldiers from the Brigade Reconnaissance Force</u> had swooped with <u>Afghan commandos</u> after a local tip-off that <u>Taliban killers</u> were making explosives.

<u>They</u> discovered that the bomb factory had been abandoned.

But as <u>they</u> moved out, <u>they</u> spotted suspicious activity at a separate compound close by — and after another gun battle unearthed 30kgs of opium, an AK-47 sub-machine gun and bundles of cash.

> Last night <u>the man in overall charge</u> of last week's 12-hour mission paid tribute to his <u>soldiers</u>, saying it was a classic example of <u>Our Boys</u> working with the local <u>security forces</u>.
> <u>Lieutenant Colonel Jasper de Quincey Adams</u>, <u>the commanding officer of 1st The Queen's Dragoon Guards</u>, said: "All of the <u>soldiers</u> and <u>airmen</u> involved in the operation worked together to deliver a high-impact effect that demonstrates the reach of the <u>Afghan government</u>.
> "This will send out a clear message to our <u>Afghan partners</u> that we will continue to offer our support however dangerous or complex the mission."
> The operation — dubbed Eagle's Shadow — was launched at first light in Nahr-e Saraj district, Helmand Province. <u>Scimitar tanks</u> first surrounded the target and trained their 30mm cannons on the enemy base.
> <u>Warthog all-terrain troop carriers</u>, armed with heavy machine-guns, reinforced the cordon before <u>two Chinook choppers</u> and a <u>US Sikorsky troop carrier</u> swept in.
> An <u>Apache attack helicopter</u> also joined the fight.
> <u>Intelligence officer 2nd Lieutenant Barnaby Smith</u> said: "This Afghan-led operation not only recovered a member of the <u>Afghan uniformed police</u> but disrupted the <u>insurgents</u> in their backyard."
> The <u>BRF</u> consists of <u>soldiers of 1st The Queen's Dragoon Guards and 1st Battalion the Yorkshire Regiment</u>, while the <u>Warthog Group</u> is manned by <u>soldiers from the Queen's Royal Hussars</u>.
>
> (*The Sun*, 11 December 2011)

In Chapter 3 we assessed this article in terms of transitivity and focussed on the role of processes in legitimising perceptions of war in general and the most recent conflict in Afghanistan in particular. We noted that the naming of participants in the article constructs a cohesive sense of professionalism by naming military equipment, noting the full names and rank of soldiers and giving the name of the operation, 'Eagle's Shadow'. Applying social actor analysis also considers how participants are named and allows us to say a good deal more about the representation of war in this article.

Firstly, there is a clear distinction in the sheer presence of the two sides of the conflict in this article. Thirty participant phrases are allocated to the British and their Afghan allies, whereas the Taliban are only named on five occasions: 'Taliban' (twice), 'terrorist gunmen', 'Taliban killers' and 'insurgents'. We can conclude therefore that the Taliban are collectivised, impersonalised, and that there are no examples of personal nomination. Functionalisation is not employed here. The Taliban are not professional soldiers with regiments and rank; instead they are identified as 'killers', 'gunmen' and 'insurgents'. This contrasts starkly with the social actor representation of the British Army and allies.

The British Army are represented in a number of ways in this article. The regiments are named in full – 'Brigade Reconnaissance Force', '1st The Queen's

Dragoon Guards', '1st Battalion the Yorkshire Regiment' and the 'Queen's Royal Hussars' – and the soldiers, who are the sole social actors with a voice in this text, are nominated and functionalised with honorifics to indicate rank and position: 'Lieutenant Colonel Jasper de Quincey Adams' and 'Intelligence officer 2nd Lieutenant Barnaby Smith'. 'Soldiers', 'commandos', 'British troops', 'airmen' and 'elite soldiers' are also examples of functionalisation, which professionalise the British Army against the insurgents and gunmen of the Taliban. Whilst they are not quoted directly, the Afghan allies of the British in this operation are also represented through functionalisation in terms like 'Afghan government' and 'Afghan partners'. The rescued prisoner is an 'Afghan cop', a 'cop', an 'Afghan policeman' and a 'member of the Afghan uniformed police'. Whilst classification identifies the nationality of the Afghan social actors, they are in all cases also functionalised to differentiate them from the Taliban. Consistent functionalisation serves to legitimise the role of the British Army and their Afghan allies; they are soldiers with rank and profession, which sets them apart from the Taliban, who have been categorised only by identification. Note also that many of the actions carried out by the British and Afghan troops are attributed to military hardware in this article rather than to the soldiers who operate Scimitar tanks or Apache attack helicopters. This is an example of a type of impersonalisation known as instrumentalisation, where 'social actors are represented by means of reference to the instrument with which they carry out the activity which they are represented as being engaged in' (van Leeuwen, 1996:60). Impersonalisation therefore is a way of backgrounding the role of individual soldiers and disconnecting them from the more unpalatable aspects of military actions.

An application of social actor analysis to this article means that we can strengthen previous conclusions drawn from a consideration of transitivity. You will find that, when using CDA to examine certain pieces of discourse, transitivity and social actor analysis are very effective analytical bedfellows; transitivity focusses on processes, participants and circumstances, and social actor analysis involves a specific focus on participants. We saw in Chapter 6 that a model such as the taxonymy for verbs of speaking can augment and provide a further level to an analysis which applies the transitivity framework by focus on a specific type of process. Social actor analysis can be utilised in a similar way, enhancing a transitivity analysis by examining how participants of all six processes are represented.

The findings of both our earlier transitivity analysis and the social actor analysis here align this article with prevailing perspectives of the Taliban within the US and UK governments in 2011; the Taliban were a terrorist, insurgent force who were unprofessional and illegitimate. In February 2020 the US and the Taliban signed a peace agreement to end hostilities with the aim of beginning talks which would also involve the Afghan government. In a White House press conference, US President Donald Trump said that US troops had been killing terrorists 'by the thousands' and that 'now it is time for someone else to do that work and it will be the Taliban and it could be surrounding countries'. Newspaper front pages the day after the signing in Doha featured a historic handshake between US special envoy Zalmay Khalizad and Mullah Abdul Ghani Baradar of the Taliban, with US Secretary of State Mike Pompeo looking on. Despite the reservations of many in the international community, including victims groups, the US was now making a clear distinction between the Taliban and terrorists, words which for so long had effectively been synonyms. Shifting contexts and changing governmental policies – in February 2020 Donald Trump was able to service a major pledge to 'bring troops home' nine months before a presidential election – reinforce much of what we already know about powerful discourse. This is never neutral and, despite ideological language's naturalisation of the Taliban as terrorists, this position is changeable should political priorities require it. Discourse is therefore not inherent and objective but subjective, interested and constructed. Following the final withdrawal of US troops from Afghanistan in August 2021, the Taliban quickly swept back to power. It is likely that the discourse representation of the group will therefore shift again in the future.

7.3 Social Actors in Representations of 'Race'

We will now consider the social actor analysis model in an area of study where critical discourse analysts have been prominent, the topic of language and 'race'.

Many works in CDA, such as van Dijk et al. (1997), present 'race' and 'racial' with inverted commas to recognise the fact that these are social rather than biological distinctions. At the risk of sounding sentimental, we all comprise the 'human race'. Distinctions within this group, traditionally based on differences of skin colour, are ideologically constructed in the social world partly through language. There is no correlation between the colour of one's skin and the strength of one's character or intelligence. Those who make these types of assumptions are reproducing racialised thinking which constructs 'race' as real. But 'race', when considered in this way, like many taken-for-granted aspects of such a heavily stratified society, is a construct. When assumptions are constructed based on stereotypes about 'race', we speak of the process of 'racialisation'. Racism is the manifestation of racialised thinking when people are subjected to discrimination in an array of forms. One of the most extreme manifestations of racist discrimination is action taken against others based on their skin colour or ethnic background, but it is important to acknowledge that racism is not limited to these more extreme manifestations. Certainly, discrimination represented by actions, from denying employment to someone based on their skin colour to violence driven by perceptions of one's ethnicity, is highly problematic. But racialised thinking is also reproduced when assumptions are made about individuals or groups of people who have a different skin colour, ethnicity or cultural background. Discourse which constructs 'race' as real and reproduces racialised thinking that links 'race' to limited characteristics can therefore be characterised as racist.

Racist discourse is a social practice with tangible and measurable outcomes. Van Dijk (2000) reminds us that social practice has a cognitive dimension, the attitudes and ideologies possessed by discourse decoders which, in the case of 'race', drives racist behaviour. Simpson, Mayr and Statham (2018:23) offer an overview of a range of theories from linguistics, anthropology and psychoanalysis which demonstrates that racialised 'difference', what Hall (1997:234) calls 'othering', has been at the heart of several longstanding intellectual positions. Many approaches from these areas of study utilise the concept of the 'other' as a way of exploring the characteristics of the 'sense of self'. In short, a sense of difference allows one to define her/his own characteristics but also can lead to an aggression against the 'other', those things which one, conceptually, is not. When one conceives difference through 'race' or ethnicity, the 'other' comes loaded with those characteristics which have been assigned to 'racial' groups through, amongst other things, the naturalisation processes of social discourse.

We have already seen some examples of how 'othering' is constructed through language, through pronoun patterns and the attribution of positive and negative judgements, for instance. We referred above to the process of exnomination, when 'whiteness' is assumed to be natural and other 'races' to be deviant to this and therefore named. Gabriel (2000) also notes the importance of 'universalisation', a similar naturalisation process which is concerned with the prominence of white European and white American principles and values. Certain discourse representations assume that these values are held by all ethnic groups and nationalities despite well-established realities to the contrary. In addition, some groups, such as political parties, might assume an absence of certain values amongst whole groups of people based on their 'race', so that 'our values' need to be defended. Extreme nationalism often calls for the universalisation of 'American values' or 'British values', for example.

Whilst it would be somewhat hard to argue that we occupy some sort of post-racial reality, especially given a seemingly new prominence of racism in politics in particular, manifested in events like Brexit and the popularity of politicians like Donald Trump, Marine le Pen or Geert Wilders, it might nonetheless seem like a focus on skin colour is not overly prominent in institutional language disseminated by most contemporary politicians or media. Certainly, when you consider the extent to which a focus on difference through skin colour and appearance has been prominent in history, such as the buffoonery attributed to 'blacked-up' actors on the minstrel stage, it would seem less frequent in contemporary society. This is equally the case in political language. When Tory and later Ulster Unionist MP Enoch Powell spoke out against the Race Relations Act in his infamous 'Rivers of Blood' speech in 1968, he lamented that 'the black man will have the whip hand over the white man' in a statement that would cause much controversy were it uttered today (we can only speculate how much thought was given to the irony of such a statement). We can also testify to comparatively rare references to skin colour in the pages of even those mainstream newspapers and news agencies hardest to the Right of the political spectrum. More blatant expressions of racism which refer to skin colour – examples of what is called 'old racism' – whilst not non-existent, are rare in the mainstream of most Western societies. Lamentably, however, we do not live in a post-racial society.

What Barker (1981, 1984) refers to as 'new racism' or 'cultural racism', where difference is constructed through reference to nationality, ethnicity, culture and religion, is fairly common. Barker's term 'pseudo-biological culturalism' acknowledges that assumed biological differences which are correlated with cultural characteristics are no more genuine than are those which equate character with skin colour. Van Dijk (1993) notes that 'elites' play a particular role in the reproduction of new racism. Elite groups and organisations are those which control policy and which construct, propagate and reinforce the concept of 'race' as real. Examples of elite groups include sections of the media, political parties and advertising agencies. We must acknowledge that the role of elites does not mitigate or excuse racism which emanates from other groups – such as far-right pressure groups and racism in lower socio-economic communities – however, the producers of this 'popular racism' do not have influence which can emulate that of powerful elite organisations. Elite racism is carried out through processes such as positive self-presentation and negative 'other' presentation in the media. Where 'race' is concerned, this occurs when a powerful and influential institution denigrates an ethnic group through pronoun patterns and overlexicalisation.

7.3.1 'Race' in the Media

Influential studies in CDA (Cottle, 2000; Gabrielatos and Baker, 2008) have demonstrated that ethnic minorities in certain sections of the media are repeatedly represented through a limited set of negative references, in particular crime and criminality, illegality, a problem of numbers and health scares. Gabrielatos and Baker (2008) constructed a corpus linguistic analysis of the representation of refugees in the British press between 1996 and 2005 and concluded that the constructions of 'foreigners' falls into eight broad categories: provenance/transit/destination, numbers, entry, economic problems, residence, return/repatriation, legality and plight (see Chapter 12 for a larger discussion of corpus linguistics). These categories demonstrate the negativity of the narratives which construct and legitimise perceptions of ethnic 'others' in the media. Apart from the limited number of categories, none of them could be conceived as positive. There is therefore only a limited media focus on features of immigration like the economic contribution of migrants, building a broader skills base or cultural enrichment and linguistic diversity.

SOCIAL ACTORS: REPRESENTING PARTICIPANTS

The article below was published in the *Daily Express* newspaper in 2014 and is representative of the discourse which composed this publication's years-long 'crusade for Britain to leave the EU'. Social actors have been underlined.

Example 7.2 <u>Migrants</u> DO take our jobs: <u>Britons</u> losing out to <u>foreign workers</u>, says official study

<u>BRITONS</u> are losing out to <u>foreign workers</u> with one in six low-skilled jobs now held by <u>an immigrant</u>

The number of <u>British-born people</u> in lowly-paid jobs has fallen by more than a million since 1997 – while <u>migrants</u> doing similar work rose by the same amount, official figures show. A Home Office study published yesterday showed the jobs boom for <u>migrants</u> was fuelled by expansion of the European Union in 2004.

More than half of the <u>new job-holders</u> in Britain are <u>eastern Europeans</u> using freedom of movement rules to seek out better wages. Of the UK's 13 million low-skilled jobs, in areas such as horticulture and food manufacturing, about 2.1 million are now held by <u>migrants</u>, the report found. Nearly half of <u>them</u>, 840,000, are <u>EU citizens</u>.

<u>Advisers on the Home Office's Migration Advisory Committee</u> who produced the research have now urged the <u>Government</u> to limit the impact of migration on <u>local communities</u>. And <u>they</u> warned <u>ministers</u> to "think carefully" about how <u>they</u> handle more EU expansion.

<u>Ukip MEP Patrick O'Flynn</u> said: "These figures demonstrate the damaging impact that mass immigration has had on the prospects of <u>ordinary Brits</u>. The low-skilled jobs market is now saturated by <u>foreign workers</u>, while <u>communities</u> have had to bear the brunt of this influx that has changed many neighbourhoods beyond recognition. <u>We</u> must leave the EU and take back control of Britain's borders."

The report said the rise in immigration over the past 15 to 20 years was "heavily influenced" by Labour's policy of dishing out more work permits, student and family visas. It found that 75 per cent of the 2.9 million rise in the <u>foreign-born population</u> in the past 10 years was concentrated in just a quarter of towns, leaving them struggling to cope with the pressure on housing and services.

"Although nationally the economic impact of immigration is very modest, the economic and social impact on particular local authorities is much stronger," the report said. It states that between 1997 and 2013 the number of <u>Britons</u> in low-skilled jobs fell by 1.1 million, while the number of <u>foreigners</u> in such roles increased by the same amount. The UK-born share of low-skilled jobs fell from 93 per cent to 84 per cent.

> Some experts say a shift by two million Britons into high-skilled work explains this change. But the UK-born share of top-level jobs also fell six per cent to 86 per cent.
> The committee raised concerns that migrants from five countries, including Turkey, that are currently negotiating to join the EU would once again find work in low-skilled occupations.
> Sir Andrew Green, of Migration Watch UK, said: "One has to ask why some people are so keen to promote mass immigration in the teeth of public opinion."
> A Home Office spokesman said: "In the past, the majority of growth in employment was taken up by foreign nationals. Under this Government, three-quarters of this growth has been accounted for by British citizens. We are working across Government to ensure immigration works for this country and will use the findings of this report to inform our approach."
>
> (*Daily Express*, 9 July 2014)

This article demonstrates several of the categories proposed by Gabrielatos and Baker with reference to provenance, numbers, legality, entry and economic problems. The dominant message is that immigration is harmful to the prospects of ordinary 'Britons'. This collectivised term identifies the 'us' element of this article – produced by a right wing British newspaper with a similar readership – through classification and is used four times in the text. Cohesion is constructed through identification in lexical items like 'Britons', 'British-born people', 'ordinary Brits' and 'British citizens'. The 'British-born' victims of immigration are set in stark contrast to opposing groups of 'foreign workers'. This collectivised term is repeated three times in the article, whilst the identifying term 'migrants' is used on five occasions. A stark structural opposition is constructed through these seemingly distinct groups. The focus is on the provenance of people and a selective interpretation of the economic impact of immigration rather than on 'old racist' features like skin colour.

We have pointed out throughout this book the importance of voices in discourse and are perhaps unsurprised that in this article no speaking rights are given to migrants despite their dominant lexical presence in the text. Ukip MEP Patrick O'Flynn and Sir Andrew Green of Migration Watch UK are formally nominated with honorifics and presented through functionalisation. As with the reference to soldiers through their rank in Example 7.1, nomination and functionalisation provide professional status and importance to these participants. O'Flynn's quotation sets up an opposition between 'foreign workers' and 'communities'. Migrants are constructed not as a part of the communities in which they live but instead are presented as bringing adverse, external effects. 'Ordinary Brits' 'bear the brunt of this influx', and O'Flynn quotes one of the most visible mantras of the anti-EU campaign which eventually resulted in Brexit, 'We must leave the

EU and take back control of Britain's borders'. The quotation at the end of the article defends the actions of the government and offers statistics on how 'this Government' is seeking to redress this apparent imbalance. This quotation, however, is attributed to a 'Home Office spokesman', an example of impersonalisation which distances the speaker from the reader. Nonetheless, this spokesperson still upholds the opposition which 'others' 'foreign nationals' from 'British citizens'. The report itself is also selectively quoted and differentiates between 'Britons' and 'foreigners'. The voices in this text are focussed on collectivised groups, both of which are represented in social actor terms through classification. The fact that this article is focussed on employment means that migrants could have been represented through functionalisation. Specific reference to the jobs and professions which migrants undertake would have afforded a level of status and respect, a sense of contribution, of 'giving' rather than 'taking'. The newspaper instead chooses to classify more than functionalise. The focus is on the 'foreignness' of these workers and is exacerbated by consistently being set against the 'Britishness' of those who are apparently 'losing out'. This 'othering' is maintained even in occasional examples of functionalisation in phrases such as 'foreign workers'.

Social actor analysis can tell us much about the ideological position being taken by this text. We can also critically consider some other aspects of the article. The economic assessment proffered by the text focusses on the proportion of 'new job-holders' who have immigrated to Britain and who are employed in Britain's 13 million 'low-skilled jobs'. The interpretation offered by the *Express* does not evaluate this employment in terms of contribution to the economy but assumes a cause-and-effect relationship which implies that 'Britons' must be unemployed as a result. Even the figures offered by the publication itself expose its ideological position: 840,000 is 40 percent of 2.1 million, yet the *Express* chooses to describe this as 'nearly half'. And 840,000 is only 6.46 percent of 13 million, so EU citizens who have been ideologically problematised here actually make up a very small portion of those employed in these jobs. Furthermore, 2.1 million is only 16.15 percent of 13 million, so the vast majority of these jobs are not done by 'foreign workers'. Consider the effect of the headline: '83.85 per cent of horticulture and food manufacturing jobs in Britain done by Britons'. This headline is just as accurate, indeed a good deal more so, than 'Migrants DO take our jobs'. Another headline might be '2.1 million migrants contributing to British economy'. However, neither of these headlines would align with the ideological position being naturalised in this article.

The statistics in the Home Office report used in this article demonstrate that only 6.46 percent of the low-skills jobs market is comprised of migrants from the EU, yet the *Express* includes Patrick O'Flynn's characterisation of this situation as 'saturated by foreign workers', utilising a metaphor of panic which conceptualises people as liquid, similar to the 'waves of immigrants' metaphor you may have encountered elsewhere. Indeed, 6.46 percent does not represent saturation in any definition of the term; however, it takes a critical discourse analyst to decipher this reality amongst the overlexicalised ideology present in this article. Green says that immigration supporters act 'in the teeth of public opinion', but no members of the public are quoted here and no statistics are offered.

Over recent decades the *Daily Express* has cast itself as a modern-day Coeur de Lion crusading against what it repeatedly characterised as inappropriate control from Brussels over the sovereign affairs of Britain. This article is one of many on the Right of the political spectrum of the press in Britain which CDA could analyse as being consistently hostile to the EU and to immigration in general. After a hugely divisive and controversial campaign, the language of which provided data for linguists (Buckledee, 2018; Jeffries and McIntyre, 2019) as well as social scientists from a range of disciplines, British voters chose to leave the EU in June 2016, and the UK ceased to be a full member of the bloc in January 2020. The front page in the *Express* the day after the referendum result declared 'World's Most Successful Newspaper Crusade Ends in Glorious Victory for Your Daily Express: We're Out of the EU'. For the right wing in British politics and media, this headline was the culmination of decades of front pages and articles like Example 7.2, which continuously represented immigration as the result of EU membership and as a root cause of unemployment, economic instability, crime and health crises, all the while leaving unscrutinised the unapologetic commitment to a poverty gap in British and Western societies generally, which is actually the primary cause of these realities. Consider the headlines below (where available online, each of the accompanying articles to these headlines would provide you with excellent data to replicate the analysis of Example 7.2 presented here and further explore the issue of language, power and 'race'):

> Every 4 Minutes a Migrant is Arrested in Britain (*Daily Express*, 4th February 2008)
> BBC Put Muslims Before You (*Daily Star*, 16th October 2008)
> Brit Kids Forced to Eat Halal School Dinners (*Daily Star*, 6th August 2010)
> EU Wants to Merge UK with France (*Daily Express*, 2nd May 2011)
> We Must Stop the Migrant Invasion (*Daily Express*, 6th June 2013)
> Draw a Red Line on Immigration (*The Sun*, 18th December 2013)
> Islamic Law Is Adopted by British Legal Chiefs (*The Daily Telegraph*, 23rd March 2014)
> Army on Alert at French Ports to Halt Migrant Invasion (*Daily Express*, 14th September 2014)
> Send in Army to Halt Migrant Invasion (*Daily Express*, 30th July 2015)
> The Great Migrant Con (*The Sun*, 28th February 2016)
> EU to Launch Kettle and Toaster Crackdown after Brexit Vote (*The Daily Telegraph*, 11th May 2016)
> Migrants Spark Housing Crisis (*Daily Mail*, 19th May 2016)

Anti-immigrant and particularly anti-Muslim hysteria, with even the quintessential staple of tea and toast seemingly at risk, has been a consistent feature of the tabloid and broadsheet press in Britain for many years. With the exception of *The Guardian*, *Daily Mirror* and *Financial Times*, which, although not immune to certain stances on immigration, were largely pro-Remain, the British media in print, online and on television was largely in favour of leaving the EU. Social media, much like it had in the Scottish independence referendum in 2014 and the British General Elections of 2016 and 2019, provided a platform where resistant voices could be heard, although in these cases it was the position of traditional media which took the day.

Summary of Chapter 7

This chapter has offered a comprehensive overview of the model of social actor analysis to demonstrate the ideological representation of immigration in the British media and has illustrated that the moral panic constructed around the migrant community in Britain has been consistently linked to the UK's membership of the European Union. Limited representations of immigration through negative narrative categories not only naturalise the notion that these categories are legitimate but also imply by extension that positive evaluations of immigration are illegitimate or non-existent. We have also exemplified that social actor analysis can be utilised to strengthen the conclusions reached by other models of analysis in CDA, such as transitivity. Chapters 8 and 9 will focus on political language and examine models of analysis to consider the persuasiveness of political speech, beginning with an examination of a speech by Donald Trump before focussing on the language of the British government during the Covid-19 pandemic.

Further Reading

Van Leeuwen, T. (1996) 'The Representation of Social Actors', in Caldas-Coulthard, C. and Coulthard, M. (eds.) *Texts and Practices: Readings in Critical Discourse Analysis*. London and New York: Routledge, pp.32–70.

Van Leeuwen, T. (2008) *Discourse and Practice: New Tools for Critical Discourse Analysis*. Oxford: Oxford University Press.

Solutions to Student Task

a. Jane Smith (personalisation, nomination); store manager (functionalisation); staff (functionalisation).
b. The company (impersonalisation); all staff (functionalisation).
c. The company (impersonalisation); customers (classification).
d. Stephanie Grisham (personalisation, nomination); White House Communications Director (functionalisation).
e. A government spokesperson (impersonalisation, functionalisation).
f. Amira Singh (personalisation, nomination); accountant (functionalisation).
g. Amira Singh (personalisation, nomination); comes from India (classification).
h. Paula Murphy (personalisation, nomination); comes from Ireland (classification).
i. 24-year-old (classification); blonde (physical identification); comes from Essex (classification).

8 Politics and Power

Analysing Political Language

KEY TERMS IN CHAPTER 8: politics, sub-politics, coercion, legitimation, representation

MODELS OF ANALYSIS IN CHAPTER 8: metaphor, metonymy, strategic functions

8.1 Introduction

It is fairly clear that all of this book is preoccupied with **politics**, and this is borne out by the analyses which we have performed in each chapter so far. Chapter 1 established that CDA itself is part of the political process. In demystifying and exposing powerful ideologies at work in institutional language, we are partaking of politics; we have a specific agenda to arm readers to see below the surface representations of discourse and to consider the motivations of text encoders of media texts, campaign leaflets or university websites.

The next two chapters will be engaged primarily with language which is produced by politicians. This chapter will explore the 'strategic functions' of political discourse proposed by Chilton and Schaffner (1997) and Chilton (2004) in an analysis of a political speech and will also set out the parameters of conceptual metaphor theory, which we have mentioned in several of our analytical discussions so far and which Charteris-Black (2004, 2014) has demonstrated play a key role in the discourse of politics. Chapter 9 will introduce the classic way to analyse political discourse given in Aristotle's *Rhetoric* and will consider how rhetoric operates in an important written document, the letter issued to all UK households by Prime Minister Boris Johnson at the beginning of the Covid-19 pandemic. In examining the language of this pandemic, which emerged in China in late 2019, was declared a pandemic in 2020 and is still ongoing at the time of writing, we are also demonstrating how CDA remains consistently relevant in its analytical focus on society. The political process and the major events which it addresses are always ongoing, so data is constantly emerging on how powerful groups use language to react to them.

It is also important to establish that politics is not the exclusive purview of political professionals. Ordinary people, for want of a better phrase, engage in politics as voters in elections and might attend protests or demonstrations or take part in industrial or other forms of collective actions like boycotts. These are all clear examples of people who are not professional politicians taking part in politics. There are a good many other examples which you might not immediately consider to be inherently 'political' but which can very easily be considered 'political statements' either by those performing them or by others who judge and evaluate them. For many, vegetarianism or veganism could be considered political – part of the process of 'lifestyle politics' – whilst choosing to walk or to take public transport instead of driving one's own vehicle might play a part in 'environmental politics'. We play 'office politics' at work and 'sexual politics' in life, although of course the boundaries here are somewhat fuzzy. It is very unlikely that anyone partaking in conventional society will not be involved in at least one of these types of **sub-politics**. Even in that unlikely event, s/he could still not be viewed as existing outside of politics. Even someone considered wholly disengaged from politics is a recipient of politics; s/he is a consumer or a taxpayer or an employee or employer, someone who contributes to or receives a pension, who uses subsidised or, perhaps more likely, unsubsidised public transport, healthcare or education. In short, whole myriads of complex networks of power, politics and policy affect the citizenry of anywhere. To be a part of society, any society, is to be amidst politics.

Before beginning an analysis of a political speech from former US President Donald Trump, the next section will discuss metaphor. Metaphor is a core component in how language users conceptualise the world around them, is pervasive in language and plays a particularly important part in political discourse.

8.2 Metaphor

At its most basic, 'metaphor' refers to mapping between two conceptual domains; it is the process through which we understand one thing in terms of another. An important point to establish immediately in any discussion of metaphor is its pervasiveness in language (Lakoff and Johnson, 1980). We are interested in political uses of metaphor in this book, but by no means is metaphor restricted to political language. There is also a well-established although wholly erroneous assumption that metaphorical constructions are exclusive to literary texts; instead, metaphors play a routine and important part in everyday conceptual thought. They are 'basic schemes through which people conceptualise their experience and their external world' (Simpson, 2014:43).

Thus metaphor, whilst undoubtedly important for persuasion and creativity, should not be thought of as exclusive to politics or to literature, but recognised as a natural part of human conception. It is by all means valid to acknowledge that some literary texts are noteworthy for their novel use of metaphor, but metaphorical transference itself is not inherently literary. Consider for example the line 'The refrigerator whinnied into silence' from the poem 'The Skunk' by Seamus Heaney, which describes an inanimate refrigerator through the verb 'whinnied', as if it were a horse. The metaphor at work here is MACHINES ARE ANIMALS (the conventional representation in conceptual metaphor theory is in small capital letters like this) and the linguistic instantiation of the metaphor in this poem is fairly novel. A more prosaic or everyday use of the same metaphor might be 'The self-service check-out barked orders at shoppers' or 'The howling burglar alarm kept the neighbours awake'. MACHINES ARE ANIMALS is quite an ingrained metaphor. These examples are less creative than Heaney's poem but they rely on the same process of transference and use the same conceptual domains.

The two conceptual domains in metaphor structure are known as the 'source domain' and the 'target domain' (Lakoff and Turner, 1989). The latter is the thing or the concept being described through the metaphor whilst the source domain is the concept drawn upon to construct the metaphor. In our examples above, ANIMALS is the source domain and MACHINES the target domain. The well-worn political metaphor 'green shoots of recovery', used to indicate improvement in times of economic downturn and usually attributed to Norman Lamont, British Chancellor of the Exchequer in 1991, expresses the metaphor THE ECONOMY IS A PLANT, where the economy is being described through the attributes of a plant. A PLANT is the source domain and THE ECONOMY is the target domain. Just like in our first example above, this metaphor can be linguistically instantiated in a range of clauses, such as 'flowering economy' or the 'roots of our financial successes'. A PLANT is also the source domain in metaphors like 'root-and-branch approach' or the 'root of an idea'.

Particular metaphorical constructions which strongly demonstrate the pervasiveness of metaphor in everyday expressions are the orientational metaphors UP IS GOOD and DOWN IS BAD. Phrases like 'on top of the world' and 'feeling low' are figurative expressions which are so ingrained they have become idiomatic fixed expressions, so their 'metaphoricity' is not always recognised. If we consider these well-established phrases more closely, however, one cannot literally be on top of the world. This sentence is an example of the UP IS GOOD metaphor.

Many metaphorical constructions perform a process known as 'concretisation' through which abstract target domains such as 'ideas' or 'life' are conceived through somewhat more physical or familiar source domains such as 'money' or 'food'. The following constructions all express the metaphor IDEAS ARE MONEY, for example: my two cents worth; a treasure trove of new ideas; the manifesto is rich in policies; there is a wealth of information here. The metaphor is constructed through a combination of references to money with a more abstract experiential domain in ideas. The phrase 'half-baked notion' expresses the metaphor IDEAS ARE FOOD, 'the root of the plan' is IDEAS ARE PLANTS, 'her mind is very sharp' expresses IDEAS ARE CUTTING INSTRUMENTS and 'the foundation of the notion' is IDEAS ARE BUILDINGS; so a target domain can be mapped onto several distinct source domains.

Charteris-Black (2004) examines metaphors which are present in the manifestos of the British Conservative and Labour parties respectively. This corpus-based analysis found that a range of metaphors drawing on source domains of CONFLICT, BUILDINGS, JOURNEYS, PLANTS and RELIGION were present in the language of both political parties although in some cases these were utilised differently. For example, Charteris-Black (2004:67) states that the 'use of conflict metaphors for the communication of value judgement is rather different for each party. While both parties defend social goals or social groups, Labour attacks social ills while the Conservative Party defends social goals or social groups that are represented as being under attack by Labour'. In sentences like 'We will continue to defend farmers and consumers', the Tories are expressing their support for groups who they perceive to be at risk from the economic and environmental policies of Labour. The Labour promise 'Labour created the National Health Service and is determined to defend it' foregrounds the fact that the NHS, Britain's state universal health service, was opposed by the Tories in its inception and has been successively underfunded and neglected on their governmental watches.

Right wing, anti-immigration language, an example of which we examined in Chapter 7, for example, often uses disaster metaphors to construct the perception of a threat around the issue of immigration. Where politically motivated discourse talks about 'swarms' of immigrants and 'waves' or 'floods' of migrants, people are metaphorically conceived as insects and water respectively. In the call to 'halt the tide of EU migrants' – a favourite rallying cry of the elements of the British media which pushed for Brexit – the PEOPLE ARE WATER metaphor is also employed. War metaphors which refer to things like the 'migrant invasion' are also common.

A process of transference related to metaphor and also prevalent across different types of discourse is 'metonymy'. Metonymy refers to a transfer within a single conceptual domain rather than drawing on one conceptual domain to describe another. One type of metonymy with which you are probably quite familiar is 'synecdoche', in which the part stands for the whole, realised in phrases such as 'hired hand' to describe an employee or 'fresh pair of eyes' when a new reader or evaluator considers a problem. Media discourse often uses a type of metonymy in which a location substitutes for an institution, such as 'Downing Street said', 'The White House issued a statement' or 'Brussels is adamant'. Small capitals are also used in an analysis to note metonymy. In the examples here we have PART FOR WHOLE and LOCATION FOR INSTITUTION. Simpson (2003, 2014) examines the role played by metonymy in the construction of 'caricature'. In terms of political discourse, this technique is most notable in the critique of politicians and political figures where they are visually represented with the satirical and hyperbolic distortion of some aspect of their physiognomy. Essentially, a grotesquely exaggerated part stands for the whole. You may be familiar with well-known British caricaturists Gerald Scarfe, Steve Bell or Ralph Steadman, who have produced illustrations for *The Times*, the *New York Times* and *The Guardian*, or with the satirical television programme *Spitting Image*, perhaps most famous for its portrayal of Margaret Thatcher with her pointed nose significantly enlarged, dressed in a gentleman's suit and often wielding an axe with which to attack her many enemies. More recent reboots of *Spitting Image* have portrayed Tony Blair through an exaggerated and disingenuous grin and Donald Trump with an extravagant comb-over and a distinctive shade of orange (Simpson [2003] provides an extended analysis of caricature).

8.3 Strategic Functions of Political Language

In this section we will present an overview of the main 'strategic functions' of political discourse proffered by Chilton and Schaffner (1997) and Chilton (2004) – **coercion, legitimation** and **representation** – and will then demonstrate these functions in action in excerpts of a speech by Donald Trump.

8.3.1 Linguistic Features

The strategic functions of political language are manifested in a number of linguistic features, most of which we have already discussed in this book, such as metaphor, pronouns, overlexicalisation and transitivity patterns. Within Chilton's framework, the analyst can examine how a speaker's intentionality to coerce, legitimate and represent is served by the use of these linguistic structures, so it is important to address these features when analysing the strategic functions in political speeches.

Simpson, Mayr and Statham (2018:43–47) outline the importance of several of these features. Pronouns, which we have already discussed in Chapters 5 and 7, are used similarly in political language to construct allegiances and oppositions. Another important feature of political language is the use of euphemism, through which unpalatable or controversial policies are described by vague and inoffensive language.

In Chapter 3 we discussed the importance of euphemism for the register of war when violent actions are expressed through Material processes which actually make little or no reference to violence. You might also be aware of certain euphemistic terms in official descriptions of war, phrases like 'extraordinary rendition' and 'enhanced interrogation', which avoid acknowledgement of, in these cases, kidnap and torture (for more on the euphemistic language of war, see Chilton [1985] and Moss [1985]). Political language is replete with euphemism, which perhaps is unsurprising given the importance of popularity in electoral politics and the fact that politicians are at the heart of many unpopular decisions. Through euphemism, politicians can find linguistic ways of softening the blow. Consider for example familiar phrases like 'rationalisation of the benefits system' used to obfuscate a policy of reducing state benefit entitlement that would further impoverish claimants. Euphemism often marks economic and foreign-policy focussed political language.

Another prominent device in political speeches is parallelism, where similar grammatical structures are used to express a range of ideas. Perhaps the best-known example of parallelism in Western politics is US President John F. Kennedy's 'Ask not what your country can do for you but what you can do for your country'.

Political language also makes extensive use of presupposition when speakers or writers presuppose threats or conditions which must then be addressed. There is abundant presupposition in the ongoing struggle between neo-liberal managers and trade union activists in higher education, which we have mentioned on several occasions in previous chapters, with management often basing cost-cutting measures like changes to pension schemes on a supposed funding gap across the university sector despite the fact that many of the institutions in question have never been more profitable. As we discuss the strategic functions of political discourse below, we will point out how these and other linguistic tactics are used to persuade audiences of political language. Table 8.1 provides a list of some presupposition triggers in English which will be useful for the discussion of the Donald Trump speech below.

We will now address in turn the three main strategic functions of political discourse: coercion, legitimation and representation.

8.3.2 Coercion

The first main strategic function of political discourse described by Chilton (2004) is 'coercion', through which people are persuaded by the power possessed by politicians. Chilton (2004:118) acknowledges that an entire speech or piece

Table 8.1 Presupposition triggers

Type of trigger	Example	Explanation
Iteratives	'This atrocity will happen again.'	Presupposes the original happening.
Factives	'We must address the problem of immigration.'	Constructs the 'problem' as fact. Look out for verbs like 'address', 'regret', 'realise'.
Cleft structures	'It is Muslims who promote this evil ideology.'	Focusses the information in the sentence, presupposes the promotion of the ideology and that it is evil.
Genitive structures	'We will build a defence against your threats.'	Presupposes ownership.

of political text could potentially be classed as coercive. Obviously, coercion in terms of how it is conventionally understood may not be necessarily viewed as linguistic. Certain regimes will coerce citizens through physical actions more so than others, for example. But for our purposes we are interested in how coercion can be achieved in language. Chilton states that there are two main types of coercion depending upon the response provoked in an audience, emotive coercion and cognitive coercion. The former refers to language which causes an audience to respond emotionally, with fear or pride, for example. Cognitive coercion operates through implied meanings in a speech or text. Audiences are coerced through presupposition and implication. For instance, if a politician presupposes that a nation has a certain societal problem, criminality or immigration, for example, this very statement implies that the problem must be addressed. In addition, and indeed perhaps more often, the presupposition allows the politician to make strong and explicit statements to this effect. Audiences are coerced into accepting that there is a problem and therefore may be much more receptive to the measures proposed to address it, which are often described as common-sense necessities.

The speech which is our focus in this analysis is widely recognised as one of the most controversial given by Donald Trump during his first campaign for the US presidency. The speech addressed issues of national security, connected consistently to immigration, and was delivered in June 2016 following a mass shooting at a Florida nightclub where forty-nine people were killed. Relevant excerpts are given below, and you can read the full speech on Donald Trump's website (www.donaldjtrump.com) or on the websites of the *New York Times*, the *Washington Post* and the political magazine *Politico*.

Given that the speech follows the atrocity in Orlando, it is perhaps unsurprising that the language at the beginning of the speech is loaded with emotive coercion:

> So many people, just hard to believe, but just so many people dead. So many people **gravely injured**. So much **carnage**. Such a **disgrace**. The **horror** is beyond description. The families of these wonderful people are totally **devastated** and they will be forever. Likewise, our whole nation and indeed the whole world is **devastated**.

Trump provokes an emotional response from the audience through highly emotive lexis, given in bold above, and there is clear cohesion between words like 'carnage', 'disgrace' and 'horror'. What is very effective about this provocation of an emotional response is that it literally tells people how they feel and, through the repetition of 'devastated', it unites the response of 'our whole nation' with 'the whole world'. Metaphorical transference attributes to 'nation' and 'world' emotions which are felt by people. Later Trump calls the attack a 'strike at the heart and soul of who we are as a nation' using the A COUNTRY IS A PERSON metaphor (a place having a 'heart' or 'heartbeat' is quite a well-established metaphor).

In this paragraph we see several of the linguistic features given above in operation. An emotional response from the audience is also achieved here through pronouns used to construct solidarity. Trump uses inclusive pronouns to make this an attack on '*our* whole nation'. He goes on to state, '<u>We</u> mourn as one people for <u>our</u> nation's loss and pledge <u>our</u> support to any and all who need it'. The message of this paragraph is also effectively communicated through parallelism, 'so many people', 'so many people dead', 'so many people gravely injured', 'so much carnage', 'such a disgrace'. The repetition of similar grammatical structures increases the force of the emotional response felt by the audience. This paragraph also demonstrates the fact that, despite the connotations of 'coercion', not all coercion is necessarily malignant. In pointing out Trump's manipulation of the audience, in the case of this section of the speech at any rate, we are also able to agree with his characterisation of this tragedy. When Trump utilises a light metaphor later in the speech, referring to the attack as a 'very dark moment' where DARKNESS IS BAD and BRIGHTNESS IS GOOD, metaphors which are as pervasive as the orientational metaphor discussed above, we are compelled to agree. How Trump rationalises the root causes of America's gun crime crisis throughout the rest of the speech is more problematic.

The paragraph below comes later in the speech, the main argumentative thrust of which is to link this shooting and by extension other instances of terrorism in the United States to immigration from predominantly Muslim countries:

> With 50 people dead and perhaps more ultimately, and dozens more wounded, we cannot afford to talk around the issues anymore. We have to address these issues head on. I called for a ban after San Bernardino and was met with great scorn and anger. But now many years and I have to say many years but many are saying that I was right to do so and although the pause is temporary, we must find out what is going on. We have to do it.

The argument structured here is an example of cognitive coercion and it makes a number of assumptions on behalf of the audience. Trump says that 'we cannot afford to talk around the issues' and 'we have to address the issues' which presupposes the 'issues', in this case a very tenuous link between immigration and gun crime, as facts which are problems. He also says that 'we must find out what is going on' and, in terms of the travel ban proposed throughout his campaign and enacted during his presidency, 'we have to do it'. The effect of the pronouns again unifies the speaker with his audience and the high modal certainty of these phrases constructs Trump's policies as necessities, as if there are no alternative choices. Trump is adamant elsewhere in the speech that 'if we don't get tough and if we don't get smart, and fast, we're not going to have our country anymore. There will be nothing, absolutely nothing left.' Apocalyptic propositions like this operate by both pronouns and abstraction; 'get tough' and 'get smart' do not provide specifics about how this ban will be enforced. We have since been provided with an insight into the human cost of Trump's immigration policies when families were detained, children separately from their parents, at the Mexican border in 2019.

Donald Trump is often noted for his less-than-polished public speaking abilities. His language is often inarticulate and rambling, such as in the penultimate sentence in this paragraph, and is frequently slated by his opponents for being ungrammatical and unsophisticated. At one point in this speech, for example, when lambasting Hillary Clinton, former US Secretary of State and the Democratic nominee for president in 2016, Trump says of her apparent lack of friendship to the LGBT community, 'And someday I believe that will be proven out bigly'. However, this type of language has conversely worked in Trump's favour with his supporters by building a perception of sincerity. Montgomery (2017:627) states that what is viewed as Trump's 'vernacular folksiness' actually builds a sense of authenticity in some quarters. The final sentences of this speech are an example of this so-called simple language:

> We'll be tough, and we're going to be smart, and we're going to do it right. America will be a tolerant and open society. America will also be a safe society. We will protect our borders at home. We will defeat ISIS overseas. We have no choice. We will ensure every parent can raise their children in peace and safety. We will make America rich <u>again</u>. We will make America safe <u>again</u>. We will make America great <u>again</u>.

In terms of coercion, the abstract mantras to 'toughness' and 'smartness' are repeated, and we get a list of all the things that America 'will' be with Trump at the helm. The speech concludes with categorical assertions which attach a sense of facticity to the promises being made, and the inclusive 'we' pronoun builds allegiance between speaker and audience.

An important element in terms of the use of presupposition through which cognitive coercion operates in this speech is the use of 'again', both in this speech and in Trump's campaign slogan 'Make America Great Again' (this was updated with a similar dollop of presupposition to 'Keep America Great' for Trump's unsuccessful 2020 campaign). 'Again' is a presupposition trigger known as an 'iterative' (see Table 8.1). In this case it presupposes that America was rich, safe and great (of course 'great' means very different things across the political spectrum). Lakoff (2017:597) calls this slogan a 'coded message' to Trump's supporters that he would return America to a time before the disturbances of the 1960s 'when the laws changed to allow others than white males entrée to all the good things America had to offer: education, jobs, power, status'. Given Trump's electoral success, it is hard for us to deny the effectiveness of this language, and it certainly fulfils the strategic functions of coercion. For Lakoff, however, Trump's promises are to 'bring America back to a time when white males could count on getting all the pie, not just their fair share of it. Back then, straight native-born white men could talk and act just as Trump did in 2016: be as racist, homophobic, xenophobic, and misogynist as America had been back when it was Great.'

8.3.3 Legitimation

Legitimation is the strategy through which politicians use language to justify themselves or their decisions and policies and positively present them to their audiences. Legitimation is also achieved by the delegitimation of political opponents. Chilton (2004:46) says that legitimation is essentially about 'establishing the right to be obeyed'. As we noted in Chapter 1, it might be possible in some contexts to exert power and obedience by physical force, but in most Western societies actors must legitimate themselves through language. Chilton (2004:46) states that 'reasons for being obeyed have to be communicated linguistically, whether by overt statement or by implication' and that the 'techniques used include arguments about voters' wants, general ideological principles, charismatic leadership projection, boasting about performance and positive self-presentation' while delegitimation includes the 'use of ideas of difference and boundaries, and speech acts of blaming, accusing, insulting'.

Donald Trump is well-known for 'boasting about performance', often asserting his own sense of superiority in terms of his apparent physical prowess and intelligence on Twitter, for example (until he was removed from the platform in January 2021). In this political speech he engages plentifully in both legitimation and delegitimation. He constructs a stark opposition in sentences like 'Hillary Clinton wants to empty out the Treasury to bring people into the country that include individuals who preach hate against our citizens. I want to protect our citizens, all of our citizens', where Clinton threatens American citizens who will instead be protected by Trump. Attacks on political opponents are a major reason why legitimation and delegitimation in political language are particularly noteworthy in election campaigns. Trump legitimates himself as a sort of 'protector-in-chief' in this speech:

> When I'm president, I pledge to protect and defend all Americans who live inside our borders. Wherever they come from, wherever they were born, I don't care. All Americans living here and following our laws, not other laws, will be protected.

Presupposing that one will be victorious is a common feature of campaign speeches. Adjuncts like 'When I am your MP' or 'When I'm president' allow candidates to legitimate themselves with an authority which they have not actually acquired yet. Trump makes a 'pledge' here which has intertextual links to the presidential oath of office ('preserve, protect and defend the Constitution of the United States').

Another way that legitimation is constructed in political speeches is through the use of figures and statistics and through reference to authoritative sources. Chilton (2004:117) notes that statistics and sources make speakers appear more 'rational' and 'objective'. The immigration into the United States of Muslims was connected to terrorism and constructed as a threat throughout this speech.

Immigration from Afghanistan into the United States has increased nearly five-fold. Five-fold. In just one year. According to Pew Research, 99 percent of the people in Afghanistan support oppressive Sharia law. We admit many more, and that is just the way it is, we admit many more from other countries in the region and I'll tell you what, they share these oppressive views and values. We want to remain a free and open society. If we do, we have to control our borders. And we have to control them now, not later. Right now.

In this section Trump offers statistics and a reputable source. These then serve to legitimate as rational his interpretation of these 'facts'. Chilton (2004:117) accurately notes that the 'speaker assumes the hearer will accept [statistics and sources used] as authoritative' and so Trump and his 'control our borders' strategy is legitimated.

Whilst members of the audience at a political rally are likely, as Chilton points out, to take as accurate the legitimating statistics offered by speakers, as critical discourse analysts we are perhaps less inclined to accept at face value 'facts' which are highly selective and are offered to an audience without very much context. In the excerpt above, Donald Trump refers to the Pew Research Center, a well-established and reputable think-tank based in Washington DC, as a way to legitimate his own expertise. Whilst he does not name the actual report, it is likely that the 99 percent referred to here is taken from a 2013 report from the Religion and Public Life division of the Pew Research Center called 'The World's Muslims: Religion, Politics and Society', the first chapter of which addresses beliefs about Sharia. It is reported here that 99 percent of Muslims in Afghanistan support making Sharia the official law of the land, so there can be no question of this statistic being one of those 'provable falsehoods' which have on other occasions emanated from the Trump campaign and the Trump White House. This is a startlingly high statistic from a reputable source which serves to legitimate Donald Trump's Muslim travel ban.

It is, however, only one statistic from a lengthy and in-depth report which, in this case, has been chosen to legitimate a key campaign position. The same report clarifies that this statistic refers to Muslims living in Afghanistan, so it is a particular conceptual leap to assume that Muslims living in the United States hold the same position. The report also states that 37 percent of Afghan Muslims do not believe that Sharia should apply to non-Muslims. Donald Trump refers to Sharia as 'oppressive' and having 'oppressive views and values', but this is somewhat of a selective interpretation. To be sure, there are those who support an extremely oppressive version of Sharia, but the same report states that in Afghanistan 29 percent of Muslims do not possess a homogenous interpretation of Sharia. It is also true that those polled may not practise or support Sharia in any case or that a single interpretation is an extreme one. A Pew report in 2017 found that 92 percent of Muslims in the United States were 'proud to be an American', that support for ISIS was very insignificant and, perhaps most relevant here given the implication of a 'five-fold' increase in immigration of Muslims from Afghanistan, that only 1.1 percent of the American population are Muslim, which could rise to 2.1 percent by 2050. The figure for those from Afghanistan would obviously be lower again.

By examining more widely statistics which are excluded from Trump's analysis, we are able to garner a somewhat more contextualised insight into his claims. Of course, this does not mean that the strategic function of legitimation has not been effectively fulfilled in this speech; most people will not be undertaking a Critical Discourse Analysis of this speech, and Trump's supporters are likely to take it at face value. In this vein Trump appears well informed and well intentioned.

Delegitimation is achieved both directly and indirectly in political discourse. In terms of the latter, an opponent is delegitimated through the very act of legitimation of oneself. More direct delegitimation is constructed by explicitly addressing and attacking opponents and their policies. Chilton (2004:46) speaks of 'blaming, accusing [and] insulting' opponents. This direct delegitimation is frequent in election campaigns, and Hillary Clinton is spoken about at length in this speech; at one point Trumps says that 'she has no clue' and at another that 'she's in total denial'. In this speech Trump presents Hillary Clinton as a defender of terrorism and as a threat to 'law-abiding Americans'.

> The bottom line is that Hillary supports policies that bring the threat of radical Islam into America and allow it to grow overseas. And it is growing. In fact, Hillary Clinton's catastrophic immigration plan will bring vastly more radical Islamic immigration into this country, threatening not only our society, but our entire way of life.

Trump describes Clinton's immigration policies as 'catastrophic'. This delegitimation of his opponent is also an opportunity for Trump to further coerce his audience through reference to dystopian certainties which will threaten 'not only our society, but our entire way of life'. Excerpts like this demonstrate that the strategic functions of political discourse do not necessarily occur in isolation but that they can be interconnected and simultaneous. Another target of delegitimation in this speech is Barack Obama, Trump's predecessor as president. By delegitimating Obama, Trump also criticises Clinton, who served in Obama's Cabinet as Secretary of State.

> Truly our president doesn't know what he's doing. He's failed us badly. Under his leadership, it will not get any better. It will only get worse. And I've been saying that for a long time. Each year the United States permanently admits 100,000 immigrants from the Middle East and many more from Muslim countries outside of the Middle East. Our government has been admitting ever-growing numbers year after year without any effective plan for our own security. In fact, Clinton's State Department was in charge of admissions and the admission process for people applying to enter from overseas.

The delegitimation of President Obama is starkly delivered here, he 'doesn't know what he's doing' and 'he's failed us badly', and used to legitimate the wisdom of Trump, 'I've been saying that for a long time'. We get an aggregated statistic to again project Islamic immigration as a major demographic and security issue which is linked directly to 'Clinton's State Department'. Census statistics note 3.45 million Muslims currently live in the United States, which equates to the 1.1 percent in the Pew report from 2017 referred to above, but phrases like 'ever-growing numbers year after year' build a somewhat different impression, and the adjunct 'without any effective plan for our own security' presupposes a link between Muslim immigrants and a threatening outcome.

Another strategy of delegitimation of a political opponent is direct quotation. Often the selected words of a rival can be used to strengthen arguments against them. Hillary Clinton is mentioned fifteen times by Donald Trump in this speech, so it is clear that delegitimation plays a significant strategic function here. She is quoted directly to further legitimate Trump's controversial positions on Muslim immigration.

> I don't know if you know this, but just a few weeks before San Bernardino, the slaughter, that's all it was, a slaughter, Hillary Clinton explained her refusal to say the words 'radical Islam'. Here is what she said, exact quote. 'Muslims are peaceful and tolerant people and have nothing whatsoever to do with terrorism.' That is Hillary Clinton. So, she says the solution is to ban guns. They tried that in France, which has among the toughest gun laws anywhere in the world, and 130 people were brutally murdered by Islamic terrorists in cold blood.

Clinton is presented throughout this speech as a defender of 'radical Islam' for refusing, from Trump's perspective, to even acknowledge its existence. Her reticence is set in contrast to Trump, who constructs himself as a politician never afraid to 'tell it like it is'. San Bernardino refers to a mass shooting in California in 2015. Clinton is conceptually linked therefore to both this massacre and the one in Orlando which has just occurred. The so-called 'exact quote' is from part of a speech given by Clinton at the Council of Foreign Relations in November 2015 and is accurate so far as it goes. The wider context of the quotation is that Clinton was attempting to articulate why she felt the term 'radical Islam' actually legitimises terrorism and was being used by certain people – including presumably Donald Trump – who are 'obsessed' with constructing a 'clash of civilizations'. The full quotation is:

> The bottom line is that we are in a contest of ideas against an ideology of hate, and we have to win. Let's be clear though, Islam is not our adversary. Muslims are peaceful and tolerant people and have nothing whatsoever to do with terrorism. The obsession in some quarters with a clash of civilizations or repeating the specific words 'radical Islamic terrorism' isn't just a distraction, it gives these criminals, these murderers, more standing than they deserve. It actually plays into their hands by alienating partners we need by our side.

It is clear, therefore, that the *carte blanche* support of Islamic terrorism attributed to Clinton by Trump is not quite accurate despite the fact that he cannot be accused of misquoting his opponent. The fact that campaign speeches are by and large given as monologues means that the speaker can selectively quote her/his opponent without being challenged in real time. Hillary Clinton's phrase 'nothing whatsoever' provides Trump with the opportunity to appropriate her words out of context in order to rally his own supporters. Clinton's point, of course, is that Islam does not predispose Muslims to terrorist acts.

Again, as critical discourse analysts we can go beyond the delegitimation in the speech and investigate further the context of the Clinton quotation appropriated by Trump. In the context of a scholarly analysis like this, we can therefore offer some resistance to the strategic function of the speaker. The audience of this speech, however, are much less likely to pursue a CDA of the candidate's words.

8.3.4 Representation

The third strategic function of political discourse is 'representation' and 'misrepresentation'. Chilton (2004:46) links mis/representation to 'political control'. This can be achieved by a number of discourse strategies including secrecy, which Chilton says is the 'inverse of censorship' as it prevents people from receiving information. Euphemism is also important in mis/representation because it is about '"blurring" and "defocusing" unwanted referents'. The 'most extreme manifestation' of mis/representation is lying, which includes omissions, evasion and denial. In the section of the speech below, Trump misrepresents America's intelligence community as constrained and even non-existent.

> When it comes to radical Islamic terrorism, ignorance is not bliss. It's deadly. Totally deadly. The Obama administration, with the support of Hillary Clinton and others, has also damaged our security by restraining our intelligence gathering. And we have just no intelligence gathering information. We need this information so badly. And he stopped it [...] As president, I will give our intelligence community, law enforcement, and military the tools they need to prevent terrorist attacks because they don't have those tools now. We need an intelligence-gathering system second to none. Second to none. That includes better cooperation between state, local and federal officials and with our allies, very importantly. I will have an attorney general, director of national intelligence, and a secretary of defense who will know how to fight the war on radical Islamic terrorism.

Misrepresentation at its most blunt is lying, and amidst the 'straight talking' and emphatic repetition above, Trump offers a key untruth, 'And we have no intelligence gathering information'. The United States has a worldwide and heavily funded intelligence network. Barack Obama did not discontinue American intelligence gathering; indeed, the Edward Snowden affair in 2013 demonstrated that the operations of the National Security Agency (NSA) were extremely widespread, if also highly questionable. Certainly, Obama exercised some oversight over US intelligence operations, but it is a huge overstatement to say that 'he stopped it'. Trump makes a general statement about an intelligence system which is 'second to none', but he does not actually offer specific information about how this ideal will be achieved. There are references to the 'tools they need' and 'better cooperation' and having personnel 'who will know how to fight the war on Islamic terrorism', but Trump's audience do not receive any specific information here.

Later in the speech Trump says, 'I want to fix our schools, I want to fix our bridges and our jobs market, we will have it rocking again. We'll make great trade deals'. Again, the plainspoken 'folksiness', what linguists refer to as interdiscursivity and conversationalisation, in 'we will have it rocking again', as well as the presupposition that it 'rocked' before, obscures the fact that no information is offered here. Trump's supporters can point to the sincerity of what he 'wants' to do, and the message is effectively delivered through parallelism, but the speech is light on details. This tendency is not exclusive to Donald Trump. Representation and misrepresentation are often achieved through obfuscation, broad generalities and even untruths in political language. In Trump's case, he cements the combative reputation which so enthrals his supporters by directly apportioning blame for supposed previous or present failures. This directness obscures the fact that, in stating that he will do the opposite, he does not tell us how. Trump says of the difference between his presidency and Barack Obama's that 'we're going from totally incompetent to just the opposite. Believe me.' He is clearly condemning of the 'incompetency' of his predecessor. This directness wins for him plaudits from supporters who are in turn distracted from the fact that how the 'opposite' will be achieved is not specifically addressed.

Student Task

The key text by Chilton (2004), drawn upon in the discussion of the Trump speech in this chapter and suggested as further reading below, analyses the strategic functions in the infamous 'Rivers of Blood' speech. This anti-immigration speech was delivered by British politician Enoch Powell in 1968 in opposition the Race Relations Act.

Read the Rivers of Blood speech and the full text of Donald Trump's speech following the massacre at the Pulse nightclub. With references to the strategic functions, what are the similarities and differences between the two speeches? Given what you have learned in this book, are you surprised by the thematic similarities between the issues addressed by Powell and Trump? Can you think of a modern-day British equivalent to Enoch Powell or a contemporary issue which was reduced to the same issues which Powell highlighted in his speech?

Summary of Chapter 8

This chapter has discussed metaphor and a number of other linguistic features which are important in the construction of persuasion in political discourse, such as presupposition and euphemism. The analysis of Donald Trump's infamous campaign speech following the Pulse nightclub shootings in Orlando examines how these features and others are used to achieve the strategic functions of coercion, legitimation and representation. This analysis also demonstrates that as critical discourse analysts you should engage with this type of language closely and with due attention to wider social contexts. In Chapter 9 an important document which addresses the lockdowns which formed a core aspect of governmental response to the Covid-19 pandemic will be analysed as a piece of political rhetoric. The discussion will also address the link between the features of rhetoric and the strategic functions we have outlined in this chapter.

Further Reading

Chilton, P. (2004) *Analysing Political Discourse: Theory and Practice*. London and New York: Routledge.

Chilton, P. and Schaffner, C. (1997) 'Discourse in Politics', in Van Dijk, T. (ed.) *Discourse as Social Interaction*. Newbury, CA: Sage, pp.206–230.

9 Political Rhetoric in a Pandemic

KEY TERMS IN CHAPTER 9: *ethos*, *pathos*, *logos*, conjunctive adjunct

MODELS OF ANALYSIS IN CHAPTER 9: political rhetoric

9.1 Introduction

In 2020 the world faced a global health emergency unprecedented in late modernity. The coronavirus Covid-19 was first detected in China in December 2019 and infected and killed millions of people as it spread around the globe (as of 27th November 2021 the global death toll was 5.2 million people and the detected cases 261 million). National economies were placed into suspended animation as governments around the world imposed 'lockdowns' in order to curtail the spread of the virus. 'Playing politics' is often constructed as somehow inappropriate in the face of a pandemic when the only focus should be on staying safe, but it would be naïve to assume that governments and politicians suspend ideological concerns in times of international crisis and even more foolish to view the ramifications of such disasters out of context with often politically motivated decisions which precede and accompany them.

In this vein, the chapter will begin to think critically about the political language of the Covid-19 pandemic. It is a safe assumption that the pandemic, its devastating human cost and its huge economic impact will be a preoccupation of scholars for decades to come. This chapter will provide a starting point for those critical enquiries by analysing the political rhetoric of a letter sent by British Prime Minister Boris Johnson to all households in the UK in March 2020 setting out the rationale for the first of several lockdowns. This analysis also demonstrates the enduring importance of CDA. As new events constantly emerge globally and locally, the discipline continues to stand ready to offer a critical linguistic analysis which drives interpretation and explanation.

The response to the pandemic varied across the world, and some countries, such as New Zealand, Australia and Vietnam, were initially much more successful at tackling the crisis than countries where the death tolls were tragically high, such as the UK, US and several countries in the EU. In the US, where the death toll was 777,000 by November 2021, Donald Trump, president until January 2021, initially ignored the seriousness of Covid-19. When the US became the epicentre of the pandemic, he bullishly rallied against China, the 'fake news' media, his own health officials and the World Health Organization (WHO), whilst he delayed the issuing of welfare cheques to 70 million people so that, in a presidential election year, his own name could be printed on them. Elsewhere he tweeted his endorsement of protests by his supporters against lifesaving lockdown measures in states which had Democratic governors. Trump's press conferences during the pandemic differed even more than usual from those of other world leaders. Whilst figures like New Zealand premier Jacinda Ardern won plaudits for compassionate reassurance, Trump's public appearances descended on several occasions into exercises in political point scoring. His mishandling of the pandemic was a major issue for Joe Biden's successful campaign to unseat Trump as president.

Of course, politicians elsewhere did not set aside politics during the pandemic despite the fact that responding to the coronavirus came to and continues to monopolise the business of governments worldwide. In Ireland, for example, Fianna Fáil and Fine Gael, parties largely on the political Right, formed a coalition government propped up by the Irish Green Party. Neither party had topped the poll in the country's general election of February 2020, but negotiations on forming a government and on a change of leadership were not halted by Covid-19. Elections were also held in South Korea, where President Moon Jae-in's Democratic Party won a landslide victory, and in New Zealand, where Jacinda Ardern's Labour Party unsurprisingly won in a landslide, although votes in other countries including Sri Lanka and Ethiopia were postponed. In the United States the primary processes and the general election proceeded in 2019 and 2020, the latter making extended use of postal voting.

Whilst there is an obvious reluctance to outwardly acknowledge the importance for electability of crisis management over, say, the importance of ensuring public safety, politicians are acutely aware that they will be judged by their responses to crises, and the Covid-19 pandemic was a largely unforeseen crisis of a significant magnitude. The initial response of the government in Britain was markedly slow, especially as the pandemic raged in other countries in Europe. Whilst lockdown was eventually imposed, the torpor of the Conservative regime's early reaction to the pandemic was criticised heavily by opponents, who also levied anger at the failure of much of the media to appropriately hold the government to account.

9.2 Political Rhetoric

As always, language was at the centre of accusations, criticisms, denials and defence during the pandemic, and politicians and other public figures utilised the strategic functions of political discourse to persuade audiences of the validity of their arguments. Alongside contemporary models for the analysis of political language, the classical approach taken in Aristotle's *Rhetoric* continues to endure for the insights which it can provide to the critical analyst. For example, Browse (2018) applies Aristotelian rhetoric to analyse audience responses to a wide range of political language. Aristotle (1962:27) states that rhetoric 'may be defined as the faculty of observing in any given case the available means of persuasion'. Persuasion, as we have seen not just in this chapter but throughout this book, is at the core of discourse which aims to legitimise and naturalise for audiences the ideologies of the powerful.

Aristotle defined three different types of rhetoric: forensic, epideictic and deliberative. Forensic rhetoric is used in broadly legal scenarios; essentially, it is about arguments surrounding justice and injustice. Epideictic rhetoric is ceremonial and focusses on concepts such as honour and dishonour. The type of language which marks a discourse event like a eulogy, where admiration is a key theme, is an example of epideictic rhetoric. The third form of rhetoric, deliberative, is the variant which is most useful in this chapter. This type of rhetoric is concerned with justifications of political decisions in terms of advantages and disadvantages. Aristotle (1962:74) states that deliberative rhetoric addresses 'the expediency or the harmfulness of a proposed course of action'. In the analysis below we will apply the components of deliberative or political rhetoric to the letter sent by British Prime Minister Boris Johnson to every household in the UK in March 2020 to 'update you on the steps we are taking to combat coronavirus'. Whilst Johnson was criticised for spending £5.7 million on this letter at a time when years of underfunding in the country's National Health Service (NHS) were moving more keenly into focus, the Prime Minister felt that the letter was an important method through which to inform citizens of the government's response to the crisis. To paraphrase Aristotle, the letter was a way to use rhetoric to persuade people of the advantages and expediency of the government's proposed actions. By extension, it was also an opportunity to foreground these proposed actions and to background the policies and failures which preceded them.

Political rhetoric is comprised of three interconnected modes of persuasion. You will likely have heard of the terms **ethos**, **pathos** and **logos** in a general sense, but in Aristotle's *Rhetoric* they have a specific meaning relative to their importance in constructing persuasion. Each mode is present in Boris Johnson's letter, and the analysis will also demonstrate how students can view a piece of discourse as political rhetoric whilst simultaneously examining its strategic functions and the linguistic methods through which these are achieved.

9.2.1 *Ethos*

The first mode of persuasion in political rhetoric, *ethos*, refers to the personal character of the speaker. An audience is more likely to be persuaded by someone with authority or expertise. Aristotle notes that *ethos* can be particularly important when strong arguments are offered for opposing positions. In such cases someone of 'good character' could swing an argument one way or another. *Ethos* is also the reason that endorsements are so important in election campaigns. *Ethos* can be linked to legitimation in terms of Chilton's strategic functions. When legitimation is achieved through the establishment of the expertise of a speaker or an organisation which they refer to in order to support a policy position, an 'ethotic argument' is being offered. Trustworthiness, expertise or authority can be established by describing the qualifications of such a participant or even just by referring to their field of expertise or including functional honorifics alongside nomination.

9.2.2 *Pathos*

Pathos refers to persuasion constructed through emotion. *Pathos* is used to construct emotional responses in an audience and refers to the many linguistic ways that this can be achieved. In the Trump speech in Chapter 8 the major emotional responses provoked are sympathy and fear; *pathos* is linked to the strategic function of emotive coercion. Trump's provocation of fear is nothing new in political discourse. It dominates foreign policy language and is addressed specifically in the *Rhetoric*:

> When it is advisable that the audience should be frightened, the orator must make them feel that they are really in danger of something, pointing out that it has happened to others who were stronger than they are, and is happening, or has happened, to people like themselves.
>
> (Aristotle, 1962:72)

This description is a very accurate synthesis of a core component of the Trump strategy in the speech analysed in Chapter 8. Despite the fact that Aristotle was writing over two millennia ago, his central insights have clearly stood the test of time.

9.2.3 *Logos*

The third component of political rhetoric is *logos*, which refers to the presentation of an argument as logical. When persuasion is pursued by offering evidence, a 'logetic' argument for acceptance is offered. In the Trump speech and in many of the discourse examples analysed in the previous chapters we have noted the use of statistical evidence, for example. In many of these cases we have also noted the selectivity of certain statistics and the omission of others. The structure of an argument also contributes to *logos*. For example, arguments can be structured in terms of a causal relationship such as 'x happens as a result of y' or 'if x happens, then y will follow'. Linking phrases like 'as a result of' and 'gives rise to' indicate the construction of an argument so that it appears logical. Comparative phrases like 'equally' and 'similarly' and symptomatic phrases like 'is evidence of' and 'is representative of' also construct the *logos* of an argument. Halliday (1994:36) identifies a set of text-building devices known as '**conjunctive adjuncts**', which correlate with the type of structures often found in logetic argumentation, briefly outlined below:

Additive: and, also, moreover
Adversative: but, yet, on the other hand
Conditional: if...then, in the event of, otherwise, if not
Causal: so, then, because, as a result of
Purposive: in order to, for, to

These phrases are also known as 'connectives' because they link sets of propositions in a sentence. Simpson (2001) and Simpson, Mayr and Statham (2018) analyse the role of conjunctive adjuncts in so-called 'reason' advertisements, where the reason to buy a product or embrace something or someone being endorsed is directly communicated to a consumer rather than constructed through implicature, which requires some cognitive decoding (known as 'tickle' advertising after Bernstein [1974], see further Chapter 10). It is interesting, although somewhat unsurprising, that the *logos* of a political argument should have linguistic structures in common with advertising discourse. After all, in both cases the element of persuasion is fundamental; whether it is a product or an idea, something is being 'sold' to the audience.

9.3 Boris Johnson's Rhetoric

Figure 9.1 is the letter sent by Boris Johnson to UK households in March 2020.

Ethos is evident from the very outset of the letter. The letterhead is comprised of the royal coat of arms and the official address of the Prime Minister, who is also categorised through functionalisation here and through nomination in his personal signature at the end of the letter. You will remember from Chapter 7 that these social actor labels can be used to establish authority and responsibility. Boris Johnson's authority also legitimates the content of the letter.

Ethos is also utilised alongside the general *logos* of the eleventh paragraph in the sentence, 'We will not hesitate to go further if that is what the scientific and medical advice tell us we must do'. The actions of the UK government are constructed as being endorsed by external 'advice', although interestingly the names or titles of these experts or their institutions are not offered. Indeed, 'scientific and medical advice' is an example of nominalisation, and the noun phrase acts as the Sayer of the process of Verbalisation 'tells'. The noun phrase through which the participant 'the scientific and medical advice' is given here implies that there is only one participant, as if there is a single, unified giver of advice.

10 DOWNING STREET
LONDON SW1A 2AA

THE PRIME MINISTER

I am writing to you to update you on the steps we are taking to combat coronavirus.

In just a few short weeks, everyday life in this country has changed dramatically. We all feel the profound impact of coronavirus not just on ourselves, but on our loved ones and our communities.

I understand completely the difficulties this disruption has caused to your lives, businesses and jobs. But the action we have taken is absolutely necessary, for one very simple reason.

If too many people become seriously unwell at one time, the NHS will be unable to cope. This will cost lives. We must slow the spread of the disease, and reduce the number of people needing hospital treatment in order to save as many lives as possible.

That is why we are giving one simple instruction – you **must** stay at home.

You should not meet friends or relatives who do not live in your home. You may only leave your home for very limited purposes, such as buying food and medicine, exercising once a day and seeking medical attention. You can travel to and from work but should work from home if you can.

When you do have to leave your home, you should ensure, wherever possible, that you are two metres apart from anyone outside of your household.

These rules must be observed. So, if people break the rules, the police will issue fines and disperse gatherings.

Figure 9.1 Boris Johnson letter

I know many of you will be deeply worried about the financial impact on you and your family. The Government will do whatever it takes to help you make ends meet and put food on the table.

The enclosed leaflet sets out more detail about the support available and the rules you need to follow. You can also find the latest advice at gov.uk/coronavirus

From the start, we have sought to put in the right measures at the right time. We will not hesitate to go further if that is what the scientific and medical advice tells us we must do.

It's important for me to level with you – we know things will get worse before they get better. But we are making the right preparations, and the more we all follow the rules, the fewer lives will be lost and the sooner life can return to normal.

I want to thank everyone who is working flat out to beat the virus, in particular the staff in our fantastic NHS and care sector across England, Scotland, Wales and Northern Ireland. It has been truly inspirational to see our doctors, nurses and other carers rise magnificently to the needs of the hour.

Thousands of retired doctors and nurses are returning to the NHS – and hundreds of thousands of citizens are volunteering to help the most vulnerable. It is with that great British spirit that we will beat coronavirus and we will beat it together.

That is why, at this moment of national emergency, I urge you, please, to **stay at home, protect the NHS and save lives.**

Figure 9.1 Continued

When examined closely, this sentence (and the eleventh paragraph in general) is somewhat vague in terms of responsibility and is representative of the sort of euphemistic language for which the British government was criticised from some quarters throughout this crisis. There are three subordinate clauses in this sentence. Complex syntactic structures can operate to obscure both agency and action in discourse; indeed, excessive subordination has been identified by linguists as a key obstacle to the comprehensibility of legal language (Charrow and Charrow, 1979). So, it is noteworthy in such an important document that simpler sentences are not more prevalent. The 'we' pronoun here is exclusive in that it refers to the government (as opposed to the inclusivity of phrases like the clichéd 'we are all in this together', which was utilised at length during the pandemic), but to 'not hesitate in going further' is pointedly unspecific and, regardless of the agency implied through the 'we' pronoun, the action will only be taken if unnamed advice 'tells us we must' take it. The modality refers to an obligation to act if there is no other option (see Chapter 4).

In Aristotle's terms, there are both logetic and ethotic arguments offered here, but specific information is scarce. The logic of adopting the 'right measures at the right time' is hard to ignore; the government represents its response to the pandemic through *logos* whilst the vagueness of the phrase itself accommodates a lack of engagement with specifics. This sentence is an example of the strategic function of representation; actions are justified through their seemingly self-evident 'rightness' instead of the measures and the timeframe themselves. When a timeframe for easing the lockdown restrictions was first outlined in the summer of 2020, it was opposed by many whose scientific advice had been useful to the government for a time. By this stage, the phrase 'the science' had been replaced by 'the best science', thereby introducing a hierarchy of science – implying that there is a 'worst science' to be ignored – and then by the even more obscure 'the data' in many ministerial statements. So far, the government's apparent dedication to the data has led to three lockdowns. Over 120,000 people died in Britain in the first year of the Covid-19 pandemic.

The language of this letter was echoed consistently in the statements, interviews and press conferences given by members of the government throughout the peak of the first wave of the pandemic. Interviewed on Sky News on 29th March 2020 about the specifics of the new regulations, Minister for the Cabinet Office Michael Gove said:

> What we have sought to do is make sure that we implement <u>the right steps at the right time</u> following appropriate <u>scientific advice</u> [...] We want to make sure that we have <u>the right steps</u> in place, to make sure that we are influencing people's behaviour in <u>the right way</u>.

Note the overlexicalised focus on this undefined 'rightness'. At the government's daily press briefing on 20th April 2020, weeks after this letter had been received by the public, Chancellor Rishi Sunak offered the following response when questioned about the fact that a quarter of a million spectators has been allowed to attend a horse racing festival at Cheltenham only days before lockdown measures were finally implemented:

> At all points we have been guided by <u>that science</u>, we have been guided by making <u>the right decisions at the right time</u>, and I stand by that.

Representation through 'rightness' and the legitimation of 'advice' were constantly to the fore in the political rhetoric of this pandemic.

One of the major criticisms levelled at Boris Johnson's government over its response to coronavirus was the failure to take appropriate lockdown measures more quickly. As the spread of the disease engulfed mainland Europe throughout February and March 2020 and the inevitability of a British outbreak became more obvious, the Conservative government increasingly justified their lack of a response through references to 'scientific and medical advice'. As the crisis deepened, facts emerged which compounded the inaction of the initial British response, including the fact that other 'scientific and medical advice' had pushed for a lockdown as early as January 2020, that Boris Johnson had consistently failed to attend emergency preparedness meetings and that facilities to expand testing for coronavirus had not been approached by the government until April 2020, by which stage the UK death toll was in the thousands. Critical Discourse Analysis of this piece of political rhetoric cannot view the letter in isolation from its context. Where robust preventative measures such as travel restrictions, contact tracing and testing for Covid-19 were appropriately pursued in places like New Zealand, the impact of the virus was controlled with much greater success. Britain had the advantage of time, but the government watched inertly from afar as the virus devastated Italy, Spain, France and other nations in Europe and beyond. Critical linguistic analysis of the political rhetoric of this pandemic must evaluate this language within its wider societal context.

One of the reasons the authorities may offer limited specifics in favour of general information in times of national crisis is to attempt to construct a collective response and to limit public panic or public non-adherence to new regulations. Johnson could argue that this letter was to 'update' and to look forward, so the failings of earlier months were now less immediate and less relevant. Again, it is hard to deny the *logos* of this position; certainly, adherence to the measures eventually imposed was now critical. This argument has the added benefit of avoiding accountability, of course. An avoidance of panic or a certain disobedient public response is a strategy pursued by the modality of the fifth to the eighth paragraphs of the letter, for example. High modal instructions – 'you must stay at home' and 'these rules must be observed' – are clearly issued here, but they bookend the softer modality of the sixth and seventh paragraphs. These paragraphs use modality to construct a conceptual space in which the measures may not be quite so extreme as they appear. There are occasions when you 'may' leave your home, you 'can' travel to work and social distancing 'should' be kept 'wherever possible'. The measures taken during the pandemic were necessarily more extensive than those ever taken in any peacetime democracy in the modern age. Their anathema to civil liberty was so extensive that in most democratic jurisdictions legislation was required to implement them, so lower modality is used here to reduce the force of higher modal instructions. These instructions both precede and follow the list of potential exceptions so that their overall importance still remains clear.

In this letter Boris Johnson makes effective use of *logos* to establish the danger of the virus and the necessity of the lockdown measures. Sentences like 'If too many people become seriously unwell at one time, the NHS will be unable to cope' (fourth paragraph) utilises a disjunctive adjunct structure, in this case a causal argument, to construct the logic of the response measures. The two additives in the sentence 'But we are making the right preparations, <u>and</u> the more we all follow the rules, the fewer lives will be lost <u>and</u> the sooner life can return to normal' (twelfth paragraph) offer the reassurance of normality as the logical result of the rules. Sentences like this also fulfil the strategic functions of legitimation and representation. By the time this letter was issued, the preparation period had been largely wasted by the indolence of the initial response, but this sentence again presents these unspecified preparations in terms of an inherent 'rightness'. If you are conducting a political discourse analysis of sentences like this, you can therefore point to their syntactic structure, logetic argumentation and strategic function, applying several models of analysis simultaneously. *Logos* is constructed through the additive and the purposive in the sentence 'We must slow the spread of the disease, <u>and</u> reduce the number of people needing hospital treatment <u>in order to</u> save as many lives as possible' (fourth paragraph). This sentence legitimates the measures through their construction as necessities.

The necessity of the measures is also established through the metaphorical construction of the coronavirus as an enemy or an opponent. Phrases like 'steps we are taking to combat coronavirus' in the first paragraph (indeed there are two metaphors with the respective source domains JOURNEY and WAR here) and 'working flat out to beat the virus' in the antepenultimate paragraph (which has an additional orientational source domain alongside WAR or SPORT) construct the virus as a conceivable entity which can be opposed. The rallying call of the letter's penultimate paragraph enhances this concept through inclusive pronouns, repetition and parallelism in the sentence 'It is with that great British spirit that we will beat coronavirus and we will beat it together'. War was invoked by many politicians in their language during the pandemic. In a speech earlier in March 2020, Johnson had called on the British people to invoke their 'Blitz spirit', and here he echoes Churchill in praising healthcare workers for 'ris[ing] magnificently to the needs of the hour' (antepenultimate paragraph). Churchillian phraseology littered the speeches of other world leaders also, such as in 'Never will so many ask so much of so few' in the Saint Patrick's Day address of Irish leader Leo Varadkar. The Taoiseach was either unaware of the irony of an Irish leader quoting Winston Churchill or, more likely, considered history less important than oratory given the weight of the crisis. For all his many failings, Churchill's language has a reputation for patriotic fervour, and politicians felt that they needed to harbour such feelings in the face of the pandemic.

Johnson's letter rightly praises the efforts of the National Health Service. The phrase with which the letter concludes – 'stay at home, protect the NHS and save lives' – was emblazoned on the podiums of the government's daily press briefings during the crisis (before 'Stay at Home' was replaced with the somewhat less clear 'Stay Alert') and the personnel of what Johnson calls here 'our fantastic NHS' (twelfth paragraph) was lauded for their heroism during this crisis. The government's construction of 'our NHS', a phrase wholly out of step with previous Tory approaches to the health service in Britain, was a core legitimating strategy of their coronavirus response. This strategy wholly ignored the root causes of why the NHS required such a level of public support at this time. The condition of the NHS as the spectre of the virus loomed towards Britain in the early months of 2020 enhances even more the heroism of NHS workers, but it also stands in stark contrast to the Conservative government's apparent goodwill towards the service during the pandemic.

Decades of Tory austerity included such measures as the closure of 17,000 hospital beds since 2010, the abolition of bursaries for trainee nurses in 2017, the downgrading of nurses' pay, a dramatic downscaling of district nursing numbers as a result of the imposition of a training fee and an exponential increase in the amount of the care budget being diverted to private health companies under the Conservatives whilst spending increases on the NHS had been reduced to just 1 percent. By 2020 the NHS had fewer doctors per 1000 patients than any other country in the EU and only half as many nurses per capita as countries like Germany. In addition, the findings of Exercise Cygnus, a pandemic preparedness drill which in 2016 accurately predicted the pressures a pandemic would place upon the health service in Britain, were ignored as part of the preparations for Brexit. The shortage of personal protective equipment (PPE) for NHS workers was a constant pressure during the crisis as stockpiles had been allowed to expire and budgetary pressures constrained their replacement. The contrast between the rhetoric of the government and their actions was noted by health officials such as Sue Hill, Vice President of the Royal College of Surgeons, who said in April 2020, 'Cabinet ministers are standing up every day, addressing us as if we're on a war footing and giving Churchillian quotes when they could be doing a few simple things like getting more bits of plastic and paper [PPE] on to wards.'

The shortfall in PPE was addressed constantly by public charity initiatives which also raised funds for the NHS throughout the emergency. Whilst these efforts were certainly born of compassion, it is worth noting that the founding charter of the NHS states the following clearly on the very first page:

> It [the 'new' National Health Service] will provide you with all medical, dental and nursing care. Everyone – rich or poor, man, woman or child – can use it or any part of it. There are no charges, except for a few special items. There are no insurance qualifications. **But it is not a "charity"**. You are all paying for it, mainly as taxpayers, and it will relieve your money worries in time of illness.
>
> (NHS, 5 July 1949)

Conservative politicians opposed the foundation of the NHS and worked against it for over 70 years. The public's support of the NHS throughout the pandemic was laudable, but the ownership of the service through phrases like 'our fantastic NHS' and 'our doctors, nurses and other carers' ring somewhat disingenuous in certain quarters. That said, the use of the inclusive pronoun contributes to the effective construction in this letter of a sense of shared responsibility.

These phrases are examples of Boris Johnson's use of *pathos* in this letter. Indeed, the government could claim that the full-throated support for the health service in their coronavirus rhetoric helped to inspire public actions of support, although, of course, these should not have been necessary. The inclusive pronouns 'we' and 'our' help to make pathotic arguments throughout the letter. The sentence 'We all feel the profound impact of coronavirus not just on ourselves, but on our loved ones and our communities' (second paragraph) provokes an emotional response through pronouns and lexical items. The patriotic language mentioned above, such as 'great British spirit', also builds an emotional response through *pathos*. Overall *pathos* is utilised somewhat less frequently than *logos* in this letter. Emotional responses are often very important for politicians, but given the goal orientation of this letter – to reduce panic but make clear the importance of the measures and to legitimate the government's response as appropriate in the face of increasing criticism – logetic arguments proved slightly more useful to Boris Johnson than emotional pleas.

An additional element important in judging the British government's initial response to the Covid-19 emergency was the role of the media in providing scrutiny of the actions of government. As was established in Chapter 6, the idealistic view of the media as forager for truth is somewhat less than accurate. The left wing commentator Owen Jones was so scathing of the BBC's favourable coverage of Boris Johnson and his government's Covid-19 response that he labelled it as 'what you'd expect of a loyal media in a tinpot dictatorship'. A particular story on the BBC website headlined '"Herculean effort" to provide NHS protective gear' (10th April 2020), which failed to offer scrutiny as to why this equipment was in such short supply in the first place, was defined by Jones as 'pro-government tub thumping'. All that we have examined in this book so far has been based on the recognition of ideology, so we are bound to acknowledge that, as a pro-Labour social democrat, Owen Jones is not to be expected to support the Tory government. However, the BBC ostensibly operates with the freedom to criticise the government also, and criticism of pro-Tory bias during the pandemic followed hot on the heels of similar accusations of its coverage of the 2019 general election.

Interestingly for students of the media, accusations of political bias at the BBC are often levelled conversely by both sides of the political spectrum, and CDA and corpus linguistics in particular can provide potential analytical avenues through which the dispute could be resolved. The Rupert Murdoch press, also addressed in Chapters 3 and 6, is usually staunchly supportive of the Conservatives, and much of its coverage was favourable during the pandemic. The headline on the front page of *The Sun* on Good Friday 2020, for example, was 'Boris is out (Now that really is a Good Friday!)' (10th April 2020), celebrating the Prime Minister's release from hospital after he contracted the virus himself. But 881 people died the day before this headline, and the British death toll stood at 7978. This made it all the more astonishing that *The Times* broke a story on 19th April which lambasted the failure of the government's preparedness for the crisis and revealed the failure of Boris Johnson to attend a raft of emergency meetings as the disease moved towards Britain. The article 'Coronavirus: 38 days when Britain sleepwalked into disaster' (19th April 2020) systematically dismantled the 'right measures at the right time' defence of a government which the publication and its owners had hitherto supported almost without question. Whether or not this article signals any sort of sea change in the relationship of the Murdoch press with the Conservative Party under Boris Johnson would be the perfect topic for a dissertation or lengthier CDA project.

Summary of Chapter 9

At the beginning of Chapter 8, we noted the fact that it is almost impossible to exist outside of politics. Even those disengaged from and uninterested in the political process are subject to politics and to the decisions of politicians and the power networks in which they operate. The coronavirus pandemic and the responses of governments and politicians to the emergency makes this point clearer than any event since the Second World War. The analysis of Boris Johnson's letter demonstrates that the idea that politics can be set aside even in the throes of international disaster is misleading. Politicians continue to utilise political rhetoric to persuade, so the responsibility of CDA and other cognate disciplines to examine the ideologies of political language remains important. This analysis engages with the letter through the parameters of Aristotle's *Rhetoric*, but you will find that other methodologies set out in this book, particularly the tripartite approach of Fairclough's model from Chapter 2, can also be effectively applied to this piece of political discourse. The analysis here also illustrates that, whilst considering argumentation in terms of *ethos*, *logos* and *pathos*, the analyst can simultaneously examine the strategic functions of the discourse and the linguistic methodologies, such as euphemism, pronoun use, parallelism and metaphor, through which these are achieved. We can anticipate that CDA and other scholarly disciplines will begin to engage with the language and politics of the pandemic on a large scale in the very near future. This chapter provides a snapshot of what those analyses might comprise.

Further Reading

Aristotle (1962) *Poetics*, J. Hutton (trans.). New York: Norton.
Aristotle (1984) *Rhetoric*, W.R. Roberts (trans.), in Barnes, J. (ed.) *The Complete Works of Aristotle*, Volume II. Princeton, NJ: Princeton University Press.

10 Multimodal Critical Discourse Analysis

KEY TERMS IN CHAPTER 10: multimodal discourse, MCDA, anatomy of advertising

MODELS OF ANALYSIS IN CHAPTER 10: visual SFL, denotation/connotation, visual social actor analysis, features of visual salience

10.1 Introduction

So far most of the analysis in this book has focussed on the ideological importance of written text but, as we know, discourse is comprised of much more than the written and spoken word. Discourse can also refer to images and sound, for example. A website or a social media post, for instance, can comprise written text, image and sound in a single discourse space. In Chapter 5 we examined visual and textual elements of meaning coming together in two different types of leaflets. CDA has been developing tools to analyse the meaning potential of modes other than the written and spoken over recent decades; in these approaches discourse is recognised as being 'multimodal'. **'Multimodal CDA'** focusses on images and other modes of communication alongside written and spoken text.

10.1.1 Types of Multimodal Discourse

Ravelli (2018:434) states that 'multimodal texts are a ubiquitous feature of today's communication landscape'; indeed, she goes so far as to assert that 'it is hard to imagine any form of communication in which English is *not* multimodal'. You might be tempted to counterargue that a discourse that contains only written text unaccompanied by images must surely be monomodal, but then this type of discourse still has a visual presence; it is arranged in a particular way on the page and has a font and a typescript; it may be even occasionally handwritten. Where images are present, be they stationary in newspapers or magazines or on billboards or hoardings or moving on television screens in your homes or placed strategically elsewhere, they are clearly a key component of the composition of discourse. Other sources of multimodal meaning include aural aspects of discourse related to music and to sound and voice quality in general, which can communicate a great deal of meaning. Linguists (Jansen, 2018; Neary, 2019; Voice and Whiteley, 2019) have been increasingly engaged with investigating meaning-making through music and its interaction with lyrics, for example. The analysis of telecinematic discourse is another area where linguists and particularly stylisticians (McIntyre, 2008; Bednarek, 2018; Hoffman and Kirner-Ludwig, 2020) have demonstrated a growing interest in multimodal aspects of communication, examining how meaning is constructed through aspects like camera shot, gaze, kinesic movements and props alongside dialogue in television and cinema. Social media, which will be the specific focus of Chapter 11, often incorporates written text, image, video and sound, and is a good example of what Ravelli (2018:434) calls a 'co-figuration of multiple modes'. Social media is also noteworthy for the use of new and emerging modes of meaning like memes and emojis, which linguists such as Lugea (2020) and Evans (2017) have investigated.

10.1.2 Multimodal Critical Discourse Analysis

In Critical Discourse Analysis we are most interested in how image, sound or video contribute to the construction of ideological meaning. Machin and Mayr (2012:10) state that Multimodal Critical Discourse Analysis (**MCDA**) is interested in how visual aspects of a text 'play a part in the communication of power relations'. In a newspaper article which includes pictures, for example, images have ideological meanings of their own as well as being meaningful in how they interact with accompanying text. Their placement in an article or on a webpage may also be significant and can contribute to how text encoders support the ideologies put forward in a text. Images in discourse are therefore highly selective.

The importance of visual discourse is perhaps no more obvious than in advertising, a type of discourse almost omnipresent in contemporary society. At its most basic, advertising operates to persuade consumers to part with their money in buying a product, but of course the medium is much more extensive and much more ideological than that. We have seen through the analysis of leaflets in Chapter 5, for example, that advertising can be used to 'sell' political parties and policies or to endorse and encourage societal behaviour which sends a highly ideological message. The messages of these examples were achieved by photographs, a conventional component of an election leaflet, and also through other visual aspects of discourse such as colour, which can construct cohesion and in some cases may have certain well-established meanings. Advertising therefore does not necessarily have to be selling a product; it can be 'non-product' advertising (Cook, 2001). Even product advertising, for that matter, is not exclusively about selling a product. It is often about selling a lifestyle and offering an indirect endorsement of features of certain lifestyles, such as what it 'means' to drive a certain vehicle, take a certain type of holiday and live in a certain area. Advertising can therefore often be viewed as doing ideological work which essentially upholds and reinforces the stratified organisation of society along economic lines. In Chapter 6 we noted the power possessed by advertising within the news media and discussed the difficulty that any media organisation might have should it reject the capitalism which lies at the heart of many examples of advertising. It is important to acknowledge that advertising itself is not inherently malignant, and we will illustrate below an example of where advertising operates for the greater good, as it were, although nonetheless much of the advertising industry is tightly tied to the maintenance of an economically organised society.

In this chapter we will utilise examples of advertising discourse and other visual images to demonstrate models in MCDA. In so doing, this chapter will also comprise an overview of advertising discourse in general and offer some important definitions and distinctions. We will revisit some of the major models of analysis which we have established earlier in the book to illustrate the fact that these models can also be thought of multimodally. The functions of Systemic Functional Linguistics (see Chapter 3) and the categories of social actor analysis (see Chapter 7) can be applied to images as well as text. We also introduce the additional model of visual salience. An appropriate awareness of the multimodality of communication will enable you to engage fully with discourse examples which use both text and image to naturalise and legitimise ideologies for text decoders.

10.2 Visual Systemic Functional Linguistics

In Chapters 3, 4 and 5 we explored the three functions of Systemic Functional Linguistics and demonstrated the important links between models of analysis in SFL and the motivations of CDA. The experiential function of language is analysed primarily through the transitivity framework, the interpersonal function analysed in Chapter 4 considers how interaction can be achieved between speaker or writer and listener or reader through mood, modality and evaluation, and the textual function is investigated through devices to construct cohesion and coherence. In this section we will outline more systematically how the models of analysis prominent in SFL can be used in a Multimodal CDA.

10.2.1 Visual SFL and Iconography in Media Images

The transitivity framework examines the experiential function of language through analysing processes, participants and circumstances. The analyst is interested in who does what to whom and how. When examining written text, we look at verb phrases, noun phrases and circumstantial adjuncts in a clause to establish meaning and patterns, and in CDA we consider how these meanings are operating socially. In MCDA we therefore consider the operation of such meanings visually, and we can start by using the same set of categories offered by Halliday (1994) to examine the visual representation of social action. We can analyse for example whether or not visual participants are represented materially as doing something or whether they are instead represented relationally as 'being', which invites a different sort of evaluation from the viewer. Certain processes like Mental process or processes of Verbalisation might be somewhat more difficult to encode visually; however, in a visual representation of the orientational metaphor discussed earlier (see further Chapter 8), a visual participant looking downward can be conceived as downbeat whilst someone looking up can appear aspirational, for example. These emotions have obvious links with Mental processes. Images can also contain visual representations of passivisation (see further Chapter 3) where an action or the result of an action might be portrayed but no perpetrator; a Goal but no Actor might be present. Circumstances such as location or time might also be relevant. Images can have meaning potential in isolation based upon the social or personal context of the viewer but usually they have more ideological weight relative to surrounding images and text in an institutional discourse scenario. Let us consider the example of the image which accompanied the article that was analysed in Chapter 2, 'Students at almost all universities may have their exams cancelled as lecturers threaten to strike over pensions dispute' (*Daily Mail*, 19th February 2018), shown in Figure 10.1.

Experientially this image reinforces the main message of the article, which is to pitch lecturers' actions as an attack upon students rather than as a reaction to profit-obsessed management practices in higher education. In this image we

Figure 10.1 Stressed student

assume the Material process of reading or writing. We cannot see the direct Goal but we assume that it is related to the pile of books on the right of the image. The generic student is obviously the Actor. In the context of this article, this image reinforces a motif of student stress; the head-in-hand pose connotes pressure and the books piled higher than the Actor herself exacerbate this impression. However, in another context, this image might have different connotations; it could be employed to promote studiousness or to indicate the importance of libraries. Rather than under pressure, the student could be concentrating and engaged. Owing to the context of the article and the ideological message which it clearly constructs, the viewer evaluates the image as one connoting stress and pressure rather than scholarly endeavour. Had this image been used in a pro-strike or pro-union leaflet, it could even be an overworked lecturer instead of an overstressed student.

Considering the connotative meanings of images adheres to the semantic theory of iconography proffered by Barthes (1973, 1977). Images can be said to 'denote' and 'connote'. The former refers to what is documented by an image, i.e. what is included in the image. Very simply, this image denotes a woman and a stack of books. Essentially, denotation refers to description. However, critical analysis must transcend description to consider not just what is documented by image but also what is *meant* by image, i.e. what an image connotes. In connotation we are interested in how an image signifies meaning, how it communicates ideas or concepts to the viewer. This image connotes through the stack of books not only the idea of scholarship but of scholarship as pressure and potential overwork, an impression supported by the head-in-hand pose of the student. In the case of the participant, she is wearing glasses, which often carry connotations of studiousness or bookishness. Sometimes students can make the mistake in a multimodal analysis of just describing the image and not foregrounding connotative meaning or, perhaps more likely, assuming that some elements of an image 'speak for themselves', as it were. Certainly, it is true that certain images have seemingly inherent connotative meanings for some viewers, and Ledin and Machin (2020:40) note the importance of 'cultural associations of elements in the image'. For example, mansions and sports cars often connote wealth and decadence. Your analysis should fully engage with these connotative meanings in an essay or a project, even if you think they seem fairly obvious. It is how established these connotative meanings have become that make them seem like this. You should fully express how meaning is achieved through 'carriers of connotation' (Ledin and Machin, 2020:42) when analysing an image

Two important carriers of connotation are object and setting. In this image the objects are the books and the student's glasses. Clothing and attire can also have connotative meaning; consider the effect of soldiers in uniform versus paramilitaries in less official garb or the meanings of a business suit versus a tracksuit, for example. In this image the clothing is fairly representative of the casual style associated with students. In another image a student might also have a laptop or a satchel or even pens and paper.

The setting of this image is somewhat unspecific, which serves to focus the viewer's attention on the objects. This is a strategy often replicated in advertisements where the setting is either empty or generic. Generic settings like a non-specific beach or meadow or city street can all contribute to the connotative meaning of an image. Settings can also be very specific, for example a particular street or a particular building. In some cases, specific settings can possess metonymic symbolism, such as when images of the Old Bailey courthouse in London stand for the justice system, 10 Downing Street for the British government or the White House or the steps of the Capitol for the US government. Buildings and settings can therefore possess iconic meaning; consider examples like the Taj Mahal, Sydney Opera House, Tiananmen Square or the Arc de Triomphe.

The **textual** function of language addresses cohesion, which, as we saw in Chapter 5, is often constructed through the linked use of colour in images. Given the relative scarcity of the props in this image, there is not a lot of internal cohesion. However, the role of the image in reinforcing the ideological stance of the article is highlighted by the fact that the image's caption is a direct repetition of the headline. So an essential part of the image is cohesive to the surrounding text through repetition, an important cohesive device (see Chapter 5 for an overview of other cohesive devices). Whilst the images in this book are reproduced in black and white, Machin (2010) reminds us that colour can operate experientially and interpersonally as well as textually, and you should attend to colour in any multimodal analysis that you carry out. Countries have national colours, for example, which are used on their flags and by extension conceptually 'stand for' the place. Colour possesses iconic meaning in most cultures. You will be aware of red being used to communicate a warning, for example. Colour is utilised in established patterns in specific contexts so that certain associated meanings can become routine. In Britain for example the highway code uses colours to denote different types of signage: red for warnings, blue for information signs, green and white for directions and distance, and brown to indicate tourist information. You should note that not all languages use colour in the same way. Linguists (Berlin and Kay, 1969) and psychologists (Winawer et al., 2007) have a longstanding interest in the meaning potential of colour. As we will see below, certain qualities of colour, such as brightness and tone, can also be important in multimodal analysis.

When an image is considered in terms of the **interpersonal** function, we are interested in how viewers and represented participants interact. Often this interaction is through a 'demand' image, where there is eye contact between viewer and participant; demand images can construct a psychological connection. The image above is an example of an 'offer' image, where there is no such eye contact and instead the viewer is invited to evaluate the participant and her/his scenario. In this case, that evaluation is driven by the ideologies communicated in the text. In a seminal work in multimodal analysis, Kress and van Leeuwen (2006) argue that visual semiotic modes such as images have a 'grammar' of their own and they outline how features of visual design can be evaluated in terms of the functions of SFL.

One element of the interpersonal function highlighted by Kress and van Leeuwen is the notion of visual modality (see Chapter 4 for an overview of textual modality). Images which are realistic are described as high modal images whilst less realistic images are low modal images. This image fits into the latter category. The background, for example, is wholly decontextualised. This not an actual student in an actual workplace but a model in front of a screen, and the image has likely been airbrushed, cropped and sharpened. Images presented in decontextualised settings like this therefore draw the attention of the viewer exclusively to the meaning potential of the represented participant and to the other objects in the image. Machin (2007) and Machin and Mayr (2012) offer a list of salient features which are manipulated in visual discourse, which we will introduce below.

The fact that this is not an actual image of a student but rather a constructed image with the potential to *represent* a 'student' in certain contexts is highly significant. The publication has chosen an image with competing potential meanings and relied on the ideological message of the written text to cause the reader to prioritise one meaning over another here. The reader of this article is not likely to look at this image and think, 'Well, study can clearly be quite a solitary process and this student is highly engaged, so this strike will have little effect on her'. The aspect of the image which allows us to quite accurately predict the motivation of the text producer in selecting it is the origin of the image itself. In the bottom left-hand corner of the image as it appears in the newspaper article we have analysed, the copyright information is given as Shutterstock/Photo Media Group. Shutterstock is an American company which provides stock images and sounds to publications which subscribe to the service. Services like Shutterstock and Getty Images, another well-known image bank company, possess the rights to vast amounts of multimodal data which is, in essence, purchased by discourse producers for use in their products. Stock image companies have revolutionised the visual composition of the media in recent decades, where it is often cheaper to use such a service than to commission or purchase images from a photographer. This process also means that the editorial staff in a media organisation can select from a large range of images exactly those which will reinforce the message of a story. Media professionals might claim that the texts they construct are free from certain forms of bias, although Chapter 6 in particular has problematised this position significantly, but they would find it difficult to proffer such an argument where images are concerned, given the process of their acquisition. Of course, many media and other discourse arenas still make extensive use of photographs of events rather than stock images, but in these cases the process of their inclusion in a piece is still highly selective, and the images are still subject to manipulation.

10.3 Salience

Certain aspects of images in discourse will be attributed more salience. This means that they are made to stand out and draw the attention of the viewer to certain symbolic meanings. Machin and Mayr (2012:54) offer a list of seven methods through which salience can be achieved: potent cultural symbols, size, colour, tone, focus, foregrounding and overlapping. We will explore these features through reference to Figure 10.2, although obviously not every image you will encounter will construct salience through all of these features. Figure 10.2 is

Figure 10.2 *The Guardian* front page

the front page of *The Guardian* newspaper on 31st January 2020, the day that Britain's departure from the European Union became official. The front page of *The Guardian*, a publication which favoured remaining in the EU, stood in sombre contrast to the triumphalism of many of the other national dailies on this highly significant date.

The first of Machin and Mayr's aspects of salience is 'potent cultural symbols', and these are obviously of particular importance in this image. The Union flag is Britain's national symbol, and here it adorns a crumbling sandcastle, a visual representation of the building-based metaphorical expression 'foundations of sand' to communicate instability and weakness. The castle also symbolically recalls the perception of Britain's former feudal or military past, a questionable 'golden era' marked by strength or importance which many Brexiteers felt could be regained by leaving the EU. This impression is starkly undermined here. The setting of this image is itself a potent cultural symbol. The famous White Cliffs of Dover, symbolic entrance to Britain, which have formed the backdrop to many homecoming narratives, are cast here as the frontier of a 'small island' which has cut itself adrift through the 'gamble' of Brexit.

In terms of 'size', the flag is small, as befits a 'small island'. This is not the grand ensign of a ship at sea or of charging cavalry but instead is more reminiscent of a plastic souvenir. Interestingly, the flag is larger than the castle, and indeed it may be the flag which has brought down the castle walls. The implication here is that the rather cheap nationalistic fervour of Brexit has brought the opposite of the strength intended by Brexiteers. Instead, it weighs too heavily and causes collapse. We are reminded of the importance of aspects of salience within the context of a text. Away from this sombre front page, this combination of symbols and disproportion of size could be construed as a sign of fortitude – the nation stands regardless of threat and ruin – but this interpretation would be at odds with the meaning constructed by this front page overall. The headline gives an interpretive lead to readers of the newspaper, which contributes to the meaning of the images.

The dominant use of 'colour' on the original front page – which is easily accessible online – is the red, white and blue of the Union flag and the white and black of the chalk and flint which compose the famous cliffs at Dover. The grey of the shingle and sky in the original cover add to the sombre mood of the image. Sometimes (and particularly in advertising) the 'tone' of an image will be enhanced so that brightness is elevated, which does not occur in this image. A brighter sky and shingle and whiter cliffs could easily be achieved by technological manipulation of this image, but this brighter tone would not fit the small-island motif. The 'focus' of this image is interesting. The flag is in sharp focus whilst the cliffs, even at their nearest point on the left-hand side of Figure 10.2, are blurred. Again, enhancement technology could easily bring the background elements into a much sharper focus, but in this image we rather suspect that the background has actually been blurred even more. These aspects of colour, tone and focus interact with the 'foregrounding' aspect of salience to emphasise the meaning of the image. The small flag and crumbling castle are in sharp focus in the foreground; they are more immediate, whilst the famous old cliffs are blurred in the background. A contrast is therefore created between the cliffs as the fading symbol of a rather more outward-looking Britain and the sandcastle and flag, which represent the small-island immediacy of Brexit. Indeed, the sandcastle itself can be construed as literally a small island separate from the bigger and more welcoming island now fading from view. *The Guardian* manipulates features of salience on this front page to construct a very specific view of Britain's departure from Europe. Figure 10.2 strikes a sharp contrast to the front page of *The Sun* shown in Figure 10.3.

This front page is from 29th March 2017, the date on which then British Prime Minister Theresa May triggered Article 50, the legislative mechanism through which Brexit was conducted. 'Overlapping', an aspect of salience which is not present in *The Guardian* example, is used here in the image of Theresa May in the bottom left-hand corner. Overlapping operates similarly to foregrounding as it places objects or people in front of other features of the image in order to enhance their importance. At this point in the Brexit process, Theresa May – 'our PM' – was still in the good graces of *The Sun* newspaper. However, the publication eventually turned on her as the difficulties of successfully negotiating a withdrawal agreement became clear in the subsequent months. Future headlines such as 'May has wrecked Brexit' (13th July 2018) and 'We're in the Brexs*it' (15th November 2018) are two examples of many headlines in *The Sun* which focussed anger on the soon-to-be former Prime Minister. This front page also uses the same potent cultural symbol of the White Cliffs of Dover but in a pointedly different way. We can see therefore that the symbolic meaning of even iconic images can be altered by surrounding textual context and aspects of visual salience. Here the tone of the cliffs has been enhanced. The brightness makes the cliffs look entirely white and interacts with the similar brightness of the sky. *The Sun* has manipulated tone in a manner wholly different from *The Guardian*. There is no contrast of focus, foregrounding or size here; the cliffs are in sharp focus, bright and large. As a symbol of Britain, they represent a strength which is not present in the faded grandeur attributed to them by *The Guardian*. The message projected onto the cliffs, 'Dover & Out', is an example of a phonological sequencing pun which constructs the separation so prized by supporters of Brexit as something to be celebrated. There is no 'small island' lament of regret here but only triumphalism and a somewhat idealistic view of the finality of Brexit.

By analysing the visual composition features of these front pages, it is clear that the meaning potential of discourse is communicated through semiotic elements in addition to written text. The use and manipulation of images by discourse producers are highly ideological and highly selective. Of course, there are other modes which can also add to meaning which we cannot express in print here, but consider, for example, how these front pages would be represented if they were moving images such as a film clip or the opening or closing segments of a

Figure 10.3 *The Sun* front page

news broadcast. We might imagine that Figure 10.2 would be shot with an initial close-up on the cliffs which eventually zooms out so that the cliffs fade and the crumbling sandcastle and Union flag come into sharp focus. A time-based discourse could even show the castle walls collapsing as they crumble under the weight of the flag. Figure 10.3, on the other hand, might be more likely to be shot from a stationary camera position. The emblazoning of the message on the cliffs could be shown in real time and the words could flash or flutter as if they themselves were a flag. Music could accompany each message and might be elegiac on one hand and celebratory on the other. If there is a British sound with a similar amount of cultural capital as the White Cliffs of Dover, it would probably be Big Ben, the bell in the clock tower at the Palace of Westminster. Interestingly, and in another example of the importance of the interaction of different semiotic modes in constructing meaning, we can imagine that the sound of Big Ben could effectively accompany both images.

10.4 Visual Social Actor Analysis of Immigration

In Chapter 7 we explored the categories of social actor analysis and examined particularly how this model could be used in the analysis of language and 'race'. Like the models of SFL discussed above, social actor analysis can also be applied to discourse which operates visually. In Chapter 7 (see 7.3.1) we presented a list of headlines from the anti-immigrant press in Britain as representative of the routine representation of immigration as a threat in certain sections of the media. One such headline was 'Army on Alert at French Ports to Halt Migrant Invasion' (*Daily Express*, 14th September 2014). The story focussed on the French port of Calais, where there were 'growing tensions about an army of migrants intent on reaching Britain', and on the newspaper's website it was accompanied by a number of images, one of which is shown in Figure 10.4.

Figure 10.4 Getty image: France-Britain-Immigration

This photograph demonstrates a number of van Leeuwen's social actor categories which contribute to the ideological construction of immigration as a threat in this article. The group of men behind the fence are collectivised, a homogenous group which represents visually the metaphorical construction of an 'invasion' in this article. Textual and visual collectivisation of migrants is present routinely in articles which use metaphorical source domains like WAR (army, invasion), WATER (waves, tide) and INSECTS (swarm). This group of men is identified through classification and physical identification; they appear to share a similar ethnic background. The police officers, on the other hand, are functionalised, represented through their professional status. Again, this image parallels the routine representation of migrants through identification and officials, such as police officers or politicians, through functionalisation in media discourse which is hostile to immigration. This book has consistently sought to point out that CDA can be strengthened by the simultaneous application of models of analysis to a single piece of textual data. The same principle applies to multimodal analysis. This image can be evaluated through the other approaches offered in this chapter as well as by social actor analysis.

10.4.1 Iconography of Immigration

In terms of the iconography proposed by Barthes (1973, 1977), the image in Figure 10.4 denotes two police officers and a number of men separated by a wire fence. The police officers are obscuring the view of another group of men standing to their left facing the opposite direction. We can focus on three aspects of the image to analyse what is connoted by this content: connotators of object, setting and pose.

Objects in this image enhance the impression of homogeneity also constructed through the collectivisation noted above, particularly in terms of attire. The men behind the fence are dressed very similarly with hats and hoods, and some are covering their face, which connotes not only a sense of similarity but also of deception. In terms of pose, many of them have their hands in their pockets. They are turned away from the camera and huddled together, focussed on a point somewhere out of the shot to the right. The connotation of deception is increased. Elements of attire and pose could of course be indicative of something much less ideological, the fact that it could be cold. Whilst you might be tempted to counterargue that it is not usually terribly cold in France in September, the copyright information provided in the article attributes this photograph to Getty, one of the image bank organisations discussed above. This photograph therefore could be construed as a high modal image in that it is not in a decontextualised setting and it does not use actors. However, it is not an image of the situation at the port of Calais on 14th September 2014. The process itself of selecting this image from the thousands available on Getty makes the image highly ideological and confirms the position of critical discourse analysts that images are selected in the media not as representations of reality but as tools to strengthen the ideological position of articles and the publications in which they appear. The uniforms of the police officers as well as their vigilant pose connote professionalism, which can be connected to the social actor category of functionalisation. We can see that the officers are armed. The sidearms are holstered rather than drawn or pointed at the group of men, but their presence connotes a sense of preparedness and characterises further the group as potentially threatening. With the exception of one man, all of the others are represented through an offer image. The viewer looks upon the participants and is invited to evaluate the threat they appear to pose but is not encouraged to psychologically engage with the men.

10.4.2 Salience of Immigration

In terms of aspects of salience, the police are in the foreground of the image (Figure 10.4), so they stand in protection between the viewer and the men behind the fence, which itself has connotations of separation and a necessity to contain, such as a fence which surrounds a prison. Owing to the position of these police officers to the left of the shot, so that we can easily see past them, and the fact that only two are included in the photograph, fewer in number than those who represent the threat, the viewer might therefore also be encouraged to perceive the situation as so potentially serious – this is apparently an 'invasion', after all – that the army should be mobilised to support the police. The colour, focus and tone of the original image do not appear to have been manipulated here. Given the technology available to many text encoders, it is also appropriate on some occasions to ask if the decision not to manipulate, sharpen or enhance an image might itself be ideological. In this case the somewhat gritty harshness of the scene is certainly clear enough.

10.4.3 Visual SFL of Immigration

Experientially this image (Figure 10.4) is rather more Relational than Material. With the obvious exception of standing, the men are *doing* very little but rather they *are* a threat. In terms of the textual function, cohesion is present in their similar attire and in its contrast to the uniforms of the police officers, and interpersonally, as stated above, we gaze upon the scene in an offer image. Kress and van Leeuwen (2006) note that visual interaction with participants in images can also be analysed through angle and length of shot. For example, close-ups and long shots have different effects, as does the viewing stance of the text decoder. If we look down upon a participant, i.e. an image is taken from above, they are perceived as less powerful, whereas the opposite effect is created when we look up at a participant. You will be aware of the orientational metaphorical expressions 'look down on' and 'look up to' when referring to criticism and admiration respectively.

This image is a medium shot rather than a close-up; the frame is about the size of the men's height. We are close enough to evaluate but not to make a psychological connection with the participants. Machin and Mayr (2012:97) state that in images 'distance signifies social relations. We keep our distance from people we do not want to "be in touch with" and "get close to people" we see as part of our circle.' In these terms, this image maintains social distance from the men and closeness to the police officers, although of course their vigilance means that their backs are to us. Experientially, the police officers are keeping watch, a Behavioural process which is more conscious than the Mental process 'to see'. The angle from which we view participants in an image is also potentially significant. We have a side view of the men behind the wire here, which constructs a sense of detachment. Because it seems that some of the men are purposely turned away from our view, their willingness to engage with us, through a frontal angle, is undermined. Our impression of them as conspiring is therefore enhanced. As we have said above, only one of the men looks at the camera, so the rest may not be aware of its presence, and pose and attire could well be explained by the fact that it is cold, but these less acrimonious interpretations are unlikely given the context of the image.

The caption of this image in the article is 'In Calais it's estimated that 100 migrants arrive every day looking to get to the UK'. Textually this is an example of interdiscursivity through the contraction and the informal use of 'looking to' to refer to intention or desire. Captions in images operate similarly to headlines in articles; they have a definitional function that states what an image portrays and directs the viewer's interpretation of the image. If the caption here was 'Desperate men united in fear at French port', our interpretation of the image might be wholly different. This analysis engages with the photograph within the context of the article and the wider ideological position of the right wing press in Britain on the issue of immigration. The analysis demonstrates that strong conclusions can be reached by a close interaction with all features of the image through the application of social actor analysis, iconography, salience and SFL. In the next section we address the role of CDA and MCDA in the analysis of advertising language.

10.5 Power and Advertising

You might be forgiven for thinking that in contemporary society advertising is everywhere. It is prominent in newspapers and magazines, it is on billboards and posters in airports, sporting venues, the sides of buses and many other everyday scenarios. Some websites are so replete with advertising that it can be difficult to locate the content. Social media feeds use complex algorithms to target advertising specifically at individual users and, with the exception of some streaming services for which users pay a subscription, advertising is ubiquitous on television and radio. In a slight corruption of the words of Robert Louis Stevenson, the world seems to be always selling something.

Critical linguistics is interested in the ways that advertising discourse uses text and images to promote certain impressions of goods and services. In CDA we are also focussed on the ideological meanings of advertising, particularly whether societal norms are upheld or challenged through various types of advertising.

10.5.1 Advertising Terminology

Cook (2001) offers a number of important distinctions which account for most of the different types of advertisements with which you will be familiar. As mentioned in the introduction to this chapter, many advertisements are aimed at selling products, but there are those which are 'non-product' adverts. Public agencies will employ non-product advertising to disseminate information, for example. During the Covid-19 pandemic the British government ran television and radio advertising campaigns encouraging people to 'Stay at Home. Save Lives'. Many large corporations will employ a mixture of non-product and product advertising, often using the former to 'soften up' consumers before 'hitting' them with product advertising. New companies might 'introduce' themselves and their apparent philosophies to the public first before concentrating adverts on specific products. This approach is linked to the second definition of advertising types, 'hard sell' and 'soft sell'. The former uses blunter and less ambiguous strategies to construct a sense of immediacy. Think of pleadings to 'buy now' and 'don't miss out' or those 'limited-time offers' (which always seem to be extended). To give something the 'hard sell' is a well-known idiom. Soft sell advertisements are more subtle; they are often more multimodal, making use of images and music in a less immediate context which uses somewhat more sophisticated forms of linguistic persuasion than ceaseless imperatives and listing product attributes. Hard sell advertising dominated in the infancy of modern advertising, whilst softer, non-product and 'tickle' advertising mark the sophisticated strategies used by more contemporary advertising agencies which began to redefine the industry in the 1960s. 'Tickle' advertising requires audiences to engage pragmatically with an advert. Often audiences have to 'work out' an advert and are hence drawn into a greater level of engagement. Bernstein (1974:104) states of tickle advertising that 'if people are intrigued and comprehension is not immediate, they may go on to participate in advertising'. Tickle advertising is therefore 'softer' than 'reason' advertising, where explicit motives to purchase are laid out for the consumer. These links are not concrete; however, there are connections between non-product, soft sell and tickle advertising and between product, hard sell and reason advertising.

'Long copy' and 'short copy' advertising is also linked to these distinctions. The latter is usually lighter on detail, particularly in written text, to elevate the requirement for cognitive engagement from the consumer. So-called 'advertorials', often article-length segments in magazines or 'infomercials' on late night television are examples of long copy advertisements which are replete with hard sell reasons to buy. A further distinction which is linked to these groups is 'slow drip' and 'sudden burst' advertisements. Slow drip advertisements compose lengthy and gradual advertising campaigns, whilst sudden burst advertisements refer to immediate offers or new releases. Modern consumers will be familiar with the concept of 'flash sales', used particularly by airlines to stimulate seat sales, as an example of sudden burst advertising. Two iconic examples of slow drip advertising were two campaigns by Oxo gravy, one of which ran for eighteen years from 1958 and the other for sixteen years from 1983. British television viewers watched the 'Oxo family' as they negotiated the intricacies of modern life around the institution of family dinner.

Many advertising campaigns carry this element of cultural iconography. For example, in Ireland advertising for Guinness almost forms part of the nation's cultural expression and is prominent at national sporting events in particular. For many, the 'Guinness Christmas ad' (there have been several, but Irish audiences inevitably know the referent) heralds the beginning of the holiday season. Perhaps the most culturally iconic Christmas advertisement for Irish and British audiences is the Coca-Cola truck lighting up wintry town scenes as it brings seasonal cheer accompanied by the famous 'Holidays Are Coming' soundtrack. Coca-Cola is also responsible for the 'Diet Coke Break', with the Etta James classic 'I Just Wanna Make Love to You' now forever associated with the tickle, slow drip, soft sell campaign. British television audiences also wait for the annual Christmas advert by the department store chain John Lewis. The cultural resonance of these campaigns (or similar campaigns which you can doubtlessly think of in your own contexts) may appear to have transcended the motivation of advertisements. They possess a certain sentimentality for cross-generational audiences; however, you should view these campaigns not just as nostalgic entertainment. The construction of this iconography is intimately linked to the profit margins of these companies. To be sure, to have constructed cultural capital for themselves is an attribute of a very successful advertising strategy, but that would not be reward enough for corporations should that cultural capital not be matched by monetary capital.

10.5.2 Analysis of Product Advertising

This section comprises a discussion of an advertisement produced by the German vehicle manufacturer Volkswagen. Volkswagen has produced many well-known and iconic advertisements, and the discussion here focusses on the 2014 advertisement for the new Beetle (or 'Bug', as the car has become known in some countries). You might be wondering why the advertisement has not been reproduced here. When approached for permission to include the advertisement in this book, the company responded that 'usage rights are not valid' for academic books. Simpson, Mayr and Statham (2018:98) note that 'the problem with powerful conglomerates is that they are ferociously protective of their "brand" and they have teams of highly paid lawyers to enforce this injunction'. From all that we have learned in this book, perhaps it is unsurprising that for-profit companies who operate at the core of the capitalist system would not invite scrutiny of their products or how they sell them. Fortunately for the critical discourse analyst (and for writers and readers of books on CDA), the refusal of companies to permit the reproduction of material cannot censor scrutiny in the age of the internet. Before reading the discussion in this section, run an online search for the advertisement. The headline of the advert is 'A gentleman takes off his hat when he meets a lady'. A lady in a blue dress is shot from the back approaching a man in sunglasses driving the new Beetle on a suburban street. The text below the image is 'The Beetle Cabriolet Karmann. A Classy Affair'. The advert is easily located, and you should read the commentary below with it on screen or printed out.

This is an example of a space-based advertisement. It appears in print rather than on television or radio or another time-based medium. Brierley (1995) notes a number of features of the **'anatomy of advertisements'**, which give us terminology when referring to certain parts of advertisements and which you should use in essays or projects in place of unwieldy phrases like the 'text at the top of the ad' or the 'picture at the bottom of the ad'. With reference to the Volkswagen advert, we can identify the headline as 'A gentleman takes off his hat when he meets a lady'. Headlines interact with or introduce the main body of an advertisement and sometimes address the viewer through some form of direct address. The main body of an advertisement is known as the 'body copy', the information-carrying component of an advert where much of the piece's persuasion takes place. The body copy in the Volkswagen advert is comprised of the images (lady, car and driver, setting), which clearly interact with the headline, and of the text 'The Beetle Cabriolet Karmann. A Classy Affair.' Many companies have recognisable 'slogans' which have been established over time. You may be familiar with 'Vorsprung durch Technik' (Audi), 'Maybe It's Maybelline' (Maybelline) or 'Every Little Helps' (Tesco). Volkswagen's international slogan is 'Das Auto', which means 'The Car' and implies therefore that Volkswagen is the very definition or epitome of the car. This accompanies the 'signature' in the bottom right-hand corner of the advert, the company logo. Signatures are usually the brand's logo and are often placed here in advertisements as a stamp of approval. Some adverts may also be accompanied by a 'testimonial', a quotation from and/or a picture of a celebrity or well-known figure endorsing the brand.

The Volkswagen advertisement is short copy, there is a limited amount of text, and the approach is soft sell. There are no lists of explicit reasons to purchase this car, for example. There are some specifications offered in very small text at the bottom, but there is not an extolling of the mechanical virtues of the vehicle. The audience is not supposed to view the Beetle Cabriolet Karmann as a tool but rather as part of a 'classy affair'. The fact that we are drawn into the narrative proposed by the advertiser and are not presented with explicit reasons to buy places this advert firmly at the tickle end of the reason–tickle continuum. Linguistically, reason advertising operates largely by entailment, the meaning of the advert is made plain for the viewer, whilst tickle advertising contains an element of implicature. Some additional meaning is implied, and the consumer must more deeply engage with the advert in order to decode this meaning, to 'work it out'.

The message of this advertisement is to define the product as sophisticated, and the text and images combine to classify 'classy' through aspects of both tradition and modernity. The headline refers to the convention of manners of a man greeting a woman by briefly removing his hat and is linked by implicature to the fact that the car has its roof down; it is a gentleman. In a somewhat casual and not overly scientific experiment, the results of which would nonetheless likely be replicated in a more stringent research exercise, I showed this advert to a seminar group of twelve undergraduates reading English (eight females and four males) and asked them what they understood to be the meaning of 'cabriolet'. The answers varied slightly, as you would expect, but the results were very useful for this analysis. One student, clearly well-versed on the subject of motor vehicles, offered a definition which would not have been out of place in the vehicle's manual. Another thought the word had been invented by the advertisers to refer to a 'classy hook-up' (which is interesting because it shows that this student had clearly bought into the implied meaning of the narrative of the advert and also accepts that advertisers can often be inventive and linguistically innovative). Six of the twelve students, a very statistically significant percentage, expressed some reaction to the message of sophistication implied by the advertisers. Two students said a cabriolet is a 'classy convertible', another said it is a 'posh convertible' and another just a 'posh car'; two students referred to class (a 'middle-class convertible' and 'what the middle classes call a convertible'). It is slightly beyond the confines of this discussion and would require a good deal more experimentation, but the answers offered by these students could form the basis for a larger project on vehicles as an expression of affluence and how this is constructed and maintained linguistically. As my one car expert student was able to point out, there is a particular definition which distinguishes a cabriolet from a convertible, but the majority instead thought that the former was a 'classy' or 'posh' way of expressing the latter. This impression has likely been driven by the advertisement itself. Given that for all but one student the actual definition of a cabriolet was unknown, many may not have been able to offer any answer at all had they not been shown the advertisement first.

Whilst traditional sophistication is constructed by the headline and a lexical field which includes 'classy', 'gentleman', 'lady' and 'cabriolet', the setting of the advert constructs this sophistication as also decidedly modern. The driver of the car through sunglasses and hairstyle and the lady in her attire and pose (remember the importance for connotation of pose, objects and setting) are the very image of modern sophistication. The scene constructed here is idealistic and highly aspirational. This idealism is reflected in the low modality of the images; the lady has been airbrushed and her contours sharpened. Colour saturation, specifically the use of shadows, is used to make the car look sleek. The setting of the encounter in the advertisement is decontextualised. This, like the models, is used to represent an ideal rather than present a reality. The scene could be set on any street in a high-end residential area with chic architecture and landscape gardens, where the residents are attractive, where slightly risqué encounters might happen but such affairs are always 'classy', and where the Beetle Cabriolet Karmann is right at the centre of everything, just as it is right in the centre of this advertisement.

We can clearly conclude quite a lot about the multimodal operation of this advertisement. As always, CDA aims to go a step further by considering how this advertisement operates ideologically. We therefore aim to expand the conclusions of the analysis by viewing the advert as a piece of institutional discourse operating in the social world. Just like the media discourse examples, the leaflets, speeches and statements we have examined throughout the book, advertising plays a societal role. It does not just reflect the desires of consumers, for example, but it constructs, legitimises and normalises these aspirations. Advertisers do not simply refer to what consumers might want but more accurately they tell consumers what they should want. Product advertising like the Volkswagen advert discussed here also involves legitimising a certain type of lifestyle and, in so doing, the overall system which maintains such lifestyles is itself legitimised. One of the great if uncomfortable successes of the advertising industry and of the strengthening of economic stratification in which it maintains an important role is the fact that accomplishment in modern society is frequently measured by materiality. Success is viewed as being able to drive a certain car, live in a certain house in a certain area, dress in a certain way, holiday in certain destinations and so on (I suspect many of you could add further to this list). The message of the Volkswagen advertisement, that driving this car is an integral part of a sophisticated, perhaps slightly risqué and certainly affluent lifestyle, legitimises the desire to attain this lifestyle and its various trappings. In this way, the ubiquity of product advertising maintains the consumer culture at the heart of capitalism. As we have discussed already, consumerism has now begun to operate even in areas traditionally committed to exposing rather than emulating these ideologies. For example, the recasting of knowledge as a product and students as consumers instead of scholars is a highly ideological, profit-driven process, and advertising is employed consistently by higher education institutions to legitimise this process.

10.5.3 Analysis of Non-product Advertising

The analysis of the Volkswagen advert does not necessarily mean that advertising as a medium is inherently misanthropic. The textual and visual capacity for persuasion in advertising can be utilised for less objectionable purposes. Many examples of non-product advertising operate to provide information which might be helpful to people, such as how to access charitable help or to donate to charities or to help the environment (of course there are bigger issues around why so many people are reliant on charity in the first place or why the environment is so damaged). As mentioned above, governments around the world have used advertising on television and radio in particular to encourage people to comply with the restrictions of movement during the Covid-19 pandemic. Figure 10.5 is from a Christmas 2011 advertising campaign by the organisation Rape Crisis Scotland. The poster appeared prominently in public spaces and on university campuses. Unlike Volkswagen, Rape Crisis Scotland granted permission for the reproduction of this advert without objection.

The main message of this advertisement contrasts with the leaflet which we examined in Figure 5.2 (see 5.3.2), where the responsibility for rape was attributed to the potential victim. In this campaign Rape Crisis Scotland utilise the power of advertising to resist constructions of sexual assault as attributable to the behaviour of victims and recast the blame for rape onto rapists. You might find it useful to revisit the analysis of section 5.3.2 to reacquaint yourself with some of the social context of this issue. Figure 10.5 is an example of several victim support campaigns which have used advertising to construct discourse resistant to the victim-blaming narratives which are prominent in the media and other powerful arenas. The organisation Help for Victims ran a campaign with a similar message ('Buying someone a drink isn't a crime…rape is!' and 'Flirting isn't a crime…rape is!'), for example. Many of these campaigns were endorsed by, and the posters disseminated in conjunction with, other powerful organisations, particularly police forces and universities. So, we have an example of powerful groups using the medium of advertising to re-educate the public and to resist dominant ideological forces. This example serves to remind us therefore that, whilst critical discourse analysts do not accept that language can be neutral and disinterested in societal contexts, we are not necessarily arguing that discourse itself is inherently malignant. Given what we know about the operation of power in society, of course it would be difficult to decouple ascendant groups and systems from their ideological positions but, in theory, discourse could be part of a process in which language is used to further somewhat more enlightened ideologies. In all cases, of course, discourse remains ideological.

Figure 10.5 is an example of non-product advertising; it is not selling a product but endorsing a principle. The poster is long copy and sudden burst. There is no slow and subtle distribution of the message here, so the piece is a clear example of reason advertising. The headline is comprised of two declarative, factual statements in parallel syntactic structures. The headline refers to a well-worn stereotype in which women who drink alcohol, especially to excess, are often condemned as unrespectable. In many rape narratives, such as Figure 5.2, a connection is constructed between alcohol and culpability (see 5.3.2). The advert in this section seeks to dismantle that connection. The parallelism which we discussed in terms of political language in Chapters 8 and 9 is also prominent in

[Figure 10.5: Rape Crisis Scotland advertisement poster with text "Drinking is not a crime. Rape is." above an image of young women, followed by "No matter how much she's drunk... No matter what she's wearing... No matter if you've already kissed... ...sex without consent is rape. If there's any doubt about whether a woman has drunk too much to give consent, assume she hasn't given it. Responsibility for rape will always lie with the rapist. Find your local Rape Crisis Centre at www.rapecrisis.org.uk or call Rape Crisis freephone helpline 0808 802 9999 (12n-2.30pm / 7-9.30pm every day)"]

Figure 10.5 Rape Crisis Scotland advertisement

advertising language and is evident again in the body copy of Figure 10.5. The three 'no matter' statements here appropriate the arguments which are prominent in victim blaming and recast them in these sentences. The arguments are all undermined by the declarative statement 'sex without consent is rape'. Clear and unambiguous statements in this poster use conjunctive adjuncts (see Chapter 9) to clearly construct the reasoning behind the main message of the advert that alcohol does not make a victim culpable in rape. Note, for example, the conditional in 'If there's any doubt about whether a woman has drunk too much to give consent, assume she hasn't given it'. These connective structures are prominent in reason advertising. We noted also in Chapters 8 and 9 that political language and advertising language share certain characteristics – such as parallelism and connectives – which should be unsurprising given that persuasion is at the core of both types of discourse. The section of the advertisement often composed of the slogan and signature in product advertising is used in this example to provide information on rape crisis centres. In some of the other iterations of this advert, this part of the poster did contain the emblems of the organisations which endorsed its message, such as police force badges and signatures of university student unions.

Figure 10.5 adheres to the Given and New structure proposed by Kress and van Leeuwen (1996) with the established information – emblematic of the 'girls' night out' – on the left and the New and more appropriate interpretation of it in the text on the right (see further Chapter 5). Kress and van Leeuwen also offer the structural definitions 'ideal' and 'real', which coincide with metaphorical meanings of 'up' and 'down'. On this poster the 'ideal' is comprised of the declarative headline, the interpretation of sexual assault which ideally should be accepted; the 'real', which composes the information in the bottom half of an image or an advert, provides factual information. The setting of the image is representative of any bar or nightclub. The objects and attire in the image, such as glasses and party dresses, represent the behaviour referenced in the textual body copy. So, there is clear cohesion between text and image. The image is an offer image and is shot in medium close-up so that the viewer has evaluative access to the scene. The clear message of the text strengthens an interpretation which views the scene as happy and carefree – it is notable that there are no men present – and not as provocative or problematic. Advertising campaigns which proffer a different message to the one prominent here and which prompt potential victims to modify their behaviour also use images of young women, drinking and dancing and dressed for a night out. Conversely, the textual messages of those adverts often promote different interpretations of these scenes as reckless and risky.

Summary of Chapter 10

This chapter has demonstrated that the discourse construction of ideology is operable across various modes. In contemporary society especially, we interact with language not just through written text but also aurally and visually. We have been focussed on the latter in the analysis here, but so-called time-based discourse is just as amenable to CDA as the images examined in this chapter. These examinations have demonstrated that approaches to language in CDA, particularly those drawn from SFL, can also be taken multimodally. Images as well as written texts have an experiential, interpersonal and a textual function. These functions are closely connected to Barthes' (1973, 1977) view of images as icons and to Machin and Mayr's (2012) list of the visually salient features of discourse. Focussing on the salient features of newspaper front pages in particular yields very in-depth critical conclusions, and a similar trajectory can be followed for the analysis of other types of front covers. Kress and van Leeuwen (1996, 2006) have been at the forefront of Multimodal CDA and provide a grammar of visual design through which we can consider the structure and composition of images. Van Leeuwen's (1996) social actor analysis also operates visually. This chapter has utilised all of these approaches to establish the importance of images in societal discourse. It is of crucial importance that models of analysis arm us to demonstrate *how* meaning is made in images. Multimodal CDA should emulate the close analytical approach taken in the examination of written text.

Further Reading

Cook, G. (2001) *The Discourse of Advertising*, 2nd edition. London and New York: Routledge.
Kress, G. and van Leeuwen, T. (2006) *Reading Images: The Grammar of Visual Design*, 2nd edition. London and New York: Routledge.
Machin, D. and Mayr, A. (2012) *How to Do Critical Discourse Analysis*. London: Sage.

11 Social Media Language and Power

KEY TERMS IN CHAPTER 11: computer mediated communication, citizen journalism, social media

MODELS OF ANALYSIS IN CHAPTER 11: Appraisal

11.1 Introduction

This chapter will address the discourse arena of the internet, particularly focussed on language on **social media** platforms. From a CDA perspective we are most interested in this book in the connection of language online with power relations and the ideological operation of discourse. The first section will discuss the role of social media and other types of **computer mediated communication** (CMC), i.e. interactions which take place online, in terms of how they may have affected or contributed to changes in power relations in society. We will consider for example if the increased ability to respond to major social events on social media increases the power possessed by the general public. The subsequent analysis will discuss the role of social media in social and political processes. Platforms like Twitter and Facebook now form an important site at which campaigns are fought. We will consider the language of two opposing campaigns which were active on Twitter in 2018, those for and against the historical movement to legislate for abortion in Ireland by a referendum to repeal the Eighth Amendment to the Irish Constitution.

11.2 Language Online: Brave New World or False Dawn

It is clear that over the last two decades the emergence of the internet and its now omnipresent role in many areas of society has contributed much to communication. For example, it seems almost surprising to reflect upon the fact that text messaging (SMS) and email, which were once revolutionary, are now viewed by some as quaint in an environment of personal and business social media networks, blogs, instant messaging services and participatory websites.

11.2.1 Online and Offline Links

Of course there is a link between online and offline discourse. Television and radio for example can be viewed or listened to online as well as through the airwaves, and programming, particularly news and current affairs programming, has online elements, with the audience able to contact a programme and comment on content through online platforms, and their responses are often integrated into a show. This is essentially an expansion of the well-established 'phone in' trope to accommodate online platforms like Twitter and Instagram. The news media also maintains a link between online and offline discourse, and newspapers now operate habitually online and on paper, so their mode of dissemination has significantly diversified in the past two decades. The newspaper articles from which examples have been drawn throughout this book are mostly available through the publications' websites (often accompanied by more advertising than could possibly be included in the physical newspaper). It is not the case that the proliferation of online content has eradicated offline forms of discourse, but certainly the internet has led to many changes in the media landscape as more and more people access news online. One significant development is the increased capacity for audience participation. Readers now often offer responses through the 'comments' option on a publication's website or through social media platforms where an article may have been shared. The textual content of the article may be the same in print and online, but the website version has a higher participatory potential. Online versions of articles are also more easily changed and updated as a story develops. When readers interact through comments on an online story, they are participating in computer mediated communication. Social media is another dominant site of CMC where users can post comments of their own, which are responded to through 'shares' or 'likes' as well as through textual responses, or they can share other content, such as a link to a newspaper website or a video or an image.

11.2.2 Computer Mediated Communication and Power

A consideration of particular importance for critical discourse analysts and other scholars who are focussed on power relations is whether or not CMC has changed the landscape of these relations. Certain emancipatory perspectives of CMC view it as paradigm-shifting; Rosen (2012:13) refers to a 'shift in power that goes with the platform shift' and states that the role of 'the people formerly known as the audience' has been fundamentally altered. Of particular importance to a view like this is the fact that, in theory, a version of the news can now be produced by any internet user – so-called **citizen journalists** or **citizen** reporters – and that this scenario represents a consequential threat to the power possessed by media institutions and other organisations. Whilst we can accept that the increased accessibility of audiences and the ability of audience members to become participators in content like online news are potentially significant factors, there are a number of caveats that must accompany the view that some version of 'people power' now outweighs traditional power bases.

Firstly, the critical view of language as discourse already recognised audiences as participants in news and other powerful discourse arenas long before the proliferation of the internet. In CDA we view listeners and readers as text decoders. Audiences are not just receivers of discourse but, in the view of the second stream of power (see Chapter 1), their consent plays a role in maintaining the ideologies which are favoured in institutional discourse. The view of CMC as having seminally shifted power relations from a vertical onto a horizontal plane – Rosen (2012:14) states that the centralised system through which audiences are connected 'up' to large media organisations has been altered by audience participation in news through the internet and has been replaced by a 'horizontal flow' that connects citizens instead to one another – neglects to address the fact that audiences have always played a part in the power networks of news. Certainly their level of direct involvement and the ability of audiences to produce news and media of their own, through 'citizen journalism' for example, has increased, but for a number of reasons it is a leap to assume that this has fundamentally altered the concentration of power.

11.2.3 Computer Mediated Communication, Power and Media

Mainstream media organisations have heavily colonised online media arenas. Newspapers for example have adapted to online news not only through the maintenance of websites and comments sections but also through live news feeds. All of the major and most of the minor print and broadcast media organisations have a presence on Facebook and Twitter, and when users on these networks 'share' news, it is very often achieved through posting a link to a story or an article produced by a mainstream news organisation. The content of these institutions is 'shared', 'liked' and 'retweeted' much more frequently than content produced by smaller institutions or by citizen reporters. Ras (2020:209) states that 'newspapers continue to be a force to be reckoned with in influencing and reinforcing widely held opinions', so we should remember that arguments which champion the internet for potentially increasing access to information must acknowledge that this information is still heavily produced by powerful groups and operates just as ideologically as if it were offline. Tagg (2020:319) acknowledges the 'continuing grip of the "old" not only in the dominance of "old media" within a new mediascape but also in the nature of the discourses and practices remediated through both old and new technologies'. So, we should not assume that audiences have been liberated from the ideological agendas which mark institutional discourse or that power relations, to use Rosen's terms, are now more 'horizontal' than 'vertical', just because this discourse is disseminated through so-called 'new media'.

Certainly we acknowledge the increased potential represented by the internet and the greater opportunities for the production of citizen journalism through blogs, vlogs and other forms of social networking, but we must also recognise that these new voices still fight for recognition in an arena which has been colonised by so-called 'old media'. Fuchs (2014:77) reminds us that larger organisations 'control more resources, such as money, decision-making powers, capacities for attention generation' than citizen journalists or independent writers or bloggers. To be sure, the internet has increased the potential of those with resistant voices to disseminate their messages, but it is still the major organisations which possess the major resources.

Looking upon the online space as having fundamentally altered the media–audience relationship also includes the misconception that citizen journalism is an invention of the internet, when the involvement of 'ordinary people' in newsworthy events is actually nothing new. Perhaps the most famous example of citizen journalism in the modern age is Abraham Zapruder's filming of the presidential motorcade as it travelled through Dealey Plaza in Dallas on 22nd November 1963 and therefore the capturing of the assassination of President John F. Kennedy. You may also be aware of George Holliday, who filmed from his balcony the police beating of Rodney King in Los Angeles in March 1991. Holliday sent the footage to local news station KTLA, and it was subsequently shown around the world, so that today we would say that it 'went viral'. What the internet has of course done for citizen journalism is increase the potential of citizens to produce and distribute much more widely sophisticated pieces of journalistic discourse, and in the 'explosion of online interactivity and user participation' (Seargeant and Tagg, 2014:2) represented by the internet the capacities of citizen journalists have doubtlessly increased. We should obviously not assume that access to requisite technologies and connectivity is universal; those in lower socio-economic groups and in less developed areas locally and globally are still heavily restrained by these circumstances, even at a time when technology and access to technology is generally more affordable and available.

11.2.4 Computer Mediated Communication, Power and Social Media

These somewhat more tempered considerations of power relations online should not be taken as a suggestion that the internet has not had a huge impact on society in general or that it does not play a significant role in many of the discourse arenas of infinite interest to critical discourse analysts. Social media has added a very influential extra dimension to politics, for example, and politicians have a very significant online presence. Before the platform finally acted upon his false claims of voter fraud in the 2020 general election and his incitement of violence at the Capitol in January 2021, Donald Trump had 80 million followers on Twitter and, perhaps to the occasional chagrin of his staff, made many more statements through social media than any other medium during his presidency. In many cases we can assume that social media accounts are delegated by politicians to communication staffers, but this was significantly not the case with @realDonaldTrump. The online element is now a massive part of political campaigns around the world, and not just those conducted by professional politicians; pressure groups, social campaigners, religious groups, community activists, almost every vaguely political actor operates online and through social media. Barack Obama's historic victory in the US presidential election in 2008 was in part facilitated by the fact that Obama's campaign developed its own social media network, my.barackobama.com or MyBo. Obama's use of the internet in 2008 was seen as revolutionary for its distribution of campaign material and its raising of donations. Fourteen years later such operations are the norm across the political spectrum.

In an analysis of relationships on social media, Thurlow (2013) nonetheless cautions against assuming that genuine interaction takes place between audiences and politicians online just because content is distributed or comments made through social media, stating that 'social media are most useful to politicians because the appearance of interaction may be achieved by the apparent use of interactive technologies' (Thurlow, 2013:236). We should not mistake 'interactivity', which refers to the fact that communication takes place online, with genuine 'interaction'.

Social activist campaigns like the Black Lives Matter movement, the Occupy movement or environmental groups like Extinction Rebellion, so lambasted by Jeremy Clarkson in the comment piece analysed in Chapter 4, have all developed social media presences. The #MeToo movement, which combats sexual harassment and sexual assault primarily in the entertainment industry, has close connections with social media. The phrase 'Me Too' as a reference to sexual abuse and harassment was initially popularised by the activist Tarana Burke on the social network MySpace in 2006 and developed into the virtual hashtag #MeToo on Twitter in 2017 when actress Alyssa Milano revived the phrase in a blog piece about the sexual abuse carried out by film producer Harvey Weinstein. #MeToo is now generally recognised as a reference to sexual assault and to survivors of sexual assault.

We know from the analysis in this book and CDA generally that reactionary positions on 'race', capitalism, the environment and gender continue to be worryingly influential, so it would be incorrect to claim that the movements mentioned here have led to fundamental societal change. Indeed, there is a certain disconnection between the popularisation of issues on social media and tangible results in society at large. Given the prominence of some campaigns and groups which often 'trend' online, it might be easy to forget just how longstanding and ingrained normalised conceptions and behaviours have become. This is owing in no small part to the role of discourse. There is also a concern that online contexts have facilitated the rise of 'slacktivism', where people consider themselves to be actively supporting a cause just by indicating approval online through a retweet or a 'like' but not actually engaging in any direct 'activism'. It is clear that increased awareness does not necessarily lead to major social change. A somewhat ironic feature of the greater accessibility afforded by online networks is that these tools can be used by all sides in a struggle, the reactionary as well as those perceived as liberating, as the analysis of the Irish abortion debate on Twitter will demonstrate. Rather than assume therefore that the internet is an inherently liberating arena, it is more accurate to consider the resistant and counter-power possibilities of online communities and social networks in terms of potential. This potential might occasionally be realised, such as in the example we will consider in the next section, but the counter-power potential of the online presence of campaigns and movements does not exist outside of wider social and political contexts any more than the advertisements, speeches or newspapers which we have examined in earlier chapters.

11.3 Evaluation on Twitter: Abortion in Ireland

Machin (2016) notes that many of the initial engagements of linguists with language online were inevitably theoretical and considered many of the issues which are overviewed here. In recent years much more work has been developed in examining the functional, semantic and pragmatic operation of language online. Twitter (Page, 2012; Zappavigna, 2012, 2015), Instagram (Veum and Undrum, 2017; Ringrow, 2020), Facebook (Tagg and Seargeant, 2016; Georgalou, 2017; Mayr and Statham, 2021) and YouTube (Lorenzo-Dus et al., 2011; Pihlaja, 2019) have all been the subject of extensive linguistic analysis using a variety of methodological approaches. Spilioti (2018) provides a good overview of social media in English Language Studies.

In this section we will present an analysis of a recent and socio-politically significant process. The campaign to legalise abortion in Ireland as well as groups which opposed the move utilised the power of social networking to build support for their positions. The path to legislating for abortion access in Ireland was a decidedly modern one for both philosophical and practical reasons. Philosophically, the process was viewed as a very important part of a growing secularism in a country which had otherwise largely been guided by religious and socially conservative dogma. In practice, campaigns both in favour of and opposed to this modernisation utilised tools from across the multimodal spectrum. Images – some very controversial – accompanied text on billboards, placards and leaflets, and, alongside traditional political campaign mediums, like rallies, marches and public speeches, political groups harnessed the increasing power of social media to distribute their messages as widely as possible.

The Eighth Amendment to the Irish Constitution enshrined the illegality of abortion in Ireland in 1983. In the decades following the adoption of the Eighth Amendment, thousands of Irish women undertook traumatic journeys to Britain to access abortion services (abortion was legalised in Britain by the Abortion Act 1967). Bouvier (2019) analyses a Twitter profile created by two Irish women who travelled to Britain for the legal termination of a pregnancy in 2016. @TwoWomenTravel documented the harrowing and yet prosaic elements of this experience, such as airports and non-descript hotel rooms, alongside the medical context, and generated 40,000 tweets over two days. The too well-trodden journey across the Irish sea was one focus of the campaign to repeal the Eighth Amendment in Ireland, which was achieved by a referendum in May 2018. The campaign to retain the amendment has been viewed as representative of an endorsement of the traditional, largely Catholic values which dominated in Ireland in the twentieth century, and the campaign to repeal it as representative of a rejection of these values in favour of more secular and socially liberal principles also represented by the legalisation of gay marriage in 2015. (For a wider discussion of the Irish abortion issue, see Earner-Byrne and Urquhart [2019]. Mullally [2018] presents an account of aspects of the campaign to repeal the Eighth Amendment from the 1980s until 2018.)

Both sides in the abortion debate utilised social media as part of their campaigns. The main pro-choice movement was known as 'Together for Yes' (@Together4Yes). The anti-choice campaign was represented by a number of largely religious groups. The 'Love Both' (@lovebothireland) campaign was led by the organisation Pro Life Campaign, a once-prominent group founded in Dublin in 1992 to resist any legislation aimed at increasing a woman's right to choose throughout the subsequent decades. Statham and Ringrow (forthcoming, 2022) analyse how each campaign used language on the social media platform Twitter in an attempt to persuade audiences of the legitimacy of their arguments utilising the Appraisal framework and conceptual metaphor theory. In this section we will reproduce some of the findings of this analysis with particular reference to the Appraisal framework (you might want to revisit Chapter 4 for a full overview of the model) to demonstrate one way in which you can conduct a CDA of social media language. The discourse arena of Twitter has certain characteristics which make the Appraisal framework an appropriate model of analysis to unlock some of the persuasive strategies at work. Appraisal is a lexical-semantic model, so it is particularly focussed on the meanings, inscribed and invoked, of lexical items. Lexis is at a premium on Twitter because posts, or 'tweets', have a 140-character limit (Twitter started to increase this limit to 280 characters for some users in 2017). Our discussion here will also comment on the use of the hashtag in these tweets.

The hashtag convention on Twitter also enhances the importance of the lexicon as it is used to mark topics and is searchable. Zappavigna (2014, 2015) has examined the use of the hashtag on Twitter at length and demonstrates that the convention, as well as marking what a post is about, has interpersonal functions.

It can 'resonate across an entire post to construe an evaluative comment' (Zappavigna, 2015:279); consider usages like #soproud or #soashamed (and all the other potential constructions), where explicit evaluation of a post or a retweet is offered. This convention now transcends Twitter and is used conversationally when people verbalise the convention by saying things like 'Hashtag so lame', perhaps in interactions viewed as quintessentially 'teenaged' or even 'Gen Z', as well as on other social networking platforms like Facebook. The hashtag can also construct connections between users who do not actually interact with one another by 'coordinating mass expression of value by focusing rallying affiliation' around a certain subject, such as #coffee (Zappavigna, 2014:151). #savethe8th featured often on the Twitter homepage of Love Both throughout the campaign, whilst #unjustbill and #amendthebill were prominent after the referendum had passed but abortion access had yet to be legislated in parliament. #repealthe8th made the opposite plea on the page of Together for Yes with messages like #together4tomorrow and #HometoVote (many Irish people living abroad returned home to vote in the referendum) also prominent.

11.3.1 Together for Yes

Statham and Ringrow (forthcoming, 2022) analyse the tweets posted by Together for Yes and Love Both on Twitter in the last five days of the referendum campaign. The discussion in this chapter is based on the last twenty tweets posted by each group before the vote. For copyright and privacy reasons only the text of these tweets is analysed, and the many retweets and endorsements posted to the page by celebrities from as diverse areas of public life as Gary Lineker, Emma Watson and Nigella Lawson and by the hundreds of private citizens who posted to the page on this date are omitted.

1. Dublin is shining #together4yes tonight. Thanks @Siptu! Tomorrow we vote together. #together2vote #together4yes [Tweet accompanied by photograph of Liberty Hall on the Dublin quays lit up in suffragette colours.]
2. This time tomorrow polls will close. Have you planned the time you will vote tomorrow? There's still time to call your family and friends and have the conversation about why a Yes vote is important. #together2vote #together4yes
3. A woman you love needs your YES tomorrow. Polls are open from 7am until 10pm. Make sure you plan to vote and bring your family with you. This is a once in a generation opportunity. Let's do this. [Tweet accompanied by video of members of the public saying, 'Vote yes' to camera and listing those for whom they are voting, such as 'My daughters' or 'My friends'.]
4. We are bowled over by the wonderful #HometoVote crowd. Look at the wonderful @repeal-clad crew arriving. #together4yes #together2vote [Tweet accompanied by video of crowds arriving at Dublin airport wearing the iconic black and white 'Repeal' jumper.]

5. Dr Marian Dyer, one of the GPs signed up to our petition, speaks about her experiences dealing with patients who, for their own reasons, end a pregnancy, and how the 8th amendment affects the care she can give them. [Tweet accompanied by interview with Dr Marian Dyer.]
6. 35 years changed nothing. One day can change everything. This is a once in a lifetime chance. Vote Yes tomorrow. #Together2Vote
7. This referendum means so much to so many. Women's health matters. Vote Yes for compassionate change.
8. As our thousands of volunteers are out across the country, one last push to bring compassion home [Tweet accompanied by video interview with leaders of Together for Yes.]
9. "Think of the women in your life and think of their lives and trust them". Thank you @davidmcw for standing up for women. #Men4Yes #Together2Vote [Tweet accompanied by video endorsement by David McWilliams, Irish economist and broadcaster.]
10. Every conversation counts. Ask your friends and family are they voting. This referendum will be tight and we need every Yes vote there is #Together4Yes #together2vote [Tweet accompanied by animation of conversations about the history of restrictions on abortion access.]
11. "I'm voting Yes for the women I love. I'm voting yes to support women and allow doctors to do their jobs. A yes means a better Ireland for women." Deidre Duffy, campaign manager's final words before the moratorium #together4yes #together2vote
12. Abortion is a reality. 9 women a day travel for an abortion. 2 women a day take pills at home, alone. Both sides agree this. This is what we are voting on tomorrow, supporting women at home, with their own doctors.
13. This is it, the final push for Yes. We have a once in a lifetime opportunity to make Ireland a safer place for women and girls. Let's do it. #Together4Yes #Together2Vote [Tweet accompanied by photograph of campaigners pushing a Yes badge up a hill.]
14. The vote tomorrow is going to be tight. We need #Men4Yes to stand with the women in their lives and to make a once in a lifetime change to improve care in this country. #Together2vote #Together4Yes
15. We're hearing about flights of Yes voters coming from all corners of the globe. 5 people are on a plane from Buenos Aires, voters are flying in from Iraq&Syria and a couple are cutting their honeymoon short to return from Japan. We are #Togethertovote [Tweet accompanied by campaign video to encourage Irish citizens to return home and the singing of the suffrage poem 'Bread and Roses' by James Oppenheim.]
16. It's time we finally addressed the reality of abortion. #together2vote #together4yes
17. By voting Yes we can finally deal with the reality that abortion happens in Ireland and ensure that we can support and care for women in Ireland who need it [Tweet accompanied by photograph of campaign directors.]
18. On May 25th we come together. Tomorrow let's do better. Be caring and compassionate. Tomorrow we vote together. Together to vote. Together

for yes [Tweet accompanied by campaign video which references lack of women's rights alongside culturally iconic features of Ireland.]
19. We need to embrace women in crisis pregnancy. We need to wrap our arms around them here in Ireland and allow our doctors to support them, a strong closing statement by @ailbhes on @BreakfastNT #together4yes #together2vote
20. Ireland is not the UK, although interestingly some who oppose repeal don't have a problem with women relying on the UK system. We need to support women at home with their own doctors @ailbhes on @BreakfastNT #together4yes #together2vote

The Appraisal analysis and examination of the use of hashtags in the tweets is carried out by assessing one-by-one how each tweet construes evaluation and by identifying connections between each tweet. In this analysis, the decision to focus on the last days of campaigning was based on the fact that opinion polls showed this campaign being very close late into the proceedings, but the pro-choice vote was eventually carried by 66.4%. It was assumed therefore that late campaigning strategies were particularly important.

These tweets demonstrate the prolific use of the hashtag convention on Twitter. Ten of these tweets include (with occasional spelling variation) both #together2vote and #together4yes, a further three use #together2vote on its own and tweet 4 (figures refer to tweets in the numbered list) uses both hashtags as well as #HometoVote. The hashtag therefore constructs cohesion across the posts on the page. These hashtags are also used frequently by the personal tweets not included here, connecting tweets through the 'rallying affiliation' noted by Zappavigna (2014:151). Most of these users are not directly interacting but they are promoting very similar messages which are unified through the prominence of the hashtag. Use of the hashtag has somewhat transcended Twitter so that this feature is now prominent across social media.

The hashtags #together4yes and #together2vote contribute strongly to the construction of solidarity by this campaign. The word 'together' appears thirty times either separately or as part of a hashtag in these twenty tweets alone and is obviously also present in the name of the campaign. 'Together' operates pragmatically as well as semantically because whilst describing solidarity it simultaneously constructs it. It is an appeal as well as a description. In terms of Appraisal, Statham and Ringrow (forthcoming, 2022) conclude that the Together for Yes campaign persuaded voters through arguments of judgement in particular and social sanction: propriety was prominent in presenting a Yes vote as the morally right action. Social sanction: propriety is at the core of arguments which call voters to create 'compassionate change' (7), 'think of the women in your life' (9), 'bring compassion home' (8), 'support women' (11), 'supporting women at home' (12), 'make Ireland a safer place for women and girls' (13), 'improve care in this country' (14), 'support and care for women in Ireland' (17), 'be caring and compassionate' (18), 'embrace women in crisis pregnancy' (19), 'wrap our arms around them here in Ireland' (19) and 'support women at home' (20). The dominant themes in the Together for Yes campaign were decidedly focussed on the lack of abortion access in Ireland as a restriction on the rights of women, and the campaign constructs 'support', 'care' and 'compassion' as moral necessities to 'improve' the lives of women in Ireland.

Social sanction: veracity is also prominent in tweets which call for the addressing of the 'reality of abortion' (16) and which state that 'abortion is a reality' (12). Campaigners to repeal the Eighth Amendment reiterated consistently throughout the campaign that the idea that the amendment meant that there was no abortion in Ireland was untruthful. They argued that abortion restrictions did not signal some form of moral superiority but rather that by forcing women to rely 'on the UK system' (20) they were hypocritical and unsafe. The journeys of Irish people coming home to vote (15, with the #HometoVote hashtag) provided a poignant counterpoint to the journeys of women travelling abroad to secure abortion access.

The referendum itself is constructed through positive appreciation: valuation. It is presented to voters as a profound and historical moment through the repetition of certain parallel constructions in 'once in a generation opportunity' (3), 'once in a lifetime chance' (6), 'this referendum means so much to so many' (7), 'once in a lifetime opportunity' (13) and 'once in a lifetime change' (14). In these phrases we can see the connection between different types of evaluation. In presenting the vote as being of profound value, the campaign also reasserts that voters have a moral responsibility to avail of the 'opportunity' the vote represents. Alongside the parallelism in these clauses, we can also note in these tweets the use of other linguistic devices prominent in the language of political persuasion (see Chapter 8), such as the recurring use of direct address and inclusive pronouns ('Let's do this', 3).

Online contexts mean that language can operate across the entire 'multimodal ensemble' (Page et al., 2014:16), and we have noted here the campaign material in different semiotic modes which accompany the tweets. Social networks allow users to attach images and videos to textual content to significantly increase the persuasive value of posts. Certainly, campaign videos are not a new phenomenon, but modern technologies allow for cheaper and more efficient production, and social networks mean that they are consistently accessible rather than being restricted to specific timeslots on radio or television. The Together for Yes campaign strengthened their messages of solidarity and citizenship through the videos attached to some of the tweets discussed here.

Tweet 3, for example, which combines the campaign's major moral messages of compassion and responsibility ('A woman you love needs your YES tomorrow') with direct address ('Let's do this', 'bring your family with you') and provides information on voting times, is accompanied by a video of 'ordinary citizens', men and women of all age groups, who compose a decidedly modern Dublin streetscape speaking directly to camera and listing the loved ones for whom they will be supporting the referendum. The video significantly enhances the ability of the accompanying text to appeal directly to voters and therefore reinforces the campaign's central messages. Tweet 15, which describes the global effort of the repeal campaign and contrasts sharply with the less hopeful journeys of Irish women travelling abroad for a termination analysed by Bouvier (2019), is accompanied by a video explaining the rights of Irish citizens abroad to vote in the referendum. The video commences by showing Irish people waking up in cities around the world, particularly in Britain and the United States, where there are large Irish communities, packing their luggage and waiting in early morning train stations and airports to go home to vote and traces their journeys to Dublin. Each person makes a direct appeal to the camera at the end of the video. An Irish version of the suffragette song 'Bread and Roses' is played as the audience travels home with the voters. This video therefore combines written text through these comments with the film and music, exploiting several modes of persuasion simultaneously. The video is linked to the celebratory scenes in tweet 4, which shows the '#HometoVote crowd' being greeted at airport arrivals. These videos, eminently analysable in their own right, add significantly to the message of solidarity constructed by the repeal campaign and were seen as a major boost for voter turnout, not always high in Irish elections but 64.13% in this referendum. Many of the comments on these tweets in particular referred to the fact that voters at home should not abstain when others were undertaking expensive journeys to support the campaign and that undecided voters should use their vote for a 'woman you love'.

11.3.2 Love Both

Below are the last twenty tweets from the Love Both Twitter account on 25th May 2018, the day of the referendum, again with personal tweets and retweets omitted.

1. To #repealthe8th would bring abortion on demand to Ireland. It means ending the lives of babies up to 3 months for any reason whatsoever. We can't let this happen. #LoveBothVoteNO #Savethe8th #TooFarForMe #8thref
2. #8thref isn't about abortion in limited cases. It's about abortion on demand for any reason. Only a NO VOTE can stop this. County Louth needs to have its voice heard. Bring your friends and family with you to #VoteNO today. #LoveBothVoteNO: loveboth.ie/voting-guide/ [Tweet accompanied by video of a single voter from Louth urging a No vote to 'make a difference'.]
3. #TooMuchForMe #8thAmendment [Tweet accompanied by sample ballot paper with email address and telephone number of Love Both attached.]
4. Find your polling place and #VoteNO: loveboth.ie/voting-guide/ [Tweet accompanied by campaign video of an ultrasound with audible foetal heartbeat and the message 'don't stop it'.]
5. #VoteNO today: loveboth.ie/voting-guide/ [Tweet accompanied by graphic of the 'facts' of a Yes vote.]

SOCIAL MEDIA LANGUAGE AND POWER

6. #8thref isn't about abortion in limited cases. It's about abortion on demand for any reason. Only a NO VOTE can stop this. County Westmeath needs to have its voice heard. Bring your friends and family with you to #VoteNO today. #LoveBothVoteNO: loveboth.ie/voting-guide/ [Tweet accompanied by video of a single voter from Westmeath describing abortion on the 'same grounds as in Britain'.]
7. Don't wait…your NO vote is needed now! Find your polling place and #VoteNO: loveboth.ie/voting-guide/ #LoveBothVoteNO #TooFarForMe #8thref #IvotedNo [Tweet accompanied by 'Vote No Today' GIF.]
8. #8thref isn't about abortion in limited cases. It's about abortion on demand for any reason. Only a NO VOTE can stop this. County Laois needs to have its voice heard. Bring your friends and family with you to #VoteNO today. #LoveBothVoteNO: loveboth.ie/voting-guide/ [Tweet accompanied by video of a single voter from Laois describing 'abortion on the same grounds as Britain'.]
9. ALERT: We need your NO vote. Find your polling location, bring three friends and #VoteNO now. #LoveBothVoteNO #TooFarForMe #8thref #IvotedNo [Tweet accompanied by 'Alert' GIF.]
10. Abortion on demand for 12 weeks is TOO extreme. #VoteNO: loveboth.ie/voting-guide/ #LoveBothVoteNO #TooFarForMe #IvotedNo [Tweet accompanied by video by a GP condemning 'Yes campaign misinformation' and 'British-style abortion'.]
11. #8thref isn't about abortion in limited cases. It's about abortion on demand for any reason. Only a NO VOTE can stop this. County Limerick needs to have its voice heard. Bring your friends and family with you to #VoteNO today. #LoveBothVoteNO: loveboth.ie/voting-guide/ [Tweet accompanied by video of a single voter from Limerick describing 'abortion on the same grounds as Britain'.]
12. The Government's plan is TOO extreme. Listen to @CllrKRedmond's viewpoint and then #VoteNO loveboth.ie/voting-guide/ #LoveBothVoteNo #TooFarForMe #IvotedNo [Tweet accompanied by video of local councillor describing the proposed bill as 'even more extreme than Britain' and 'just too extreme'.]
13. Many local newspapers around the country have been showing a big interest in the NO vote. Thank you! #LoveBothVoteNo #TooFarForMe [Tweet accompanied by photographs of newspaper interviews with citizens and healthcare professionals who oppose 'abortion on demand'.]
14. #LoveBothVoteNO #TooFarForMe #IvotedNo [Tweet accompanied by image of 'It's Too Extreme' election advertisement.]
15. Cycling lovers are asking voters who cycle to polling stations to take a photo of their bicycles and post it on social media using the hashtag #IbikeIVote #LoveBothVoteNo #prolifeProBike
16. #8thref isn't about abortion in limited cases. It's about abortion on demand for any reason. Only a NO VOTE can stop this. County Offaly needs to have its voice heard. Bring your friends and family with you to #VoteNO today. #LoveBothVoteNO: loveboth.ie/voting-guide/ [Tweet

accompanied by video of a single voter from Offaly describing abortion 'on the same grounds as Britain'.]
17. #TooFarForMe #IvotedNo [Tweet accompanied by photograph of and quotation from a No voter for whom 'abortion up to 12 weeks is too far'.]
18. "If we voted No we will force the Government to put in place a proper strategy to support all women and families facing unwanted or crisis pregnancies." @CoraSherlock huffingtonpost.co.uk/entry/irish-abortion #LoveBothVoteNo #8thAmendment [Tweet accompanied by image link to article from which quotation is taken.]
19. The Government's proposal is far too extreme. #VoteNO today: loveboth. ie/voting-guide/ RETWEET and tweet #TooFarForMe to help spread the word! #LoveBothVoteNo #IvotedNo [Tweet accompanied by a graphic of the 'facts' of a Yes vote.]
20. #8thref isn't about abortion in limited cases. It's about abortion on demand for any reason. Only a NO VOTE can stop this. County Donegal needs to have its voice heard. Bring your friends and family with you to #VoteNO today. #LoveBothVoteNO: loveboth.ie/voting-guide/ [Tweet accompanied by video of a single voter from Donegal describing abortion 'on similar grounds to Britain'.]

The tweets from Love Both also demonstrate a significant use of the hashtag; #LoveBothVoteNo is used in sixteen of the twenty tweets here, and #TooFarForMe features in ten tweets in this sample. Again, the hashtag constructs cohesion across the tweets here by connecting the official tweets of the campaign to the individuals who post to the page using the hashtag and in turn constructs affiliation between these users. The more general #8thref is also used ten times in these tweets, which is significant given that the hashtag is a searchable feature of Twitter. Users who therefore use this hashtag to search for information on the referendum without explicitly expressing a position, through #LoveBoth or #Together4Yes for example, will have these tweets included in the search results. This hashtag therefore is a potential way through which Love Both can increase the interaction of undecided voters or other observers – such as people from outside Ireland, for example – with their campaign material.

#TooFarForMe refers to a central tenet in the anti-choice movement's arguments against repealing the Eighth Amendment. They claimed that the proposal to legalise abortion up to twelve weeks of pregnancy was 'too extreme'. This was a major theme in their campaign literature, both online and in general; one infamous placard declared that the legislation was a 'licence to kill'. The phrase 'abortion on demand' invokes negative social sanction: propriety for conservative or religious voters and is present eight times in these twenty tweets. The government's proposal is consistently condemned as 'extreme' (tweets 10, 12, 14 and 19). This might be a negative judgement of social esteem: normality in some contexts, but Statham and Ringrow (forthcoming, 2022) classify 'too extreme' as negative social sanction: propriety given the seriousness of the context here.

Tweet 1 invokes strongly negative social sanction: propriety, for example in the sentence 'It means ending the lives of babies up to three months for any reason whatsoever'. The use of a foetal image in tweet 4 also aims to invoke a strong moral response. Foetal images appeared on a range of campaign material from the various No camps during the referendum campaign. Some showed images of aborted foetuses and were extremely controversial. Both campaigns therefore make strong moral arguments through social sanction. Tweet 10 is accompanied by a video interview with a GP who negatively judges 'Yes campaign misinformation' through social sanction: veracity.

Whilst the morality of Together for Yes is focussed on the rights of women, the Love Both campaign focusses instead on the effects of the legislation on pregnancies. The anti-choice movement faced a difficult task in arguing that they also represented women, despite the claim that retention of the amendment represented 'both' woman and child. The Eighth Amendment acknowledged the 'right to life of the unborn' on an equal footing with pregnant women and therefore severely limited the potential remit of any abortion legislation (there were several very limited bills in Dáil Éireann, the Irish parliament, between 1983 and 2018). Retention of the amendment meant that there would very little opportunity to 'make a difference', despite the claims of the video in tweet 2, for example. The quotation from Cora Sherlock, one of the leaders of the Pro Life Campaign, in tweet 18, whilst acknowledging 'unwanted or crisis pregnancies', refers euphemistically to a 'proper strategy to support', which therefore includes the presupposition that this will not equate to abortion access. Whilst there was a clear avenue through which the Yes campaign in the referendum could demonstrate that the amendment restricted the rights of women, the No campaign faced a conceptual problem here. Despite arguments in some campaign material, we can conclude that Love Both chose clearly to focus linguistically on 'babies' rather than pregnant women. References to the rights of women, which are abundant in the tweets from Together for Yes, are wholly absent in this sample from Love Both.

A particular comparison is drawn in the videos which accompany tweets 6, 8, 10, 11, 12, 16 and 20 with the legislative situation for abortion in Britain. This provides a recognisable comparison for potential voters, and phrases like 'even more extreme than Britain' (12) again use negative social sanction to condemn the proposed legislation. References to Britain by the anti-choice movement utilise the strategic function of misrepresentation (see Chapter 8) and contribute to the moral argument that the proposed legislation goes 'too far' by introducing 'abortion on demand'. Whilst the Yes campaign focussed on a healthcare-at-home message which called for the improvement of healthcare in Ireland, Love Both vilified the legislative arrangements for abortion access abroad. This strategy was effectively countered by Together for Yes, which consistently reminded voters of the 'reality of abortion' represented by Irish women forced to travel to Britain for a termination. Owing to its fairly consistent inability to offer an alternative to repeal – demonstrated by the euphemism of Cora Sherlock in tweet 18 and the lexical absence of women throughout its tweets – Love Both instead attacked the alternatives which did exist. Statham and Ringrow (forthcoming, 2022) point out that the overlexicalised focus on Britain reinforced a nationalistic agenda often used by conservative forces in Ireland to equate social change with being 'too British', which can invoke strongly negative judgements of social sanction given Britain's long colonial occupation of Ireland.

Love Both tweets also focussed heavily on the concept of the local, as opposed to the international focus of Together for Yes. Rather than focus on far-flung cities and airports, the content on Love Both's page is decidedly more prosaic. Tweet 15 calls for cyclists to post photographs of themselves with the hashtag #prolifeProBike, for example. The videos which accompany tweets 2, 6, 8, 11, 16 and 20 situate the Love Both campaign within Irish communities. The speakers are local people who attempt to draw on a county-based consensus which is strong in other aspects of Irish life, particularly sport. In an attempt to counter the tendency to equate the No campaign with conservative ideologies typically attached to older voters, the videos all feature younger members of the electorate, most of whom are women. On Love Both's page on the day of the referendum, seven similar tweets, with the same identical text and similarly focussed videos, were posted, in addition to the six featured in this sample. There was therefore a concerted effort to foreground the concept of Love Both as an example of community activism through these tweets and their accompanying videos.

This campaign was new territory for the anti-choice movement, which had generally enjoyed the support of very powerful Irish church and state apparatuses throughout the previous decades. By 2018 progressive movements like those for repeal of the Eighth Amendment and the legalisation of gay marriage, for so long hegemonically maligned in Ireland, had eclipsed their more conservative opposition movements in terms of both public and political support. Interestingly, the videos for the other thirteen Irish counties entitled to vote in the referendum do not feature on Love Both's page on the day of the referendum, a choice probably driven by certain electoral mathematics such as turnout and 'likely voter' figures. The videos for counties Dublin and Roscommon are unique in that, rather than young women, they are presented by men. Roscommon (as part of the Roscommon-Galway constituency) was the only area to oppose gay marriage in 2015, so the anti-choice movement may have been attempting to appeal to an ostensibly more traditional electorate (Roscommon-Galway supported repeal by 57.2%).

Like Together for Yes, we can see that Love Both utilised the potentiality of social media platforms to present campaign material in a range of linguistic modes. Indeed, they make a greater use of graphics and sample ballots, and they consistently refer the audience to the additional range of material on their website. The link loveboth.ie/voting-guide is included in twelve tweets in this sample. The ability of social media to embed URLs which link to other relevant or supporting content is a particular advantage which online platforms possess over offline contexts. Certainly, a physical newspaper or leaflet, for example, can contain a website address, but this content is much more readily accessible whilst a reader is already online.

11.4 Social Media in Context

The success of the movement for women's reproductive rights in Ireland must be set in historical, political and social context, particularly rising secularism and the decline of the influence of religious organisations in Ireland following decades of scandal and controversy. We should not underestimate the role of the internet in these processes, and social media platforms allowed the voices of Irish abortion rights campaigners to be heard much more widely than ever before. But also for the first time in Ireland the message of the campaigners found support in other places, such as in 'old media' and in political parties which are decidedly less progressive in other ways, particularly economically. Other movements which we have referred to in this book, such as the Remain campaign in Britain during the Brexit debate, have also had a significant online presence, but this did not prove decisive in the face of the influence possessed by traditional power bases when they held opposing positions. The same can be said of the referendum for Scottish independence in 2014 and the British general election in 2019, where the role of traditional media continued to hold sway. Online contexts represent significant potential for resistant forces to use language to further their aims, but ascendant groups have themselves adapted and also make importance use of language on the internet. The Twitter presence of Together for Yes and Love Both were influential parts of their respective campaigns. The success of the former in the referendum was aided by discourse online, and this should be viewed in context of the growing support for women's bodily autonomy in Ireland in general.

Summary of Chapter 11

The analysis of the sample tweets from Together for Yes and Love Both demonstrates the importance of social media in contemporary political campaigns. The analysis in turn should serve as a reminder that use of the internet is not the sole purview of reformers but is embraced equally by reactionary forces. These campaigns also directly illustrate some of the important points raised in the initial discussions of this chapter, particularly the fact that neither the pro-choice nor the anti-choice movements in Ireland emerged as the result of the internet but rather social media was utilised as an important site for furthering the agenda of these campaigns. The internet and social media platforms represent discourse arenas through which campaigns can enhance and increase their persuasiveness through text, images and video. The internet itself is not necessarily always a decisive factor in the emergence of such movements but it can be significant in increasing their sphere of influence and the avenues through which they can reach their audiences.

Further Reading

Martin, J.R. and White, P.R.R. (2005) *The Language of Evaluation: Appraisal in English*. Basingstoke: Palgrave Macmillan.
Mullally, U. (2018) *Repeal the 8th*. London: Unbound.
Earner-Byrne, L. and Urquhart, D. (2019) *The Irish Abortion Journey 1920–2018*. Basingstoke: Palgrave Macmillan.

12 Critical Discourse Analysis
Detractors and Defenders

KEY TERMS IN CHAPTER 12: corpus-assisted CDA, ethnomethodology, cognition

12.1 Introduction: Summarising the Book

The first chapter of this book provides a rationale for Critical Discourse Analysis, sets the discipline in context with the social and political theories which underpin it, particularly those established by Marx ([1933] 1965) and Gramsci (1971), and demonstrates how their views of 'ideology' and 'hegemony' relate to the construction, distribution and reinforcement of power. The sections of Chapter 1 discuss how power connects to language and illustrates through the manifesto for CDA offered by Fairclough and Wodak (1997) the dialogical relationship between language and the social world, in which language is recognised for the ideological role it performs in its operation as 'discourse'. In Chapter 2 we demonstrate how language is used by powerful institutions to legitimise and normalise one set of principles over another in the discourse construction of social events by applying CDA in practice. The subject of the marketisation of higher education, an issue to which we return at several points in the book (see in particular Chapter 5), gives university students who are reading the book an immediate and recognisable point of contact with its aims and with the type of material which is addressed in the analysis throughout.

Chapters 1 and 2 could be read together as a treatise on CDA, addressing theory and practice and demonstrating that the elements of CDA's three-pronged approach to analysing power in language – by description, interpretation and explanation – require the analyst to engage fully with socio-political contexts when considering the operation of discourse. Each of the subsequent chapters demonstrate the scope of CDA by illustrating the range of models of analysis through which the critical focus of CDA is maintained. The book also makes clear just how many discourse arenas (and there are others which we have not been able to investigate here) are targeted by CDA and is welded throughout to the critical focus of the discipline. Fowler (1996:10) is clear that critical linguistic analysis must include 'full descriptions of context and its implications for beliefs and relationships'. Each chapter of this book, from the examination of the representation of industrial action in higher education in the British media in Chapter 2 to the analysis of persuasive language in the campaigns for and against reproductive rights in Ireland in Chapter 11, has engaged fully with the political contexts of the often controversial topics which form our data examples.

Chapter 3 investigates the representation of war in the press and links these constructions with the ideological agendas of powerful figures in government. Chapter 4 discusses environmental campaigns and political speeches. The analysis of two leaflets in Chapter 5 addresses political campaigns and the social construction of sexual assault. These Systemic Functional Linguistics chapters establish the methodological rigour which is provided to CDA by a focus on the experiential, interpersonal and textual functions of language, both respectively and simultaneously. They also remain committed to the importance of fully examining the role of discourse in society. Chapter 6 demonstrates how to assess the use of sources and voices in discourse and expands upon the discourse arena of the media, assessing the role of advertisers, owners and institutional practices. When we engage as readers or viewers with the language of the media – in print, on television or online – we are engaging with a product which carries with it a vast array of political features. Chapter 7 considers language and 'race' and looks forward to the extensive analysis of the political speech from Donald Trump which comprises Chapter 8. Chapter 9, on the political rhetoric of the Covid-19 pandemic, demonstrates how you can apply several models of analysis to discourse examples in a way that is rigorous linguistically and still fully cognisant of context. Some of the conclusions in this chapter in particular may be somewhat uncomfortable given the immediacy of the data. As pointed out in Chapter 1, it is our responsibility as critical discourse analysts to 'expose misrepresentation and discrimination in a variety of modes of public discourse' (Fowler, 1996:5), and we must not shy away from our part in the political process. This 'variety of modes' is set out in Chapter 10, and again rigorous analysis is used to fully address the ideological operation of the images which are discussed. Chapter 11 demonstrates how CDA has been applied to the most recently emerging multimodal discourse arena, social media.

12.2 The Development of CDA: Responding to the Critics

This book has aimed to be both a comprehensive example of Critical Discourse Analysis in theory and practice and an advocate for the discipline as both linguistically rigorous and politically motivated. The critical focus of CDA is unapologetic in terms of this motivation and, when considered alongside the wide range of models of analysis which fall under the scope of CDA, perhaps it is not surprising that the discipline has occasionally caused some 'friction among scholars'

(Pihlaja, 2018:385). This section will address some of the criticisms which have been levelled at CDA and outline ways in which the discipline has developed in recent years in response to these criticisms.

Most of the criticisms of CDA are interconnected and relate to both the composition and the form of the analysis carried out by critical discourse analysts. Firstly, there are those detractors who view CDA as an exercise in selective interpretation of 'fragmentary and exemplificatory data' (Hart, 2014:39). Other discontents claim that CDA is too qualitative, that it does not engage sufficiently with real readers and listeners and that it is ultimately too ambitious in terms of its quest for social change (Machin and Mayr, 2012:208). Some of these criticisms might seem immediately problematic if you are coming to this chapter having engaged fully with the eleven chapters which have come before it. Others will require some additional discussion and explanation. In some cases, proponents of CDA have acknowledged the shortcomings of certain aspects of the discipline and, like scholars in most fields of academic endeavour, have continuously sought to improve the methods used by critical discourse analysts.

12.2.1 Selection and Interpretation of Data

Firstly, let us consider the criticism of data, that the discourses which comprise CDA are too selective and qualitative. This relates to the notion that CDA selects data for analysis with certain *a priori* motivations intact so that the conclusions which ostensibly result from linguistic analysis are predetermined because the analyst has chosen an obviously contentious text to suit her/his purposes. This criticism implies in turn that certain patterns in the text may be ignored in favour of those which support predetermined conclusions. Widdowson (2004:102), one of the most outspoken critics of CDA, says that too often texts for analysis are 'cherry picked' and that they therefore may not be representative. In addition, Stubbs (1997) questions the rigour of CDA, which focusses on individual texts rather than larger data sets.

Certainly, there might seem to be validity to some of these claims when considering the analysis in this book. The texts chosen in certain topics have been selected to demonstrate a number of problematic ideologies, such as racism in the right wing press (Chapter 7) or the normalisation of victim blaming in sexual assault cases (Chapter 5), for example. We look at two pieces of political discourse from millions in Chapters 8 and 9, and only at a limited number of images in Chapter 10. However, this is a textbook and has as one of its main purposes to be as illustrative and instructive as possible when presenting models of analysis. There would be very little point in a textbook which aims to inform students about models of analysis and set out those models in detail, and then does not select texts which contain an abundance of certain features.

12.2.2 Examples of Real-world Discourse in CDA

More particularly, and this point relates both to this book and to CDA more generally, the texts which are presented for analysis are real and not invented examples of social discourses. One of the main shortcomings identified in certain fields of linguistic analysis, particularly in early work in linguistic pragmatics such as the conversational cooperation model of Grice (1975) or early iterations of speech act theory (Austin, 1962), even though these are recognised as trailblazing and continue to be applied, is that they do not use examples of real text but rather engage with invented examples. A similar criticism cannot be levelled at CDA or at critical linguistics generally, which has demystified real-language examples right from its origins in *Language and Control* (Fowler, Hodge, Kress and Trew, 1979). It is a rather simple point, perhaps, but it is also worth pointing out the ready availability of texts for CDA. There are plentiful texts available for analysis which demonstrate the operation of ideologies that uphold the unfair organisation of society largely along economic lines. Of course, this is at least partly down to the prominence of this lack of fairness in society in the first place. Even the loudest detractors of CDA presumably would not deny the stranglehold of free market capitalism or the prominence of classism, racism and misogyny. Certainly CDA is motivationally preoccupied with exposing and indeed standing against the myriad of malignant principles by which society has largely been organised. The prominence of these principles is the result of the power relations explained in Chapter 1. We can accept that CDA approaches the analysis of texts with a particular set of aims in mind; as Fowler (1996:5) puts it, 'The goals of critical linguists are in general terms defamiliarisation or consciousness-raising', and we are concerned with raising consciousness of inequality. You should remember that these inequalities are seemingly omnipresent, that their exposure is something worth pursuing and that those responsible for them sit at the apex of power.

This is not to suggest that the detractors of CDA position themselves as defenders of society. They do not explicitly suggest that the inequalities exposed by CDA do not exist, only that critical discourse analysts allow them to influence their selection and interpretation of texts. In response, we acknowledge that CDA is indeed politically motivated but argue that there are other clarifications required here both in terms of data and analysis. Hart (2014:41) points out that many of the 'well-founded criticisms' of CDA tend to be disproportionately directed at early analyses of the discipline and are less relevant when one accounts for the developments in linguistic analysis more generally which have been embraced by CDA.

12.2.3 Corpus-assisted CDA

One of those significant developments has been the growth in corpus linguistics, the expansion of which has been the direct result of technological developments in recent decades. Corpus linguistics allows for the efficient collection and analysis of very large bodies of texts and can therefore be used to confirm the presence of certain ideologies across very large data sets, such as articles from a single or multiple newspapers over a period of years or all of the political speeches of a single politician or political party. These quantitative methods of analysis mean that the analyst can compare the content of a single text or of a specific corpus (say of newspaper articles) with a larger reference corpus – such as the British National Corpus (BNC), which contains 100 million words of spoken and written text, or the Corpus of Contemporary American (COCA), which contains 450 million words – to determine similarities and deviations. The technological developments which have given rise to the collection of large corpora have also accommodated the emergence of specific tools to investigate certain aspects of these word banks. For example, analysts can examine individual words and their collocates by carrying out a 'key word in context' (KWIC) analysis, which focusses on a selected window of words which accompany a key word in a corpus. In the context of some of the analysis in this book, it might be interesting to examine how often in his political speeches Donald Trump uses the word 'Muslim' and which words appear most frequently alongside it, or we could construct a corpus of the language of university websites and consider how often and with which collocates words like 'innovation' and 'enterprise' are present. A corpus on global institutions could be constructed, as well as individual corpora for institutions in different jurisdictions, so we could investigate deviations between the text for Zayed University (Chapter 5) and other higher education organisations in the Middle East and those in Europe, for example.

Therefore corpus linguistic analysis gives us 'some very broad, yet rigorous, analyses of sometimes eye-watering swathes of textual material' (Simpson, 2014:47) and can also provide utilisations which answer some of the specific criticisms directed at CDA. Garzone and Santulli (2004:73) note that CDA could have 'the problem of the representativeness of the sample of language analysed and the need to check the hypotheses developed in a qualitative analysis against empirically verifiable data'. Corpus linguistics can provide a solution to both issues, and critical discourse analysts have been consistent in their adoption of corpus linguistic techniques to strengthen the discipline so that a growing number of **'corpus-assisted critical discourse analysis'** (Baker et al., 2008) works have emerged. Gabrielatos and Baker (2008) constructed a corpus of British newspaper representations of refugees over a ten-year period, and the analysis in Chapter 7 located a number of the broad categories identified by this corpus in an article from the *Daily Express*. Gabrielatos and Baker's quantitative methodology by definition did not engage specifically with one newspaper over another but rather offered eight categories for the media construction of refugees across the spectrum of the press. The location of these categories within the article analysed in Chapter 7 strengthens the conclusions reached by the analysis because we can make a claim of representativeness based on the verifiable data in the corpus. This is an example of how quantitative and qualitative analysis can be married in CDA. Another example of corpus-assisted CDA is the use of preexisting databases when selecting data for analysis. Statham (2016) carries out a corpus exercise using the newspaper database Nexis UK in order to establish the representativeness of data before undertaking qualitative analysis of a range of media constructions of crime using established methods in CDA. As this work is focussed on how certain types of crime are defined in the media, a search of the database focusses on newspaper headlines which explicitly mention crimes like 'robbery' and 'murder', and the subsequent analysis then applies CDA to individual articles which can be offered as representative of, in this case, British and American media in general.

Despite the additional verifiability offered to CDA by corpus linguistics, Gabrielatos and Baker (2008:33) acknowledge that the analyst must still 'make sense of the linguistic patterns thrown up via the corpus-based processes'. It would not be accurate therefore to claim that the interestedness of the analyst is eliminated by corpus-assisted CDA; we know that CDA does not make claims on unachievable objectivity in any case. In addition, Fairclough (2015) notes that, whilst corpus linguistics offers statistical findings on features of texts and the use of lexical items within them, it is not in and of itself an analytical method which makes sense of the statistics; this is for the analyst to do. In the development of the discipline of 'critical stylistics', Jeffries (2010, 2014) somewhat detaches analytical methods from the more politically motivated intentions of CDA by setting out how to locate ideologies in a text whether or not the analyst approves of them. Machin and Mayr (2012:216) state that the adoption of corpus linguistics has been the 'most marked change in CDA' in recent decades, and it provides a robust response to those who have criticised the discipline for a lack of representativeness and for being overly qualitative. It should be noted that, whilst the adoption of corpus linguistic methods has strengthened the conclusions of CDA, it has not fundamentally altered them. As pointed out above, the inequalities exposed by CDA remain plentiful. Corpus linguistics assists CDA in this exposure and makes the resultant conclusions stronger.

12.2.4 Analytical Rigour in CDA

A criticism closely connected to the notion that data in CDA is too selective is that conclusions which emerge from the analysis are too interpretive. Widdowson (1995:159) has gone so far as to state that in CDA 'interpretation of belief takes precedence over analysis in support of theory'. The essence of this complaint is that critical discourse analysts privilege certain meanings over others when carrying out an analysis. As we have noted already, a similar apprehension has been raised in terms of the selection of data, and the adoption of corpus linguistic techniques also offers part of the solution to the interpretive criticism. Analysts who employ corpus-assisted CDA do not simply select texts which they know to be contentious in the first place. This of course only goes some of the way in addressing the accusation of excessive interpretation, because, of course, a quantitative-qualitative analysis could choose to disproportionately focus on one part of a text even if the selection of that text has been determined by a corpus exercise. This would obviously be more difficult for an exercise which is entirely quantitative, although even in these cases the parameters of the search are set by the analyst. We have noted already that the elimination of the analyst's motivation is neither entirely possible nor desirable within CDA anyway, although it is still somewhat disingenuous to claim that the discipline lacks rigorous explanation.

We can offer a number of points to support this statement. Firstly, CDA is consistently focussed on comparative analysis and potential alternative meanings, and many established works in CDA focus on competing discourse constructions of the same occurrence. Comparative analysis has been a bedrock of critical linguistic methodology from the seminal examination offered by Trew (1979) of articles in *The Times* and *The Guardian* (see further Chapter 1) and is utilised often by critical discourse analysts in both research and pedagogical contexts. Comparative analyses demonstrate the analyst's awareness of divergent ideologies, and this goes some way to reduce subjectivity. What is most important in this vein is the fact that critical discourse analysts are consistent – as this book has stated often – in their recognition of the fact that no discourse example exists outside of ideology or that it can offer a neutral or disinterested perspective. This applies to discourse with which broadly socialist proponents of CDA might find affinity and to those which contain ideologies which we might find disagreeable.

A similar principle guides examinations of texts which offer alternative textual representations to those we are analysing. At several times in this book it has been pointed out that discourse examples could have been lexically or grammatically different, for example. This method is a core trajectory by which CDA questions legitimised elements of discourse. As Fowler (1996:4) puts it, critical linguistics 'challenges common sense by pointing out that something could have been represented some other way, with a very different significance'. CDA goes beyond accusations of bias by arguing that this is really only an inevitable aspect of discourse. Even the texts with which we might agree are ideological, and these ideologies can be equally uncovered by linguistic analysis. Fowler (1996:4) confirms that 'there is not necessarily any true reality that can be unveiled by critical practice'. Critical discourse analysts do not criticise the discourse of politicians or media organisations as 'untruthful' and then claim to provide 'truth' ourselves; instead we expose the ideologies which are operable in the texts we target for analysis. Corpus linguistics can increase the representativeness of those texts, whilst carrying out comparative analysis of multiple texts or offering alternative constructions to the linguistic make-up of texts reduces subjective or singular interpretations of the discourse representation of events in the social world.

12.3 The Role of the Reader

A significant development in CDA in recent years which specifically answers one of Widdowson's (1995, 1996) core complaints about the discipline is the use of **ethnomethodological approaches**. Widdowson has argued that CDA is overly dependent on the ideology of the analyst and that analyses ignore the experience of real readers. Obviously, all of the analyses included in this book have referred consistently to the reader/listener experience, and the theory outlined in Chapter 1 explains why these examinations can draw conclusions about reader/listener interpretations. However, Widdowson would argue that this is insufficient as real readers have not been consulted.

12.3.1 Ethnomethodology in CDA

CDA has acknowledged the potential to further enhance verifiability by engaging with reader response and other types of relevant data and has adopted certain ethnomethodological approaches to strengthen conclusions. Machin and van Leeuwen (2007) included interviews with designers of video games, and Machin and Niblock's (2008) work on the visual marketing of newspapers includes interviews with text producers and editors. We must remember that ethnomethodology is not just about readers and listeners but also about writers and speakers. In terms of readers, Benwell (2005) for example analyses reader responses to men's lifestyle magazines. This type of analysis has become more straightforward with the advent of computer mediated communication. Many news websites in particular now allow readers to comment on stories, so the analyst has access to a depository of reader-response data which might previously have been practically more difficult to acquire. The element of anonymity offered to readers in online contexts and the fact that they are in more natural rather than controlled environments, say in a lecture theatre, might also enhance the reliability of their responses. We saw, albeit in a limited way, in the discussion of the Volkswagen advertisement in Chapter 10 that reader/viewer impressions of a piece of discourse can be very useful in an analysis. Other linguistic disciplines, particularly literary linguistics, have also increased their interactions with reader-response data in recent years (Whiteley and Canning, 2017).

12.3.2 Cognition in CDA

Another way in which CDA and related disciplines, again stylistics and literary linguistics in particular (Stockwell, 2020), have increasingly engaged with the role of the reader is through **cognitive linguistics**. Hart (2014:41) states that cognitive linguistics can 'reduce subjectivity and demonstrate cognitive import by grounding analyses in psychologically plausible, potentially testable models', acknowledging that by examining cognition, the way that readers understand text, we can appropriate perspectives from psychology to strengthen the conclusions reached by linguistics. Van Dijk (see particularly Chapter 7) is a major figure in CDA who offers longstanding arguments that the discipline should pay more attention to socio-cognitive elements which mediate between discourse and the social world. The 'discourse-historical approach' of Wodak is also interested in reader interpretations alongside several other elements of methodology which essentially attempt to strengthen textual analysis by a comprehensive engagement with historical and ethnomethodological information. Like much of van Dijk's work (1991, 1993), the discourse-historical approach has been particularly interested in the cognitive component of racism (Van Leeuwen and Wodak, 1999).

In the development of a critical-forensic linguistic interface for the analysis of the concept of trial by media, Statham (2016) attempts to reconcile some perceived mismatches between CDA and cognitive approaches to language. Fairclough (2001:9) has argued that some studies in cognition lean too heavily towards individualism and have given 'little attention to the social origins or significance of MR'. 'MR' refers to Fairclough's concept of 'members' resources', the representations which readers/listeners have stored in their long-term memory and use when understanding and interpreting language and events. Classic studies in cognition (Schank and Abelson, 1977; Schank, 1982) are focussed on the role of memory in the process of understanding and do not focus on the social roles of language, although they do acknowledge the importance of context in interpretation, whilst critical linguistic approaches are obviously very focussed on these. Analyses which are interested in the processes through which people understand events and which also acknowledge that the mental representations, usually called schemata, possessed by language users are partly the result of how events in society are constructed and reinforced by discourse bring cognitive and critical linguistics together in a way which pays attention to both social contexts and the mental role of the reader. Fowler (1996:11) envisaged such a relationship in stating that if 'we give the reader a more prominent role in our model [critical linguistics], it will be appropriate to look at the various kinds of schemata which have developed in cognitive psychology and Artificial Intelligence'. It is exactly these types of analysis which have developed through works like Statham (2016), Browse (2018), which utilises cognitive linguistics to analyse audience reception of political discourse, and Koller and Ryan (2019), which analyses metaphor in media coverage of the Brexit referendum. Metaphor (see further Chapter 8) involves mapping between two conceptual domains and is another important example of where CDA has engaged with cognitive methodologies to consider the role of the reader. Charteris-Black (2004) combines corpus and cognitive linguistics in a critical metaphor analysis of party political manifestos and Charteris-Black (2014) analyses metaphor in political speeches.

12.4 Methodological Diversity of CDA

CDA therefore has engaged heavily with the role of the reader through ethnomethodology and cognitive linguistics, and work in corpus-assisted CDA demonstrates attendance to concerns about representativeness and partiality of data. You will note that many of the references to work in this chapter are more recent than those that have looked to point out apparent flaws in CDA, which is itself an indication of the willingness of the discipline to address some well-founded criticisms.

Some of these criticisms recall concerns from within critical linguistics itself, particularly around the need for linguistic methodologies to be as rigorous and replicable as possible. Fowler (1996:6) expresses the concern that critical linguistic work 'in the hands of practitioners of diverse intellectual persuasions will come to mean loosely any politically well-intentioned work on language and ideology' and that the technical method must be consolidated to ensure against such as scenario. Widdowson (1998:137) states that CDA is a 'kind of ad hoc bricolage which takes from theory whichever concept comes usefully to hand'. Given the range of models presented in this book alone, for example, you might somewhat acknowledge arguments that CDA is too diverse or that some of the models utilised by critical discourse analysts are too divergent from others. You should remember, however, that this is not in and of itself problematic and that it is important that diversity is not simply taken to mean a lack of rigour. There are, after all, many disciplines within linguistics and other fields of study which utilise a very wide range of models. In the right circumstances, this is generally accepted as a mark of in-depth scholarly endeavour and not as an indicator of inconsistency. Diversity of approaches to analysis should not be seen as problematic where clear models are outlined and applied. Fowler warns that methodological diversity should not give rise to merely casual application of language models. He also reminds us that any work which seeks to expose ideology in text does not automatically count as 'critical linguistics'. The work must be linguistically rigorous. If you consult the works which have been referenced in this book and consider the models which we have applied in the last eleven chapters, it is clear that CDA does not merely pay lip service to rigorous analysis. These models are replicable and can be applied to a range of texts. Indeed, it has been demonstrated here that conclusions are strengthened when a discourse is examined by multiple models.

Summary of Chapter 12

Each of the texts analysed in this book have been subject to close, modelled analyses alongside an extensive consideration of their societal operation. Critical discourse analysts are clear that it is essential that we view discourses as being operable in the social world and being at the crux of the maintenance of often problematic ideologies. Part of the mission of CDA is to expose the ideologies through which power is concentrated in privileged institutions and organisations. It is for this reason that so many of the texts which are chosen for analysis confirm the presence of these problematic ideologies. We are also clear, however, that the same models can be used to demystify those texts with which we might have an ideological affinity. No piece of social discourse is neutral. Texts which uphold the misanthropic principles by which too much of society is organised on multiple levels are as dangerously plentiful as the ideologies they uphold. In order to stand against these principles, it is essential that analyses fully engage with context; the describe-interpret-explain structure of CDA therefore strengthens the conclusions that are reached, and we are clear that engaging each of these steps is crucially important in CDA.

References

Aldridge, M. and Luchjenbroers, J. (2007) 'Linguistic Manipulations in Legal Discourse: Framing Questions and "Smuggling" Information', *Speech, Language and the Law* 14(3): 85–107.

Anderson, I. and Beattie, G. (2001) 'Depicted Rapes: How Similar Are Vignette and Newspaper Accounts of Rape?', *Semiotica* 137: 1–21.

Aristotle (1962) *Poetics*, J. Hutton (trans.). New York: Norton.

Aristotle (1984) *Rhetoric*, W.R. Roberts (trans.), in Barnes, J. (ed.) *The Complete Works of Aristotle*, Volume II. Princeton, NJ: Princeton University Press.

Austin, J. (1962) *How to Do Things with Words*. Oxford: Clarendon Press.

Baker, P., Gabrielatos, C., Khosravinik, M., Krzyzanowski, M., McEnery, T. and Wodak, R. (2008) 'A Useful Methodological Synergy? Combining Critical Discourse Analysis and Corpus Linguistics to Examine Discourses of Refugees and Asylum Seekers in the UK Press', *Discourse and Society* 19(3): 273–306.

Barker, M. (1981) *The New Racism*. London: Junction.

Barker, M. (1984) 'Het Nieuwe Racisme' [The New Racism], in Bleich, A. and Schumacher, P. (eds.) *Nederlands Racisme* [Dutch Racism]. Amsterdam: Van Gennep, pp.62–85.

Barthes, R. (1973) *Mythologies*. London: Paladin.

Barthes, R. (1977) *Image, Music, Text*. London: Paladin.

Bednarek, M. (2018) *Language and Television Series*. Cambridge: Cambridge University Press.

Bell, A. (1991) *The Language of News Media*. Oxford: Blackwell.

Benwell, B. (2005) '"Lucky This Is Anonymous!" Men's Magazine and Ethnologies of Reading: A Textual Culture Approach', *Discourse and Society* 16(2): 147–172.

Berlin, B. and Kay, P. (1969) *Basic Color Terms*. Berkeley, CA: University of California Press.

Bernstein, D. (1974) *Creative Advertising*. London: Longman.

Bloor, M. and Bloor, T. (2007) *The Practice of Critical Discourse Analysis*. London: Hodder Arnold.

Bourdieu, P. (1997) 'The Forms of Capital', in Halsey, A.H., Lauder, H. and Brown, P. (eds.) *Education: Culture, Economy, Society*. Oxford: Oxford University Press, pp.46–58.

Bouvier, G. (2019) 'How Journalists Source Trending Social Media Feeds: A Critical Discourse Perspective on Twitter', *Journalism Studies* 20(2): 212–231.

Brierley, S. (1995) *The Advertising Handbook*. London: Routledge.

Brown, P. and Levinson, S. (1987) *Politeness*. Cambridge: Cambridge University Press.

Browse, S. (2018) *Cognitive Rhetoric: The Cognitive Poetics of Political Discourse*. Amsterdam and Philadelphia: John Benjamins.

REFERENCES

Buckledee, S. (2018) *The Language of Brexit: How Britain Talked Its Way Out of the European Union*. London and New York: Bloomsbury.

Caldas-Coulthard, C. (1988) 'Reported interaction in narrative: a study of speech representation in written discourse', PhD thesis, University of Birmingham.

Caldas-Coulthard, C. (1994) 'On Reporting Reporting: The Representation of Speech in Factual and Factional Narratives', in Coulthard, M. (ed.) *Advances in Written Text Analysis*. London and New York: Routledge, pp.295–308.

Caldas-Coulthard, C. (1997) *News as Social Practice: A Study in Critical Discourse Analysis*. Florianópolis, Brazil: Federal University of Santa Catarina Press.

Cameron, D. (2001) *Working with Spoken Discourse*. London: Sage.

Charrow, R. and Charrow, V. (1979) 'Making Legal Language Understandable: A Psycho-linguistic Study of Jury Instructions', *Columbia Law Review* 79: 1306–1974.

Charteris-Black, J. (2004) *Corpus Approaches to Critical Metaphor Analysis*. Basingstoke: Palgrave Macmillan.

Charteris-Black, J. (2014) *Analysing Political Speeches: Rhetoric, Discourse and Metaphor*. Basingstoke: Palgrave Macmillan.

Chilton, P. (ed.) (1985) *Language and the Nuclear Arms Debate: Nukespeak Today*. London: Frances Pinter.

Chilton, P. (2004) *Analysing Political Discourse: Theory and Practice*. London and New York: Routledge.

Chilton, P. and Schaffner, C. (1997) 'Discourse in Politics', in Van Dijk, T. (ed.) *Discourse as Social Interaction*. Newbury, CA: Sage, pp.206–230.

Clark, K. (1992) 'The Linguistics of Blame', in Toolan, M (ed.) *Language, Text and Context*. London and New York: Routledge, pp.208–224.

Cole, P. and Harcup, T. (2010) *Newspaper Journalism*. London: Sage.

Cook, G. (2001) *The Discourse of Advertising*, 2nd edition. London and New York: Routledge.

Cotterill, J. (ed.) (2007) *The Language of Sexual Crime*. Basingstoke: Palgrave Macmillan.

Cottle, S. (ed.) (2000) *Ethnic Minorities and the Media*. Buckingham: Open University Press.

Coulthard, M. (1992) 'Forensic Discourse Analysis', in M. Coulthard (ed.) *Advances in Spoken Discourse Analysis*. London and New York: Routledge, pp.243–258.

Coulthard, M., Johnson, A. and Wright D. (2016) *An Introduction to Forensic Linguistics: Language in Evidence*, 2nd edition. London and New York: Routledge.

Cutting, J. (2014) *Pragmatics*, 3rd edition. London and New York: Routledge.

Eades, D. (1997) 'Language in Court: The Acceptance of Linguistic Evidence about Indigenous Australians in the Criminal Justice System', *Australian Aboriginal Studies* 1: 15–27.

Earner-Byrne, L. and Urquhart, D. (2019) *The Irish Abortion Journey 1920–2018*. Basingstoke: Palgrave Macmillan.

Eggins, S. and Slade, D. (1997) *Analysing Casual Conversation*. London: Continuum.

Ehrlich, S. (2001) *Representing Rape: Language and Sexual Consent*. London and New York: Routledge.

Evans, V. (2017) *The Emoji Code: The Linguistics Behind Smiley Faces and Scaredy Cats*. London: Picador.

Fairclough, N. (1989) *Language and Power*. London: Longman.

Fairclough, N. (1992) *Discourse and Social Change*. Cambridge: Polity.

REFERENCES

Fairclough, N. (1995) *Critical Discourse Analysis: The Critical Study of Language*. London: Longman.

Fairclough, N. (2000) *New Labour, New Language?* London and New York: Routledge.

Fairclough, N. (2001) *Language and Power*, 2nd edition. London: Longman.

Fairclough, N. (2010) *Critical Discourse Analysis: The Critical Study of Language*, 2nd edition. London and New York: Routledge.

Fairclough, N. (2015) *Language and Power*, 3rd edition. London and New York: Routledge.

Fairclough, N. and Wodak, R. (1997) 'Critical Discourse Analysis', in van Dijk, T. (ed.) *Discourse as Social Interaction*. London: Sage, pp.258–285.

Fowler, R. (1991) *Discourse in the News: Language and Ideology in the Press*. London and New York: Routledge.

Fowler, R. (1996) 'On Critical Linguistics', in Caldas-Coulthard, R. and Coulthard, M. (eds.) *Texts and Practices: Readings in Critical Discourse Analysis*. London and New York: Routledge, pp.3–14.

Fowler, R., Hodge, R., Kress, G. and Trew, T. (1979) *Language and Control*. London and New York: Routledge.

Fuchs, C. (2014) *Social Media*. London: Sage.

Gabriel, J. (2000) 'Dreaming of a White…', in Cottle, S. (ed.) *Ethnic Minorities and the Media*. Buckingham: Open University Press, pp.67–83.

Gabrielatos, C. and Baker, P. (2008) 'Fleeing, Sneaking, Flooding: A Corpus Analysis of Discursive Constructions of Refugees and Asylum Seekers in the UK Press, 1996–2005', *Journal of English Linguistics* 36(1): 5–38.

Galtung, J. and Ruge, M.H. (1965) 'The Structure of Foreign News', *Journal of International Peace Research* 1: 64–90.

Garzone, G. and Santulli, F. (2004) 'What Can Corpus Linguistics Do for Discourse Analysis?', in Partington, A., Morley, J. and Haarmaan, L. (eds.) *Corpora and Discourse*. New York: Peter Lang, pp.71–88.

Gibbons, J. (2003) *Forensic Linguistics: An Introduction to Language in the Justice System*. Oxford: Blackwell.

Georgalou, M. (2017) *Discourse and Identity in Facebook*. London and New York: Bloomsbury.

Gramsci, A. (1971) *Selections from Prison Notebooks*, Hoare, Q. and Nowell-Smith, G. (eds. and trans.). London: Lawrence & Wishart.

Grice, H.P. (1975) 'Logic and Conversation', in Cole, P. and Morgan, J. (eds.) *Syntax and Semantics 3: Speech Acts*. New York: Academic Press, pp.41–58.

Hall, S. (1997) 'The spectacle of the "Other"', in Hall, S. (ed.) *Representation: Cultural Representations and Signifying Practices*. London: Sage, pp.223–297.

Halliday, M.A.K. (1978) *Language as a Social Semiotic*. London: Arnold.

Halliday, M.A.K. (1979) 'Modes of Meaning and Modes of Expression: Types of Grammatical Structure, and Their Determination by Different Semantic Functions', in Allerton, D., Carney, E. and Holdcroft, D. (eds.) *Function and Context in Linguistic Analysis*. Cambridge: Cambridge University Press, pp.57–79.

Halliday, M.A.K. (1985) *An Introduction to Functional Grammar*. London: Arnold.

Halliday, M.A.K. (1994) *An Introduction to Functional Grammar*, 2nd edition. London: Arnold.

Halliday, M.A.K. and Matthiessen, G. (2014) *An Introduction to Functional Grammar*, 4th edition. London and New York: Routledge.

Harcup, T. and O'Neill, D. (2001) 'What Is News? Galtung and Ruge Revisited', *Journalism Studies* 2(2): 261–280.

Hart, C. (2014) *Discourse, Grammar and Ideology: Functional and Cognitive Perspectives*. London and New York: Bloomsbury.

Hodge, R. and Kress, G. (1988) *Social Semiotics*. Cambridge: Polity.

Hodge, R. and Kress, G. (1993) *Language and Ideology*. London and New York: Routledge.

Hoffman, C. and Kirner-Ludwig, M. (eds.) (2020) *Telecinematic Stylistics*. London and New York: Bloomsbury.

Hunston, S. and Thompson, G. (eds.) (2000) *Evaluation in Text*. Oxford: Oxford University Press.

Iarovici, E. and Amel, R. (1989) 'The Strategy of the Headline', *Semiotica* 77(4): 441–459.

Jansen, L. (2018) '"Britpop Is a Thing, Damn It!": On British Attitudes Toward American English and an Americanized Singing Style', in Werner, V. (ed.) *The Language of Pop Culture*. London and New York: Routledge, pp.116–137.

Jeffries, L. (2010) *Critical Stylistics: The Power of English*. Basingstoke: Palgrave Macmillan.

Jeffries, L. (2014) 'Critical Stylistics', in Burke, M. (ed.) *The Routledge Handbook of Stylistics*. London and New York: Routledge, pp.408–420.

Jeffries, L. and McIntyre, D. (2019) 'The Devil Has All the Best Tunes: An Investigation of the Lexical Phenomenon of Brexit', in Page, R., Busse, B. and Norgaard, N. (eds.) *Rethinking Language, Text and Context: Interdisciplinary Research in Stylistics in Honour of Michael Toolan*. London and New York: Routledge, pp.103–122.

Jewkes, Y. (2011) *Media and Crime*, 2nd edition. London: Sage.

Keeble, R. (2006) *The Newspapers Handbook*, 2nd edition. London and New York: Routledge.

Koller, V. and Ryan, J. (2019) 'A Nation Divided: Metaphors and Scenarios in the Media Coverage of the 2016 British EU Referendum', in Hart C. (ed.) *Cognitive Linguistic Approaches to Text: From Poetics to Politics*. Edinburgh: Edinburgh University Press, pp.131–157.

Kress, G. (1990) 'Critical Discourse Analysis', *Annual Review of Applied Linguistics* 11: 84–99.

Kress, G. and van Leeuwen, T. (1996) *Reading Images: The Grammar of Visual Design*. London and New York: Routledge.

Kress, G. and van Leeuwen, T. (2006) *Reading Images: The Grammar of Visual Design*, 2nd edition. London and New York: Routledge.

Lakoff, G. and Johnson, M. (1980) *Metaphors We Live By*. Chicago: University of Chicago Press.

Lakoff, G. and Turner, M. (1989) *More than Cool Reason: A Field Guide to Poetic Metaphor*. Chicago: University of Chicago Press.

Lakoff, R. (2017) 'The Hollow Man: Donald Trump, Populism, and Post-truth Politics', *Journal of Language and Politics* 16(4): 595–606.

Larcombe, W. (2002) 'The "Ideal" Victim v. Successful Rape Complainants: Not What You Might Expect', *Feminist Legal Studies* 10(2): 131–148.

Ledin, P. and Machin, D. (2020) *Introduction to Multimodal Analysis*, 2nd edition. London and New York: Bloomsbury.

Lorenzo-Dus, N., Garcés-Conejos Blitvich, P. and Bou-Franch, P. (2011) 'On-line Polylogues and Impoliteness: The Case of Postings Sent in Response to the Obama Reggaeton YouTube Video', *Journal of Pragmatics* 43(10): 2578–2593.

REFERENCES

Lugea, J. (2020) 'The Pragma-stylistics of "Image Macro" Internet Memes', in Ringrow, H. and Pihlaja, S. (eds.) *Contemporary Media Stylistics*. London and New York: Bloomsbury, pp.81–107.

Machin, D. (2007) *An Introduction to Multimodal Analysis*. London: Arnold.

Machin, D. (2008) 'News Discourse I: Understanding the Social Goings-on behind News Texts', in Mayr, A. *Language and Power: An Introduction to Institutional Discourse*. London: Continuum, pp.90–115.

Machin, D. (2010) *Analysing Popular Music*. London: Sage.

Machin, D. (2016) 'The Need for a Social and Affordance-driven Multimodal Critical Discourse Studies', *Discourse and Society* 27(3): 322–334.

Machin, D. and van Leeuwen, T. (2007) *Global Media Discourse*. London and New York: Routledge.

Machin, D. and Niblock, S. (2008) 'Branding Newspapers: Visual Texts as Social Practice', *Journalism Studies* 9(2): 244–259.

Machin, D. and Thornborrow, J. (2003) 'Branding and Discourse: The Case of *Cosmopolitan*', *Discourse and Society* 14(4): 453–471.

Machin, D. and Mayr, A. (2012) *How to Do Critical Discourse Analysis*. London: Sage.

Martin, J.R. (2000) 'Beyond Exchange: Appraisal Systems in English', in Hunston, S. and Thompson, G. (eds.) *Evaluation in Text*. Oxford: Oxford University Press, pp.142–175.

Martin J.R., Matthiessen, G. and Painter, C. (1997) *Working with Functional Grammar*. London: Hodder Arnold.

Martin, J.R. and White, P.R.R. (2005) *The Language of Evaluation: Appraisal in English*. Basingstoke: Palgrave Macmillan.

Marx, K. [with Frederick Engels] ([1933] 1965) *The German Ideology*, Ryazanskaya, S. (ed. and trans.). London: Lawrence & Wishart.

Mautner, G. (2005) 'The Entrepreneurial University: The Discursive Profile of a Higher Education Buzzword', *Critical Discourse Studies* 2(2): 95–120.

Mayr, A. (2008) *Language and Power: An Introduction to Institutional Discourse*. London: Continuum.

Mayr, A. and Statham, S. (2021) '"Free Mo Robinson": Citizen Engagement in Response to a Crime Event on Social Media', *Social Semiotics* 31(3): 365–385.

McIntyre, D. (2008) 'Integrating Multimodal Analysis and the Stylistics of Drama: A Multimodal Perspective on Ian Mckellen's *Richard III*', *Language and Literature* 17(4): 309–334.

Montgomery, M. (2017) 'Post-truth Politics? Authenticity, Populism and the Electoral Discourses of Donald Trump', *Journal of Language and Politics* 16(4): 619–639.

Mooney, A. (2007) 'When Rape Is (Not Quite) Rape', in Cotterill, J. (ed.) *The Language of Sexual Crime*. Basingstoke: Palgrave Macmillan, pp.198–216.

Moss. P. (1985) 'Rhetoric of Defence in the United States: Language, Myth and Ideology', in Chilton, P. (ed.) *Language and the Nuclear Arms Debate: Nukespeak Today*. London: Frances Pinter, pp.45–63.

Mullally, U. (2018) *Repeal the 8th*. London: Unbound.

Neary, C. (2019) '"Please Could You Stop the Noise": The Grammar of Multimodal Meaning-making in Radiohead's "Paranoid Android"', *Language and Literature* 28(1): 41–60.

Page, R. (2012) *Stories and Social Media: Identities and Interaction*. London and New York: Routledge.

REFERENCES

Page, R., Barton, D., Unger, J. and Zappavigna, M. (2014) *Researching Language and Social Media*. London and New York: Routledge.

Pihlaja, S. (2018) 'Discourse Analysis: Studying and Critiquing Language in Use', in Seargeant, P., Hewings, A. and Pihlaja, S. (eds.) *The Routledge Handbook of English Language Studies*. London and New York: Routledge, pp.379–391.

Pihlaja, S. (2019) '"Hey YouTube": Positioning the Viewer in Vlogs', in Page, R., Busse, B. and Norgaard, N. (eds.) *Rethinking Language, Text and Context: Interdisciplinary Research in Stylistic in Honour of Michael Toolan*. London and New York: Routledge, pp.254–266.

Ras, I.A. (2020) 'Child Victims of Human Trafficking and Modern Slavery in British Newspapers', in Ringrow, H. and Pihlaja, S. (eds.) *Contemporary Media Stylistics*. London and New York: Bloomsbury, pp.191–214.

Ravelli, L.J. (2018) 'Multimodal English', in Seargeant, P., Hewings, A. and Pihlaja, S. (eds.) *The Routledge Handbook of English Language Studies*. London and New York: Routledge, pp.434–447.

Richardson, J. (2007) *Analysing Newspapers: An Approach from Critical Discourse Analysis*. Basingstoke: Palgrave Macmillan.

Ringrow, H. (2020) '"This is a Sponsored Post But All Opinions Are My Own": Advertising (Re)Tellings on Social Media', Lambrou, M. (ed.) *Narrative Retellings: Stylistic Approaches*. London and New York: Bloomsbury, pp.163–180.

Rosen, J. (2012) 'The People Formerly Known as the Audience', in Mandiberg, M. (ed.) *The Social Media Reader*. New York: New York University Press, pp.13–17.

Schank, R.C. (1982) *Dynamic Memory*. Cambridge: Cambridge University Press.

Schank, R.C. and Abelson R.P. (1977) *Scripts, Plans, Goals and Understanding*. Hillsdale, NJ: Erlbaum.

Scott, J. (2001) *Power*. Cambridge: Polity.

Seargeant, P. and Tagg. C. (eds.) (2014) *The Language of Social Media: Identity and Community on the Internet*. Basingstoke: Palgrave Macmillan.

Simpson, P. (1993) *Language, Ideology and Point of View*. London and New York: Routledge.

Simpson, P. (2001) '"Reason" and "Tickle" as Pragmatic Constructs in the Discourse of Advertising', *Journal of Pragmatics* 33: 589–607.

Simpson, P. (2003) *On the Discourse of Satire*. Amsterdam and Philadelphia: John Benjamins.

Simpson, P. (2014) *Stylistics*, 2nd edition. London and New York: Routledge.

Simpson, P. and Mayr, A. (2010) *Language and Power*. London and New York: Routledge.

Simpson, P., Mayr, A. and Statham, S. (2018) *Language and Power*, 2nd edition. London and New York: Routledge.

Spilioti, T. (2018) 'The Language of Social Media', in Seargeant, P., Hewings, A. and Pihlaja, S. (eds.) *The Routledge Handbook of English Language Studies*. London and New York: Routledge, pp.310–324.

Statham, S. (2016) *Redefining Trial by Media: Towards a Critical-forensic Linguistic Interface*. Amsterdam and Philadelphia: John Benjamins.

Statham, S. and Ringrow, H. (forthcoming, 2022) '"Wrap Our Arms Around Them Here in Ireland": Social Media Campaigns in the Irish Abortion Referendum', *Discourse and Society*.

REFERENCES

Stockwell, P. (2020) *Cognitive Poetics*, 2nd edition. London and New York: Routledge.

Stubbs, M. (1997) 'Whorf's Children: Critical Elements on Critical Discourse Analysis (CDA)', in Ryan, A. and Wray, A. (eds.) *Evolving Models of Language*. Clevedon: Multimodal Matters, pp.100–116.

Tabbert, U. (2016) *Language and Crime: Constructing Offenders and Victims in Newspaper Reports*. Basingstoke: Palgrave Macmillan.

Tagg, C. (2020) 'Contemporary Media Stylistics: The Old, the Remediated and the New', in Ringrow, H. and Pihlaja, S. (eds.) *Contemporary Media Stylistics*. London and New York: Bloomsbury, pp.317–329.

Tagg, C. and Seargeant, P. (2016) 'Facebook and the Discursive Construction of the Social Network', in Georgakopoulou, A. and Spilioti, T. (eds.) *The Routledge Handbook of Language and Digital Communication*. London and New York: Routledge, pp.339–353.

Temkin, J. (2000) 'Prosecuting and Defending Rape: Perspectives from the Bar', *Journal of Law and Society* 27(2): 219–248.

Thomas, L., Wareing, S., Singh, I., Peccei, J.S., Thornborrow, J. and Jones, J. (2004) *Language, Society and Power: An Introduction*, 2nd edition. London and New York: Routledge.

Thompson, G. (1996) *Introducing Functional Grammar*. London: Arnold.

Thurlow, C. (2013) 'Fakebook: Synthetic Media, Pseudo-sociality and the Rhetorics of Web 2.0', in Tannen, D. and Trester, A.M. (eds.) *Discourse 2.0: Language and New Media*. Washington, DC: Georgetown University Press, pp.225–249.

Tiersma, P. (2007) 'The Language of Consent in Rape Law', in Cotterill, J. (ed.) *The Language of Sexual Crime*. Basingstoke: Palgrave Macmillan, pp.83–104.

Trew, T. (1979) 'Theory and Ideology at Work', in Fowler, R., Hodge, R., Kress, G. and Trew, T. *Language and Control*. London and New York: Routledge, pp.94–116.

Van Dijk, T. (1991) *Racism and the Press*. London and New York: Routledge.

Van Dijk, T. (1993) *Elite Discourse and Racism*. Newbury Park, CA: Sage.

Van Dijk, T. (2000) 'New(s) Racism: A Discourse Analytical Approach', in Cottle, S. (ed.) *Ethnic Minorities and the Media*. Buckingham: Open University Press, pp.33–49.

Van Dijk, T., Ting-Toomey, S., Smitherman, G. and Troutman, D. (1997) 'Discourse, Ethnicity, Culture and Racism', in van Dijk, T. (ed.) *Discourse as Social Interaction: Discourse Studies, Vol. 2: A Multidisciplinary Introduction*. Newbury, CA: Sage, pp.144–181.

Van Leeuwen, T. (1996) 'The Representation of Social Actors' in Caldas-Coulthard, C. and Coulthard, M. (eds.) *Texts and Practices: Readings in Critical Discourse Analysis*. London and New York: Routledge, pp.32–70.

Van Leeuwen, T. (2008) *Discourse and Practice: New Tools for Critical Discourse Analysis*. Oxford: Oxford University Press.

Van Leeuwen, T. and Wodak, R. (1999) 'Legitimizing Immigration Control: A Discourse-historical Analysis', *Discourse Studies* 1(1): 83–118.

Veum, A. and Undrum, L. (2017) 'The Selfie as Global Discourse', *Discourse and Society* 29(1): 86–103.

Voice, M. and Whiteley, S. (2019) '"Y'all Don't Wanna Hear Me, You Just Wanna Dance": A Cognitive Approach to Listener Attention in Outkast's "Hey Ya!"', *Language and Literature* 28(1): 7–22

REFERENCES

Weber, M. ([1914] 1978) *Economy and Society: An Outline of Interpretive Sociology*, Roth, G. and Wittich, W. (eds.), Fischoff, E. (trans.). Berkley, CA: University of California Press.

West, C. (1990) 'Not Just "Doctor's Orders": Directive Response in Patients' Visits to Women and Men Physicians', *Discourse and Society* 1(1): 85–112.

Whiteley, S. and Canning, P. (2017) 'Reader Response Research in Stylistics', *Language and Literature* 26(2): 71–87.

Widdowson, H. (1995) 'Discourse Analysis: A Critical View', *Language and Literature* 4(3): 157–172.

Widdowson, H. (1996) 'Reply to Fairclough: Discourse and Interpretation: Conjectures and Refutations', *Language and Literature* 5(1): 57–69.

Widdowson, H. (1998) 'The Theory and Practice of Critical Discourse Analysis', *Applied Linguistics* 19(1): 136–151.

Widdowson, H. (2004) *Text, Context, Pretext*. Oxford: Oxford University Press.

Winawer, J., Witthoft, N., Frank, M.C., Wu, L., Wade, A.R. and Boroditsky, L. (2007) 'Russian Blues Reveal Effects of Colour Discrimination', *PNAS* 104(19): 7780–7785.

Young, L. and Fitzgerald, B. (2006) *The Power of Language: How Discourse Influences Society*. Sheffield: Equinox.

Young, L., Fitzgerald, M. and Fitzgerald, S. (2018) *The Power of Language: How Discourse Influences Society*, 2nd edition. Sheffield: Equinox.

Zappavigna, M. (2012) *Discourse of Twitter and Social Media*. London: Continuum.

Zappavigna, M. (2014) 'Coffee Tweets: Bonding Around the Bean on Twitter', in Seargeant, P. and Tagg, C. (eds.) *The Language of Social Media: Identity and Community on the Internet*. Basingstoke: Palgrave Macmillan, pp.139–160.

Zappavigna, M. (2015) 'Searchable Talk: The Linguistic Functions of the Hashtag', *Social Semiotics* 25(3): 274–291.

Index

Note: References to figures, images and illustrations are indicated by page citations in *italics*. References to tables are indicated by page citations in **bold**.

Abelson, R. P. 217
abortion 1, 191–208; anti-choice campaign 197, 204–7; foetal images 202, 205; Irish referendum, Twitter campaign 1, 191–207; legalise, campaign to 196; #LoveBothVoteNo campaign 202–4; #together4yes campaign 198–202
accountancy 16
activism 2, 71–2, 90, 143, 195–6, 206
additives 158, 163
Adern, J. 155
adjectives 42, 46, 64, 70, 78
adjuncts 52, 147, 150, 154, 158, 162, 170, 188
adverbials 38
adverbs 46, 61, 63–4, 80, 87
adversatives 158
advertising 10, 22, 24, 81, 87–8, 91, 116–17, 131, 158, 167–9, 175, 181–3, 185–90, 192; advertisements 80, 85, 88, 116–17, 158, 172, 182–9, 196, 203, 216; advertisers 14, 19, 30, 42, 100, 115–18, 185–6, 210; advertorials 182; anatomy of 184; news financing 115–17; non-product advertising, analysis of 186–9; power and 181–9; product advertising, analysis of 183–6; Rape Crisis Scotland advertisement *188*; space-based 116, 184; terminology 182–3; *see also* billboards
aesthetic evaluation 66, 70, 74

affect 66–8; appraisal and 66, 70, 75; examples 68; positive and negative features **67**; *see also* appraisal
Afghanistan 49–53, 126–9, 148–9; Helmand province 49–50, 127
Africa 101
aggregation 119, 122, *125*
airlines 183
airmen 50, 127–8
airports 181, 197–8, 202, 206
Al Nahyan, Sultan 77, 81
alcohol 91–5, 187–8
Aldridge, M. 59
Amel, R. 26
anaphora 76, 81–2; *see also* cataphora
ANC 11
Anderson, I. 94–5
anthropology 130
appraisal: applying the framework 70–2; evaluation and 64–75; inscribed 67–8; invoked 67–8; model 66; *see also* affect; appreciation; inscribed appraisal; invoked appraisal; judgement
appreciation 73–4; appraisal framework 66, 75; aesthetic value, of 66; positive 74, 201; positive and negative features **73**; *see also* appraisal
aristocracy 10, 123
Aristotle 138, 156–7, 161, 166
assertives 110
attitude 16, 56, 95–6, 130
attributive processes 46–7

INDEX

Audi 184
austerity 17–18, 164; anti-austerity protestors 108; measures 108
Austin, J. L. 212
Australia 68, 101, 115, 154
Austria 18, 112, 116
authenticity 85, 88, 146
auxiliaries *see* modal verbs

backgrounding 11, 41, 128
Baker, P. 131, 133, 213–14
bankers 17
Baradar, M. A. G. 129
Barclays 117
Barker, M. 131
Barnier, M. 46–7
barristers 59, 95–6
Barthes, R. 171, 179, 189
BBC (British Broadcasting Corporation) 104–5, 115, 165
Beattie, G. 94–5
Bednarek, M. 168
behavioural processes 39, 43–4, 49, 181
belief systems 10, 61, 71, 214
Bell, A. 26, 30
Bell, S. 142
benefits, state 26, 143; *see also* welfare state/system
Benwell, B. 216
Berlin, B. 172
Bernstein, D. 158, 182
Biden, J. 63, 155
billboards 167, 181, 196
Bin Laden, O. 117
Blair, T. 17, 53–4, 142
blogs/bloggers 192, 194–5
Bloor, M. 14
Bloor, T. 14
bombs 49, 51, 126
Boothroyd, B. 108
Bottomley, P. 108
Bourdieu, P. 15
bourgeoisie 10
Bouvier, G. 197, 202
boycotts 139
brands 115, 184

Brexit 57–8, 60, 67, 73, 130, 133, 135, 141, 164, 175–6, 207, 217
bricolage 218
Brierley, S. 184
Brigade Reconnaissance Force (BRF) 49–50, 126–7
British National Corpus (BNC) 213
broadsheets 32, 102, 136
brochures 78
Brown, P. 60–1
Browse, S. 156, 217
Buckledee, S. 135
bulletins 105, 111
bureaucracy 5

Caldas-Coulthard, C. 45–6, 99, 109–11, 113
Cameron, D. 17
Cameron, David 74, 107
Campbell, G. 108
Canning, P. 216
capitalism 2, 15, 17–19, 31, 33, 43, 62, 116–17, 122, 124, 169, 184, 186, 195, 212; advertising and 169, 186; corporate 117; free market 15, 62, 122, 212; neo-liberal 18; new 17; unchecked 43
carbon footprint 85
caricature 141–2
cataphora 76, 82; *see also* anaphora
categorisation 119, 123, 125; nomination and 123; social actor category, as a *125*
Catherine, Duchess of Cambridge 123
censorship 102, 151
Census data 150
chains: definition 76–7; vocabulary 78–80, 89–90, 93
Chancellor of the Exchequer 18, 140
Charrow, R. 160
Charrow, V. 160
Charteris-Black, J. 138, 141, 217
Chilcot Inquiry (2016) 53
children 62, 105, 145–6; middle-class 71, 73
Chilton, P. 138, 142–4, 147–9, 151–2, 157
China 84, 101, 138, 154–5
Chinook choppers 50–1, 127

229

INDEX

Churchill, W. 163; Churchillian phraseology 163–4
cinema 168; *see also* film
circumstances 34–5, 38–9, 43, 50, 52, 66, 80, 86, 119, 128, 169–70, 194, 218; circumstantial elements 39–41, 46–7, 52, 170; definition 38–9; experiential function 38–9, 43, 86; social 35; social actors 119, 128; topical themes 80; visual SFL 169–70
citizen journalism 193–4
citizenship 201
civic responsibility 77, 84
civil disobedience 11, 107
civil liberty 162
civil service 8
civil society 7
civilians, innocent 41–2, 49
civilizations: clash of 150
Clark, K. 95
Clarkson, J. 70–3, 195
classism 2, 16n4, 19, 212
Clinton, H. 150
clothing 171
CNBC 116
coalition government 17–18, 90, 155
Coca-Cola 183
coercion 7, 64, 138, 142–6, 153, 157; cognitive 144–6; emotive 144, 157; institutional 7; political discourse 64, 142–6; strategic functions 146, 153
cognition 43, 58, 73, 92, 209, 216–17; in CDA 216–17; classic studies 217; cognitive approaches 2, 88, 130, 144–6, 158, 182, 216–18; mental processes and 43, 58, 73, 92
coherence 76–98; innovative education 77–84; sexual assault, language of 93–7; SFL in CDA 84–93
cohesion 76–98; innovative education 77–84; sexual assault, language of 93–7; SFL in CDA 84–93; *see also* cohesive devices; lexical cohesion
cohesive devices 76, 80–2, 89, 93, 172; anaphoric reference 81; *see also* cohesion
Cole, P. 116

collectivisation 119, 121–2, 125, 179; individualisation and 121–3; social actor category, as a 119, *125*; textual and visual 179
colonialism 11
Comcast Corporation 115–6
commercialism 83
common-sense principles 72, 99
communism 6, 62
computer-mediated communication (CMC) 191, 216; media and power 193–4; power and 192–3; social media and power 194–6
conjunctions 80, 187
conjunctive adjuncts 154, 158, 188
connectives 158, 188
connotation 42, 48, 120, 125, 145, 167, 171, 179–80, 185; carriers of 171; coercion 145; connotative meaning of images 171–2; deception 179; ideological 48, 125; immigration 180; innocence 42; semantic meaning 120; sophistication 185; *see also* denotation
conservative ideology/conservatism 11, 70, 102, 108, 112, 196, 204, 206
Conservative Party (UK) 17–18, 53, 67, 72, 90, 102, 107–8, 113, 130, 141, 155, 162, 164–6
constructionism: social 34
consumerism 10, 79, 186
consumption: production and 22–3, 30, 33, 91
conversationalisation 73, 92, 152
Cook, G. 116, 168, 182
copyright 173, 179, 198
Corbyn, J. 67–8, 104
coronavirus *see* Covid-19 pandemic
corpora *see* corpus linguistics
corporatisation 116
corporatism 115–16
Corpus of Contemporary American (COCA) 213
corpus linguistics 2, 131, 165, 212–15; cognitive linguistics and 217; corpus-assisted CDA 209, 212–15, 218; corpus-based analyses 141, 214; key word in context (KWIC) analysis 213

Cottle, S. 131
Coulthard, M. 17, 59
courtroom discourse 59, 94–5, 97
Covid-19 pandemic 17, 103, 112, 154–66; advice, scientific and medical 158, 161–2; background 154–5; Boris Johnson's letter to UK households 138, 154, 158; Boris Johnson's rhetoric 158–66; Exercise Cygnus 164; lockdown restrictions 153–5, 161–2; PPE (personal protective equipment) 164
criminality 131, 144, 150
criticisms of CDA 210–15; analytical rigour 214–15; corpus-assisted CDA 212–14; data interpretation 211; data selection 211; real-world discourse in CDA 212
culturalism: pseudo-biological 131
culture: discourse and 15–16
Cutting, J. 61

Dacre, P. 53
Dáil Éireann (Irish parliament) 205
Daily Mail 12–14, 24, 26–7, 30–2, 35–6, 53, 74, 102, 106–9, 115, 135, 170
Daily Mirror 102, 136
Daily Telegraph 32, 102, 135
deception 69, 179
declaratives 37, 40, 57–60, 87, 92, 187–9
decontextualised settings 87, 173, 179, 186
defamiliarisation 212
delegitimation 147, 149–51
'demand' image 76, 87–9, 172
democracy 4–5, 15, 90, 162
Democratic Unionist Party (DUP) 60
denotation 167, 171; *see also* connotation
Department of Health, Social Services and Public Safety (DHSSPS) 91, 93
description: definition 22
dictatorship 165
discourse: historical nature of 16; ideology and 7–10, 16; power and language 4–5; social action, as a form of 16–17; society and culture 15–16

discourse analysis: explanatory nature of 16; interpretive nature of 16
discourse-historical approach 217
discrimination 129, 210
discursive practice 30–1
disease 161, 163, 166; *see also* Covid-19 pandemic
disjunctive adjunct structure 162
Disney 115
doctors 43, 164, 199–200; doctor–patient communication 17
Dorries, N. 112
drugs 91, 95
drunkenness *see* alcohol
Duffy, D. 199
dummy subject 48
Dyer, M. 199

Eades, D. 17
Earner-Byrne, L. 197
education: cohesion and coherence 77–84; higher/university *see* higher education; innovative 77–84; underperformance in Scotland 113
effectiveness, linguistic 36, 90, 146
Ehrlich, S. 59
elections 4, 85, 90, 102, 136, 139, 155, 202
elites 105, 131
ellipsis 76, 81, 87; elliptical constructions 87
email 191, 202
emblems 188
emojis 168
emotions 16, 47, 65–6, 144, 157, 170; emotional responses 66, 68, 144–5, 157, 165
employability 32
employment 74, 83, 129, 133–4
endophora 82; endophoric references 82
endorsements 157, 198
enhancement technology 88, 175
entailment 185
enterprise 78, 213
entertainment industry 102, 105, 115, 183, 195; *see also* cinema; film; music; streaming services; television

entrepreneurship 32, 78
environmental activism 1, 72, 85, 90, 97, 139, 141, 195, 210
epideictic rhetoric 156
equality *see* gender: equality
ethics 66, 68, 70, 77; ethical issue 6, 66, 68–9
Ethiopia 155
ethnic groups/minorities 129–31, 179
ethnicity 124, 129–31
ethnomethodology 2, 209, 216–18
ethos 154, 156–8, 166
ethotic argument 157, 161
eulogy 156
euphemism 52, 142–3, 151, 153, 166, 205
evaluation: appraisal and 64–75; *see also* appraisal
Evans, V. 168
exams, university 24–5, 28, 35, 170
existential processes 39, 48–9
exnomination 124, 130
exophoric references 82, 89
experiential function 34, 38–54, 58, 76, 80, 89, 93, 97, 140, 169, 189, 210; behavioural processes 44; existential processes 48–9; material processes 39–43; mental processes 43; political leaflets 85–6; public service leaflets 91–2; relational processes 46–8; verbal processes 44–6; *see also* transitivity
explanation: definition 23
exploitation 16
Extinction Rebellion 71–3, 195

Facebook 89, 191, 193, 196, 198
facticity 32, 111, 146
factives 143
Fairclough, N. 4, 10, 13–18, 20–4, 29, 33–4, 36, 52, 64, 73, 91, 94, 97, 109, 166, 209, 214, 217
fake news 155
fascism 62
Fianna Fáil (Ireland) 155
film 56, 176, 202; *see also* cinema
financial crisis, global (2008–9) 18
Financial Times 136

financing news: advertisers and owners 115–17
Fine Gael (Ireland) 155
Fitzgerald, B. 76–7
Fitzgerald, M. 36, 56–8, 60–1, 83
Fitzgerald, S. 36, 56–8, 60–1, 83
folksiness 146, 152
font 93, 167
foregrounding 11, 47, 141, 171, 174–6
foreign nationals 133–4
foreignness 134
forensic linguistics 217; forensic rhetoric 156
for-profit companies 184
Fowler, R. 11, 38, 52, 64, 209–10, 212, 215, 217–18
France 18, 135, 150, 162, 178–9; French ports, migration issue 135, 178, 181
fraud, voter 195
freedom of movement 132
freesheets 116
Fuchs, C. 194
functionalisation 119, 123–8, 133–4, 137, 158, 179–80; social actor category, as a 125
functions of language *see* experiential function; interpersonal function; Systemic Functional Linguistics (SFL); textual function

Gabriel, J. 130
Gabrielatos, C. 131, 133, 213–14
Galtung, J. 103–5
Garzone, G. 213
gay marriage: legalisation of 197, 206
gender: equality 74; female behaviour, stereotypes of 94; female politicians 74; female victims 95; 'think female' approach 125; *see also* gay marriage; LGBT community; rape; sex; sexual assault
genitive structures 143
geographical spectrum 99, 101
Georgalou, M. 196
Germany 112, 116, 164
Gibbons, J. 59

Given information 88, 189; *see also* New information
Gove, M. 161
Gramsci, A. 6–7, 209
Green Party (Ireland) 85–90, 155
Grice, H. P. 82, 212
The Guardian, The 9, 11–13, 53, 74, 102, 108–9, 116–17, 136, 142, 174–6, 215
Guinness 183

Hall, S. 130
Halliday, M. A. K. 22, 28, 34–8, 56, 61, 64–5, 120, 158, 170
harassment: sexual 195
Harcup, T. 104–5, 116
Hart, C. 37, 64, 211–12, 216–17
hashtags 195, 197–8, 200–1, 203–4, 206
healthcare 87, 122, 139, 163, 203, 205
Heaney, S. 140
hegemony 6–7, 90, 206, 209
heroism: theme 163–4
higher education: academic excellence 77–9, 81; industrial action 12, 14, 24–32, 116, 121, 210; innovation model of 78–9, 83–4; institutions 10, 78, 83, 186, 213; leadership and 77–80, 83–4; 'learning-to-earn' 29, 31; management practices 170; marketisation/commodification of 1, 10, 12, 29–33, 36, 78, 97, 209; Middle Eastern 38, 213; pension dispute 14, 24, 27; social practice 31–3; trade union activism 143; tuition fees 18–19, 32; UK university expenditure 78–9; university lecturers 12–14, 24, 26–30, 32–3, 35–6, 43, 170
Hinds, D. 26
history: discourse and 16
Hodge, R. 11, 13, 212
Hoffman, C. 168
homophobia 146
honorifics 125, 157
horizontal power relations 193–4
horticulture 132, 134
hospitals 16, 88, 163–5; *see also* NHS (National Health Service)
housing 86, 132, 135

HSBC 117
humanitarianism 53
humanities research 78
Hunston, S. 65
Hunt, S. 26, 30–1
Hussein, S. 53
hyperbole 141

Iarovici, E. 26
iconic images 172, 176, 183, 198, 200
iconography 169, 171, 179, 181, 183, 189
idealism 62, 186
ideational function 37, 68, 80; *see also* experiential function
identification *125*
ideology: centre-left 9, 117; discourse and 7–10, 16; left-leaning press 11, 29, 116; Left–Right spectrum 102; power and language 4–5
immigration 18, 45, 81, 119, 122–3, 131–6, 141, 143–5, 147–50, 152, 178–81; anti-immigration 81, 136, 141, 178; Calais port/Anglo-French 178–9, *178*, 181; iconography of 179–80; salience of 180; visual SFL and 180–1; *see also* migrants; migration; refugees
imperatives 37, 57, 60, 86–7, 89, 92, 94, 113, 182
impersonalisation 120–1, 125, 127–8, 134, 137; personalisation and 120–1; social actor category, as a *125*; *see also* personalisation
implicature 82, 158, 185
impoliteness 60; *see also* politeness
India 124, 137
individualisation 119, 122, 125; collectivisation and 121–3, 125; social actor category, as a *125*
individualism 17, 217
industrial disputes 85, 122, 139; civil service 8; higher education 12, 14, 24–32, 116, 121, 210; media 1; news reports 43; walkouts 12–13
influenza 103
infomercials 183
innovation 77–81, 83–4, 213

inscribed appraisal 56, 74, 197; inscribed evaluation 70; invoked appraisal distinguished 67–8; judgement and 69, 71; *see also* appraisal
Instagram 105, 192, 196
instant messaging 192
institutional practices: media sources and 98–100, 103, 106–7, 114, 210; text and society, link between 16
instrumentalisation 128
intelligence-gathering 151
interdiscursivity 21–3, 73, 152, 181
internet: emancipatory potential 1, 97, 192
interpersonal function 34, 37, 54, 56–8, 64–5, 75–6, 80, 84, 86–7, 89–90, 92–3, 97, 169, 172–3, 189, 197, 210; political leaflets 86–8; public service leaflets 92
interpretation: definition 22–3
interrogation 142
interrogatives 37, 57–60, 83, 87, 92
intertextuality 16, 21–3, 30–1, 52, 63, 93, 147; definition 22–3; historical nature of discourse 16
interviews 15, 30, 95, 101, 122, 125, 161, 199, 203, 205, 216
invoked appraisal 197; inscribed appraisal distinguished 67–8; invoked evaluation 68–70, 72; judgement and 71; positive appreciation 74
involuntary action 40, 51
Iraq 53–4, 199
Ireland 60, 89–91, 101, 112, 115–16, 124, 137, 183, 191–2; abortion referendum *see* abortion; Catholic Church 197; Constitution 191, 197; political campaigning 85–90, 155; *see also* Dáil Éireann (Irish parliament)
irony 5, 131, 163, 196
ISIS (Islamic State of Iraq and Syria) 146, 148
Islam 149–51; anti-Muslim hysteria 136; immigration 149–50; Islamic law 135; Muslim community 135, 143, 147–51; Muslim countries 145; Muslim immigration to the US 148–50, 213; *see also* Sharia law
Islamic terrorism 151–2
Italy 6, 18, 116, 162

Jae-in, M. 155
James, E. 183
Jansen, L. 168
Japan 199
Jeffries, L. 135, 214
Jewkes, Y. 105
John Lewis (retail chain) 183
Johnson, A. 59
Johnson, B. 40, 43–4, 67–8, 112–13, 138, 154, 156, 158–66
Johnson, M. 139
Jones, O. 165
journalism 106, 114, 116–17, 191, 193–4; journalists 26, 30, 100, 102–3, 106–7, 114, 116, 192, 194; journalistic discourse 56, 194; *see also* citizen journalism; news production
judgement 56, 66, 68–72, 75, 84, 92, 120, 141, 200, 204; appraisal and 68–9; positive and negative features **69**; social esteem **69**; *see also* appraisal
justice system 97, 156, 172

Kay, P. 172
Kennedy, J. F. 143, 194
key word in context (KWIC) 213
Khalizad, Z. 129
kidnapping 142
killing, military 42, 48, 117, 128
kinesic movement 168
kinship 124
Kirner-Ludwig, M. 168
knife crime 71, 73
knighthoods 123
knowledge-based economy 78–9
Koller, V. 217
Korea 102, 155
Kress, G. 11, 13, 21, 24, 87–8, 172–3, 180, 189, 212
KTLA news station 194

Labour Party (UK) 17, 53, 67, 104, 132, 141, 155
Lakoff, G. 139–40, 146
Lamont, N. 140
Larcombe, W. 96
Lawson, N. 198
leadership: academic *see* higher education; political 17, 106, 147, 149, 155
leaflets 1, 76, 85, 87–99, 116, 138, 167–8, 186, 196, 210; *see also* political leaflets; public service leaflets
Ledin, P. 171
legal discourse: witness cross-examination 59; *see also* barristers; courtroom discourse
legitimation 64, 138, 142–3, 147, 149, 153, 157, 161, 163; delegitimation and 147–51; political discourse 64, 138, 142–3, 147, 153, 157, 161; strategic functions 163
legitimisation process 4, 7, 51, 53
Levinson Inquiry 53, 115
Levinson, S. 53, 60–1, 115
lexical cohesion 21, 27, 30, 79, 89; *see also* cohesion
lexical-semantic model 12, 57, 65, 197
lexico-grammar 36, 90, 97
lexicon 28, 36, 197
lexis 68, 144, 197
LGBT community 146; *see also* gender
Liberal Democrats (UK) 90
liberal principles 117, 197
liberalism 102
libraries 39, 83, 171
licence fees 115
lifestyle 118, 168–9, 186; magazines 47, 88, 125, 216; politics 139; risqué 186
Lineker, G. 198
lobby system (UK) 107
lockdown restrictions *see* Covid-19 pandemic
logetic argumentation 157–8, 161, 163, 165
logos (brand identity) 93
logos (political rhetoric) 154, 156–8, 161–3, 165–6

Lorenzo-Dus, N. 196
low-skilled jobs 132–4
Luchjenbroers, J. 59
Lugea, J. 168
lying 69, 151

Machin, D. 8, 24, 28, 44, 88, 106, 110–12, 116, 120, 168, 171–5, 181, 189, 196, 211, 214, 216
magazines 47, 88, 115, 122, 125, 144, 167, 181, 183, 216
managerialism 16, 79
manifestos 10, 15, 20–1, 24, 140–1, 209, 217
manufacturing industries 132, 134, 183
marches 196
marketisation 1, 10, 30, 33, 78, 209; *see also* higher education
marriage *see* gay marriage
Martin, J. R. 37, 57, 65–9, 73, 79
Marx, K. 10, 209
Marxism 10
masculinity 47, 94
massacres (US) 150, 152
materiality 52, 186
Matthiessen, G. 57, 79
Mautner, G. 78
May, T. 45, 176
Maybelline 184
Mayr, A. 8, 17, 24, 28, 44, 47, 59, 79, 88, 110–12, 120, 130, 142, 158, 168, 173–5, 181, 184, 189, 196, 211, 214
McCann, M. 104
McIntyre, D. 135, 168
McKinstry, A. 87, 89
McVey, E. 74
McWilliams, D. 199
memes 168
memory 217
mental processes 38, 42–4, 49, 58, 73, 92, 96, 170, 181, 217
metalinguistic verbs 110–11, **110**
metaphor 22, 29, 35, 113, 122, 134, 138–42, 144–5, 153, 163, 166, 170, 197, 217; conceptual domains 139–41, 163, 179, 217; source and target domains 140–1, 163

INDEX

metapropositional verbs 45, 110–11, **110**, 113
methodological diversity of CDA 218
metonymy 138, 141
#MeToo movement 195
Metropolitan Police (UK) 108–9
Mexican border dispute 145
migrants 122, 131–6, 141, 178–9, 181
migration 132–3; *see also* immigration
Milano, A. 195
military hardware 51, 128
misanthropy 186, 219
misinformation 203, 205
misogyny 146, 212
misrepresentation 151–2, 205, 210
misuse of power 14
Mitchell, A. 105
mnemonic devices 92–3, 96
modal verbs 27, 61, 63, 87–8, 145, 162, 173, 179
modality 1, 27, 37, 56–7, 61–4, 75, 87–8, 161–2, 169, 173, 186; modalisation and 64; modelling 64; modulation and 64; political speeches 61–4; *see also* modal verbs
modernity 10, 29, 124, 154, 185
monarchy 105, 123, 125
monologues 151
Montgomery, M. 85, 146
mood 1, 37, 56–61, 64, 75, 86–7, 89, 92, 94, 169
Mooney, A. 94
morality 66, 68, 205
Moss. P. 142
MSNBC 116
Mullally, U. 197
multifunctionality of language 34
multimodal discourse 1, 24, 56, 87, 167–9, 171–3, 179, 182, 186, 189–90, 196, 201, 210; types 167–8
Multimodal Critical Discourse Analysis (MCDA) 167–90; *see also* advertising; multimodal discourse; salience; visual SFL; visual social actor analysis
murder 18, 59, 70, 150, 214
Murdoch, R. 53–4, 115, 165–6
music 168, 178, 182, 202; songs 202

Muslim community *see* Islam
MyBo 195
MySpace 195

National Security Agency (NSA) 152
National Union of Students (NUS) 32–3
nationalism 130, 175, 206
nationality 124, 128, 130–1
naturalisation 7, 95, 129–30, 134
naturalness 3, 7
Neary, C. 168
negativity 72, 131
neo-capitalism 15; neo-liberal capitalism 18, 31, 143
neo-liberalism 17
Netherlands 17–18, 112
neutrality of news 106–7
New information 88, 189; *see also* Given information
news production 100–9; financing news 115–17; geographical spectrum of the news 101–2; political spectrum of the news 102; sourcing the news 106–9
newsworthiness 23, 99, 102–6, 113, 117, 194
Nexis UK 214
NHS (National Health Service) 108, 141, 156, 162–5
Niblock, S. 216
nightclubs 93, 189; Pulse nightclub shootings, Florida 144, 152–3
nominalisation 34, 48, 52, 158
nomination 119, 123, 125, 127, 133, 137, 157–8; semi-formal 123, 125
normalisation 211
NUIG (National University of Ireland Galway) 89
nurses 164

O'Flynn, P. 132–4
O'Neill, D. 104–5
O'Neill, T. 104
Obama, B. 60, 62–3, 125, 149–52, 195
objectivity 14, 214
'offer' image 76, 87, 172, 180, 189
OneGalway 89
one-party governmental systems 102

opium 49, 51, 126
Oppenheim, J. 199
Osaka, N. 68
Osborne, G. 18
'othering': concept 124, 130, 134
overlexicalisation 21, 27–9, 72, 81, 93, 108, 131, 135, 142, 161, 206

Page, R. 196, 201
Painter, C. 57, 79
Pakistan 117
pandemic *see* Covid-19 pandemic
paralinguistic features 110–11
parallelism 143, 145, 152, 163, 166, 187–8, 201
participants 38–9, 43, 46, 119–20, 128, 169–70, 180–1; participant roles 42–4; *see also* Sayer; Receiver; Verbiage
passivisation 11, 30, 34, 41, 50, 120, 170
pathos 154, 156–7, 165–6
patriarchal institutions 74, 94–6
patriotism 84, 163, 165
paywalls 101
pensions 12, 14, 24–31, 35, 139, 143, 170
personalisation 91, 125, 137; *see also* impersonalisation
persuasion 5, 10, 65, 139, 153, 156–8, 182, 184, 187–8, 201–2
persuasiveness 136, 139–40, 207
petitions 199
phonology 8, 176
Photo Media Group 173
photographs 88, 179–81, 198–9, 204
physiognomy 141
Pihlaja, S. 196, 211
Pistorius, O. 59
placards 60, 85, 196, 204
PMQs (Prime Minister's Questions) 112–13
poetry 140, 199
polarity 37
politeness 60–1; *see also* impoliteness
political language 138–53; coercion 143–6; legitimation 147–51; linguistic features 142–3; metaphor 139–42; presupposition features **143**; representation 151–2; strategic functions 142–52; *see also* Covid-19 pandemic; PMQs (Prime Minister's Questions); political leaflets; political rhetoric; political speeches
political leaflets: experiential function 85–6; Green Party leaflet 86; interpersonal function 86–8; SFL and CDA 85; textual function 88–90
political rhetoric 155–8; *ethos* 156–7; *logos* 157–8; *pathos* 157; *see also* Covid-19 pandemic
political spectrum 9, 99, 101, 116, 146, 165, 195; elitism 104; press/print media 101–2, 109, 131, 135
political speeches: modality and 61–4
politics: discourse *see* political language; political leaflets; political rhetoric; political speeches; ideology and *see* ideology; political spectrum; parliamentary discourse/power 5, 90, 107, 113; sub-politics 138–9; *see also* elections; presidential election campaigns (US)
polling/polls 67, 198, 200, 202–3
Pompeo, M. 129
populism 18, 70
Portugal 104
poverty gap (UK) 135
Powell, E. 130, 152
power 4–7; domination and 5–7; language and 3–20; persuasion and 5–7; power relations, discursive nature of 15; *see also* discourse; ideology; principles of CDA
practice of CDA 21–33; *see also* discursive practice; social practice; text; three-dimensional model of CDA
pragmatics 212
pregnancy 105, 197, 199–200, 204–5; *see also* abortion
prejudice 14
presidential election campaigns (US) 60, 102, 129, 147, 155, 194–5
Press Gazette 114
presupposition 113, 143–4, 146, 152–3, 205

principles of CDA 10–19; contemporary perspectives 17–19; manifesto for CDA 15–17; *see also* discourse; ideology; power
privacy 198
privatisation policies 19, 122
probability 57, 61, 63–4, 75
professionalism 51, 107, 127, 180
pronouns 22, 30, 81–2, 92–4, 130–1, 142, 145–6, 161, 163–6, 201
prosody 110–11, 113
protests 107–8, 139, 155
Psaki, J. 123
pseudo-biological culturalism 131
psychoanalysis 130
psychology 44, 87, 172, 180–1, 216–17
public bodies 1, 93
public sector 9
public service leaflets: experiential function 91–2; interpersonal function 92; PSNI leaflet 91; textual function 93; victim blaming 91–3
publicity 32, 78

qualitative methods of analysis 211, 213–4
quantitative methods of analysis 213, 215
quotations 30, 32, 45, 52, 99, 106, 108, 114

race 1, 22, 122, 124, 126, 129–30, 152, 178, 195, 210; media representation 131–6; representations and social actors 129–36; *see also* 'whiteness'
racism 2, 16, 18–19, 81, 129–31, 133, 146, 211–12, 217
radio 100–1, 182, 184, 187, 192, 201
raids, bombing 49, 126
rallies 60, 148, 151, 196
rape 91–2, 94–7, 187–8; alcohol, effect of 92–4, 187–8; conceptual construction 96–7; crime of 94, 97, 187; crisis centres 188; date rape drugs 91; narratives 187; perceptions 94; Rape Crisis Scotland campaign 187–8, *187*; sex *vs.* 96, 188; victims 94–5, 188; *see also* sexual assault

Ras, I. A. 193
Ravelli, L. J. 167–8
reader, role of 216–17; cognition in CDA 216–17; ethnomethodology in CDA 216; reader-response data 216
Reagan, R. 17
Receiver 44–5; *see also* participants: participant roles
recycling 85
referendum campaigns 1, 57, 135–6, 191, 197–9, 201–2, 204–7, 217; *see also* abortion; Brexit
refugees 131, 213; *see also* migrants; migration
relational processes 28, 39, 46–9, 86, 89–92, 124–5, 180
religion 124, 131, 141, 148; religious values/beliefs 63, 195–7, 204, 207
repetition 27, 76, 78, 80–1, 89–90, 144–5, 151, 163, 172, 201; excessive 93
representativeness 213–15, 218
reproductive rights *see* abortion
Rhodesia 11
Ringrow, H. 196–8, 200, 204–6
riots 11, 71, 104, 107–8, 117, 120, 122
Rivers of Blood speech (E. Powell) 130, 152
Rosen, J. 192–4
royalty *see* monarchy
RTÉ (Ireland) 115
Ruge, M. H. 103–5
Russell Group 25, 27
Ryan, J. 217
Ryanair 117

salience 167, 169, 173–6, 180–1; features 173–8; foregrounding 175; *The Guardian* front page *174*; immigration, of 180; overlapping 176; *The Sun* front page *177*; visual, features of 167, 169
Salisbury riots 11
sanctions 54; *see also* social sanction
Santulli, F. 213
sarcasm 72
satire 141–2
Saudi Arabia 105

Sayer 44–5, 50, 158; *see also* participants: participant roles
saying *see* verbs of saying
scandal 207
Scandinavia 101
Scarfe, G. 142
Schaffner, C. 138, 142
Schank, R. C. 217
schemata 217
Scotland 108, 113, 187–8; Scottish independence referendum (2014) 136, 207; underperforming education system 113
Scotland Yard 108
Scotsman 68
Scott, J. 5–6
Scottish National Party (SNP) 112–13
Seargeant, P. 17, 194, 196
secrecy 151
secularism 196, 207
self-presentation 131
semantic analysis/semantics 8, 11, 26, 35, 83, 85, 87, 119–20, 171, 196
semiotics 22, 24, 34, 88, 172, 176, 178, 201
sensationalist news 102, 108
sex 92, 95–6, 105, 125, 188; *see also* gender
sexism 2, 16n4, 19; sexist language 17
sexual assault 93–8; advertising campaigns 187–9; crime of 76; danger 92; language of 93–7; #MeToo movement 195; social construction of 1, 210; trauma 91; trials 59, 95–6; victim blaming 91–3, 96–7, 211; *see also* rape
SFL *see* Systemic Functional Linguistics (SFL)
shareholders 117, 121
Sharia law 148; *see also* Islam
Sherlock, C. 205
shootings 49, 144–5, 150, 153
Shutterstock 173
Sikorsky troop carriers (US) 50–1, 127
Simpson, P. 8, 17, 38, 41, 44, 47–9, 59, 61, 88, 130, 139, 141–2, 158, 184, 213
sincerity 146, 152

Sinn Féin 60
situational context 58, 83, 93
social actor analysis 120–9; categories 120–6; categorisation 123–6; collectivisation 121–3; impersonalisation 120–1; individualisation 121–3; model *125*; nomination 123–6; personalisation 120–1; race, media representations of 129–36; textual examples 126–9; visual *see* visual social actor analysis
slacktivism 196
slogans 67, 146, 184, 188
Smith, B. 50, 127–8
Snowden, E. 151
social action: discourse as a form of 16–17
social actor analysis 119–36
social constructionism 34
social media 191–208; CMC and 194–6; context 207; language online 191–6; online and offline links 192; Twitter, and abortion debate 196–207; *see also* computer-mediated communication (CMC); Facebook; Instagram; Twitter; YouTube
social networking 194, 196, 198
social practice 31–3; explanation and 23; gender equality and 74; higher education and 28, 31–3; language as a form of 13–14; racist discourse as 130; three-dimensional CDA model 22, *23*, 31–3, 116
social problems 15
social sanction 69–73, 200–1, 204–6
socialism 107–8, 215
society: discourse and 15–16; text, relationship to 16
socio-cultural context 6, 9, 16
socio-economic context 131, 194
sociology 5, 8
socio-political context 1, 11, 102, 106, 196, 209
sociosemantic inventory 125
soldiers 39–42, 44, 49–51, 62, 126–8, 133, 171
solidarity 122, 145, 200–2

Spain 112, 116, 162
speech reporting verbs *see* verbs of saying
speeches 22, 61–4, 85, 99, 142–3, 147, 151–2, 163, 186, 196, 210, 213, 217; *see also* political speeches
speechwriters 64
Spilioti, T. 196
sport 68, 171, 181, 183, 206
Sri Lanka 155
Statham, S. 7–8, 17, 59, 64, 88, 95–6, 117, 130, 142, 158, 184, 196–200, 204, 206, 214, 217
statistics 27, 32, 78, 122, 134–5, 147–50, 157, 185, 214
Steadman, R. 142
Steenkamp, R. 59
stereotypes 85, 94, 129, 187
Stevenson, R. L. 182
Stockwell, P. 216
strategic functions 142–52; *see also* political language
strategic partnerships 83
streaming services 181
Stubbs, M. 211
style guides 113–14
stylistics 168, 216; critical 214
sub-editors 26, 106
sub-headlines 26–7
subject-initial position 11, 41
subjectivity 215–16
subject-verb-object (SVO) 29
sub-politics *see* politics
Suffragette movement 198, 202
supervention 39–40, 42, 51
Sweden 112
Switzerland 116
symbolism 172
synecdoche 141
synonyms 43–4, 48, 129
syntax 11, 28, 36; syntactic construction 11, 41, 59, 160, 163, 187
Syria 199
Systemic Functional Grammar (SFG) 34
Systemic Functional Linguistics (SFL) 15, 22, 34–8, 41–2, 54, 56, 74–6, 79–80, 84–5, 89–90, 93–4, 97, 109, 167, 169, 172, 178, 180–1, 189; CDA and 34–7, 84–93; functions of language 37–8; visual *see* visual SFL

Tabbert, U. 117
tabloids 70, 73, 102, 125, 136
Tagg. C. 17, 193–4, 196
Taj Mahal (India) 172
Taliban 49–53, 126–9
taxation systems 7
telecinematic discourse 168
telephone 202
television 18, 70, 100–1, 104–5, 115–16, 136, 142, 167–8, 181–4, 187, 192, 201, 210
Temkin, J. 95–6
terrorism 49, 51–2, 126–9, 145, 147, 149–52; *see also* Islamic terrorism; war
Tesco 184
testimonials 184
testimony/testimonials 59, 115, 184
text 26–30; decoders 30, 56, 75, 79, 130, 169, 180, 193; encoders 30, 56, 75, 79, 81, 114, 120, 138, 168, 180; society, relationship to 16
text messaging (SMS) 191
textual function 54, 75, 79, 97, 210; definition 37, 76; political leaflets 88–90; public service leaflets 93; SFL model 34, 37–8, 76, 84, 88–91, 93; visual SFL 169, 172, 180, 189
Thatcher, M. 17, 122, 142; Thatcherism 15
Themes 79–80; chains *vs.* 76–7; 'Interpersonal' 80, 84; 'Rheme' *vs.* 80; 'Textual' 80; 'Topical' 80, 89
think-tanks 148
Thomas, L. 52
Thompson, G. 65
Thornborrow, J. 88
three-dimensional model of CDA 20, 22–37, 52, 109, 166; application 24–33; description 22; explanation 23; interpretation 22–3; model 23
Thunberg, G. 71–2
Thurlow, C. 195
Tiananmen Square (China) 172
Tiersma, P. 96

time-based discourse 24, 116, 177, 184, 189
'tinpot' dictatorship 165
topics 78, 94, 197, 210–1
Tories *see* Conservative Party (UK)
torture 142
transdisciplinary analysis 14, 94, 97
transitivity 1, 23, 34, 37–54, 73, 80, 85, 91–3, 95, 109, 113, 119–20, 127–8, 136, 142, 169; in action 49–54; processes *49*; *see also* experiential function
transparency 78
transport, public initiatives 85, 139
Treasury (UK) 147
Trew, T. 11, 13, 212, 215
trials, sexual assault 59, 95–6, 98
tribal cultures 124
Trinity Mirror 115
triumphalism 175–6
troops, military 49–51, 53, 126–9
Trump, D. 18, 45, 60, 63, 85, 128–30, 136, 139, 142–53, 155, 157, 195, 210, 213
trustworthiness 88, 157
truthfulness 41
tuition fees 18–19, 25, 29; compensation of 25, 29
Turkey 133
Turner, M. 140
Tusk, D. 46–7
Twitter 1, 85, 105, 108, 147, 191–3, 195–8, 200, 202, 204, 207; abortion referendum debate (Ireland) 196–207; announcements 105; evaluation on 196–207; hashtag convention 197–207; Irish abortion referendum campaign 1, 191; #LoveBothVoteNO campaign 202–7; mainstream media organisations *vs.* 193; #MeToo movement 195; online and offline discourse 192; political comments 108; #together4yes campaign 198–202; 'trending' news stories 105; Trump, Donald, and 85, 147, 195; *see also* abortion; social media

Ukip (UK Independence Party) 133
Ulster Unionist Party (UUP) 130

underfunding 18, 141, 156
understanding: interpretive and explanatory discourse analysis 16n7, 35; media power 13; memory, role of 217; text, of the 35
Undrum, L. 196
unemployment 18, 134–5
unexpectedness 103–4
unions: student 188; trade 8–9, 15, 89, 122
United States (US): Constitution 63, 147; politics *see* Obama, B.; presidential election campaigns (US); Trump, D.; war
universalisation of values 130
Universities UK (UUK) 29, 31–2, 121
University and College Union (UCU) 25–7, 30–3
Urquhart, D. 197

Van Dijk, T. 16, 21, 129–31, 217
van Leeuwen, T. 24, 87–8, 119–20, 123–5, 128, 172–3, 179–80, 189, 216–17
Varadkar, L. 163
veganism 139
vegetarianism 139
verbal processes 12, 24, 39, 44–6, 50, 89, 103
verbalisation processes 44, 49, 108–9, 112–13, 158, 170
Verbiage 44–5, 109, 113; content-type 45; *see also* participants: participant roles
verbs of saying 109–14; speech reporting verbs, types of **110**; style guides 113–14
vernacular language 146
Veum, A. 196
victim-blaming 94–5, 187; *see also* public service leaflets
Vietnam 154
violence 52, 96, 105, 108–9, 129, 142, 195
viral news 194
visas 132
visual salience *see* salience
visual SFL: iconography in media images 169–73; immigration 180–1; stressed

student *170*; visual social actor analysis and 180–1; *see also* social actor analysis; Systemic Functional Linguistics (SFL)

visual social actor analysis: France-Britain immigration *178*; iconography of immigration 179–80; immigration 178–81; salience of immigration 180; visual SFL and 180–1; *see also* social actor analysis

vlogs 194

vocabulary 27, 78–80, 84, 89–90, 93

Voice, M. 168

voices in discourse 99–118; *see also* news production; verbs of saying

Volkswagen 183–4, 186–7, 216

volunteers 121, 199

voter turnout 202, 206

wages 132

war: Afghanistan 52–3, 127; constructions of 1; euphemistic language 142; Global War on Terror 52–3; 'high-impact effect' 50, 52, 127; innocence, connotations of 42; Iraq War (2003) 53; metaphors 141, 163–4, 179; official descriptions 142; perceptions of 127; press representations 127, 210; radical Islamic terrorism 151–2; register of 142; *see also* terrorism; World War II

Warthog Group 50–1, 127

Washington Post 144

Watson, E. 198

wealth distribution 3, 5, 19, 124, 171

web designers 56

Weber, M. 5–6

Weinstein, H. 195

welfare state/system 18, 112, 122, 155; *see also* benefits, state

West, C. 17

wh-interrogatives 58–9

White, P. R. R. 37, 57, 65–9, 73

Whiteley, S. 168, 216

'whiteness' 130; *see also* race

Widdowson, H. 211, 214, 216, 218

Wilders, G. 130

Winawer, J. 172

Wodak, R. 15–16, 21, 209, 217

workplace interactions 60, 74, 81–2, 173

World War II 107, 164, 166; 'Blitz spirit' during Covid-19 163

Wright, D. 59

wrongful legal convictions 17

xenophobia 81, 146

Yemen 105

YouGov 32

Young, L. 36, 56, 58, 60–1, 76–7, 83

YouTube 196

Zappavigna, M. 196–8, 200

Zapruder, A. 194